The Architecture of the
Language Faculty

Linguistic Inquiry Monographs
Samuel Jay Keyser, general editor

The Architecture of
the Language Faculty

Ray Jackendoff

The MIT Press
Cambridge, Massachusetts
London, England

This book was set in Times Roman by Asco Trade Typesetting Ltd., Hong Kong

Printed and bound in the United States of America.

Library of Congress Cataloging-in-Publication Data

Jackendoff, Ray S.
  The architecture of the language faculty / Ray Jackendoff.
    p.   cm. — (Linguistic inquiry monographs ; 28)
  Includes bibliographical references.
  ISBN 0-262-10059-2. — ISBN 0-262-60025-0 (pbk.)
  1. Grammar, Comparative and general. 2. Thought and thinking.
I. Title. II. Series.
P151.J25   1996
415—dc20   96-25903
                                                                          CIP

Contents

Contents

Series Foreword

We are pleased to present this monograph as the twenty-eighth in the series *Linguistic Inquiry Monographs*. These monographs will present new and original research beyond the scope of the article, and we hope they will benefit our field by bringing to it perspectives that will stimulate further research and insight.

Originally published in limited edition, the *Linguistic Inquiry Monograph* series is now available on the much wider scale. This change is due to the great interest engendered by the series and the needs of a growing readership. The editors wish to thank the readers for their support and welcome suggestions about future directions the series might take.

Samuel Jay Keyser
for the Editorial Board

Preface

"But it comes time to stop and admire the view before pushing on again." With this remark, intended mainly as a rhetorical flourish, I ended *Semantic Structures*, my 1990 book on conceptual structure and its relation to syntax. The present study is in large part a consequence of taking my own advice: when I stepped back to admire the view, I sensed that not all was well across the broader landscape. This book is therefore an attempt to piece together various fragments of linguistic theory into a more cohesive whole, and to identify and reexamine a number of standard assumptions of linguistic theory that have contributed to the lack of fit.

The architecture developed here already appeared in its essentials in my 1987 book *Consciousness and the Computational Mind*, where I situated the language capacity in a more general theory of mental representations, connected this view with processing, and stated the version of the modularity hypothesis here called Representational Modularity. At that time I assumed that the architecture could be connected with just about any theory of syntax, and left it at that. However, two particular issues led to the realization that my assumption was too optimistic.

The first concerns the nature of lexical insertion. In 1991, Joe Emonds published a critique of my theory of conceptual structure, in which it seemed to me that much of the disagreement turned on differing presuppositions about how lexical items enter into syntactic structure. Around the same time, the very same presuppositions surfaced as crucial in a number of intense discussions with Daniel Büring and Katharina Hartmann. Consequently, in replying to Emonds, I found it necessary to unearth these presuppositions and decide what I thought lexical insertion is really like. A fortuitous invitation to the 2nd Tilburg Idioms Conference gave me the opportunity to expand these ideas and work out their implications for idioms, coincidentally bringing me back to questions of lexical content that I had thought about in connection with my 1975 paper on lexical redundancy rules, "Morphological and Semantic Regularities in the Lexicon."

The second major impetus behind this book was the appearance of Chomsky's Minimalist Program, whose goal is to determine how much of the structure of language can be deduced from the need for language to obey boundary conditions on meaning and pronunciation. I found myself agreeing entirely with Chomsky's goals, but differing radically in what I considered an appropriate exploration and realization. Bringing these concerns together with those of lexical insertion led to a 1994 paper entitled "Lexical Insertion in a Post-Minimalist Theory of Grammar." This paper was circulated widely, and I received (what was for me at least) a flood of comments, mostly enthusiastic, from linguists and cognitive scientists of all stripes. As a consequence, the paper grew beyond a size appropriate for a journal, hence the present monograph.

Many of the ideas in this study have been floating around in various subcommunities of linguistics, sometimes without contact with each other. The idea that a grammar uses unification rather than substitution as its major operation, which I have adopted here, now appears in practically every approach to generative grammar outside Chomsky's immediate circle; similarly, most non-Chomskian generative approaches have abandoned transformational derivations (an issue about which I am agnostic here). The idea adopted here of multiple, coconstraining grammatical structures appeared first in autosegmental phonology of the mid-1970s and continues into the syntax-phonology relation and the syntax-semantics relation in a wide range of approaches.

What is original here, I think, is not so much the technical devices as the attempt to take a larger perspective than usual on grammatical structure and to fit all of these innovations together, picking and choosing variations that best suit the whole. In fact, for reasons of length and readability, I have not gone into a lot of technical detail. Rather, my intent is to establish reasonable boundary conditions on the architecture and to work out enough consequences to see the fruitfulness of the approach. My hope is to encourage those who know much more than I about millions of different details to explore the possibilities of this architecture for their own concerns.

Acknowledgments

I must express my gratitude to those people who offered comments on materials from which the present work developed, including Steve Anderson, Mark Aronoff, Hans den Besten, Manfred Bierwisch, Daniel Büring, Patrick Cavanagh, Marcelo Dascal, Martin Everaert, Yehuda Falk, Bob Freidin, Adele Goldberg, Georgia Green, Jane Grimshaw, Ken Hale, Morris Halle, Henrietta Hung, Paul Kay, Paul Kiparsky, Ron Langacker, Joan Maling, Alec Marantz, Fritz Newmeyer, Urpo Nikanne, Carlos Otero, Janet Randall, Jerry Sadock, Ivan Sag, André Schenk, Lindsay Whaley, Edwin Williams, Edgar Zurif, and various anonymous referees. A seminar at Brandeis University in the fall of 1994 was of great help in solidifying the overall point of view and developing the material in chapters 5 and 6; its members included Richard Benton, Piroska Csuri, Judi Heller, Ludmila Lescheva, Maria Piñango, Philippe Schlenker, and Ida Toivonen.

Correspondence with Noam Chomsky has been extremely helpful in clarifying various basic questions. Pim Levelt encouraged me to mention psycholinguistic issues sufficiently prominently; Dan Dennett and Marcel Kinsbourne, to include neuropsychological and evolutionary viewpoints. Beth Jackendoff's energy and enthusiasm in collecting the *Wheel of Fortune* corpus was an important spur to the development of chapter 7. Katharina Hartmann read an early draft of most of the book and suggested some important structural changes. Comments on the penultimate draft from Robert Beard, Paul Bloom, Daniel Büring, Peter Culicover, Dan Dennett, Pim Levelt, Ida Toivonen, and Moira Yip were instrumental in tuning it up into its present form. Anne Mark's editing, as ever, smoothed out much stylistic lumpiness and lent the text a touch of class.

My first book, *Semantic Interpretation in Generative Grammar*, acknowledged my debt to a number of individuals in reaction to whose work my own had developed. I am pleased to be able to thank again two of the central figures of that long-ago Generative Semantics tradition, Jim McCawley and Paul Postal, for their many insightful comments on aspects of the work presented here. It is nice to know that collegiality can be cultivated despite major theoretical disagreement.

I also want to thank three people with whom I have been collaborating over the past few years, on projects that play important roles in the present study. Work with Barbara Landau has deeply influenced my views on the relationship between language and spatial cognition, and consequently my views on interfaces and Representational Modularity (chapter 2). Peter Culicover and I have been working together on arguments that binding is a relationship stated over conceptual structure, not syntax; I draw freely on this work in chapter 3. James Pustejovsky's work on the Generative Lexicon, as well as unpublished work we have done together, is a major component in the discussion of semantic composition (chapter 3) and lexical redundancy (chapter 5).

It is a pleasure to acknowledge financial as well as intellectual support. I am grateful to the John Simon Guggenheim Foundation for a fellowship in 1993–1994 during which several parts of this study were conceived, though not yet molded into a book; this research has also been supported in part by National Science Foundation grant IRI 92-13849 to Brandeis University.

Finally, as usual, Amy and Beth are the foundation of my existence.

Chapter 1
Questions, Goals, Assumptions

Much research in linguistics during the past three decades has taken place in the context of goals, assumptions, and methodological biases laid down in the 1960s. Over time, certain of these have been changed within various traditions of research, but to my knowledge there has been little thorough examination of the context of the entire theory. The problem of keeping the larger context in mind has been exacerbated by the explosion of research, which, although it is a testament to the flourishing state of the field, makes it difficult for those in one branch or technological framework to relate to work in another.

The present study is an attempt to renovate the foundations of linguistic theory. This first chapter articulates some of the options available for pursuing linguistic investigation and integrating it with the other cognitive sciences. In particular, I advocate that the theory be formulated in such a way as to promote the possibilities for integration. Chapter 2 lays out the basic architecture and how it relates to the architecture of the mind more generally. The remaining chapters work out some consequences of these boundary conditions for linguistic theory, often rather sketchily, but in enough detail to see which options for further elaboration are promising and which are not.

One of my methodological goals in the present study is to keep the arguments as framework-free as possible—to see what conditions make the most sense no matter what machinery one chooses for writing grammars. My hope is that such an approach will put us in a better position to evaluate the degree to which different frameworks reflect similar concerns, and to see what is essential and what is accidental in each framework's way of going about formulating linguistic insights.

1.1   Universal Grammar

The arguments for Universal Grammar have by now become almost a mantra, a sort of preliminary ritual to be performed before plunging into the technical detail at hand. Yet these arguments are the reason for the existence of generative grammar, and therefore the reason why most of today's linguists are in the profession rather than in computer science, literature, or car repair. They are also the reason why linguistics belongs in the cognitive sciences, and more generally why linguistics concerns people who have no interest in the arcana of syllable weight or exceptional case marking.

These arguments are due, of course, to Chomsky's work of the late 1950s and early 1960s. Far more than anyone else, Chomsky is responsible for articulating an overall vision of linguistic inquiry and its place in larger intellectual traditions. By taking Universal Grammar as my starting point, I intend to reaffirm that, whatever differences surface as we go on, the work presented here is down to its deepest core a part of the Chomskian tradition.

1.1.1   The Mentalist Stance

The basic stance of generative linguistics is that we are studying "the nature of language," not as some sort of abstract phenomenon or social artifact, but as the way a human being understands and uses language. In other words, *we are interested ultimately in the manner in which language ability is embodied in the human brain.* Chomsky makes this distinction nowadays by saying we are studying "internalized" language (I-language) rather than "externalized" language (E-language). Generative grammar is not the only theory of language adopting this stance. The tradition of Cognitive Grammar adopts it as well, Lakoff (1990), for instance, calling it the "cognitive commitment." On the other hand, a great deal of work in formal semantics does not stem from this assumption. For instance, Bach (1989) asserts Chomsky's major insight to be that language is a formal system—disregarding what I take to be the still more basic insight that language is a psychological phenomenon; and Lewis (1972), following Frege, explicitly disavows psychological concerns.

What about the abstract and social aspects of language? One can maintain a mentalist stance without simply dismissing them, as Chomsky sometimes seems to. It might be, for instance, that there are purely abstract properties that any system must have in order to serve the expressive purposes that language serves; and there might be properties that language has because of the social context in which it is embedded. The mentalist stance would say, though, that we eventually need to investigate how such properties are spelled out in the brains of language users, so that *people* can use language. It then becomes a matter of where you want to place your bets methodologically: life is short, you have to decide what to spend your time studying. The bet made by generative linguistics is that there are some important properties of human language that can be effectively studied without taking account of social factors.

Similar remarks pertain to those aspects of language that go beyond the scale of the single sentence to discourse and narrative. Generative grammar for the most part has ignored such aspects of language, venturing into them only to the extent that they are useful tools for examining intrasentential phenomena such as anaphora, topic, and focus. Again, I am sure that the construction of discourse and narrative involves a cognitive competence that must interact to some degree with the competence for constructing and comprehending individual sentences. My assumption, perhaps unwarranted, is that the two competences can be treated as relatively independent.

Chomsky consistently speaks of I-language as the speaker's *knowledge* or *linguistic competence*, defending this terminology against various alternatives. I would rather not make a fuss over the terminology; ordinary language basically doesn't provide us with terms sufficiently differentiated for theoretical purposes. Where choice of terminology makes a difference, I'll try to be explicit; otherwise, I'll use Chomsky's terms for convenience.

1.1.2 The Notion of Mental Grammar

The phenomenon that motivated Chomsky's *Syntactic Structures* was the unlimited possibility of expression in human language, what Chomsky now calls the "discrete infinity" of language. In order for speakers of a language to create and understand sentences they have never heard before, there must be a way to combine some finite number of memorized units—the words or morphemes of the language—into phrases and sentences of arbitrary length. The only way this is possible is for the speaker's knowledge of the language to include a set of principles of combination that determine which combinations are well formed and what they mean. Such principles are a conceptually necessary part of a theory of language.

The finite set of memorized units is traditionally called the *lexicon*. The set of principles of combination has been traditionally called the *grammar* (or better, *mental grammar*) of the language; in recent work Chomsky has called this set the *computational system*. Alternatively, the term *grammar* has been applied more broadly to the entire I-language, including both lexicon and computational system. Given that many lexical items have internal morphological structure of interest, and that morphology has traditionally been called part of grammar, I will tend to use the term *mental grammar* in this broader sense. How the lexicon and its grammatical principles are related to the extralexical (or phrasal) grammatical principles will be one of the topics of the present study.

Now we come to Bach's point. The major technical innovation of early generative grammar was to state the combinatorial properties of language in terms of a formal system. This confers many advantages. At the deepest level, formalization permits one to use mathematical techniques to study the consequences of one's hypotheses, for example the expressive power (strong or weak generative capacity) of alternative hypothesized combinatorial systems (e.g. Chomsky 1957; Chomsky and Miller 1963) or the learnability of such systems (e.g. Wexler and Culicover 1980). At a more methodological level, formalization permits one to be more abstract, rigorous, and compact in stating and examining one's claims and assumptions. And, as Chomsky stressed in a much-quoted passage from the preface to *Syntactic Structures*, a formalization uncovers consequences, good or bad, that one might not otherwise have noticed.

But formalization is not an unmitigated blessing. In my experience, an excessive preoccupation with formal technology can overwhelm the search for genuine insight into language; and a theory's choice of formalism can set up sociological barriers to communication with researchers in other frameworks. For these reasons, I personally find the proper formalization of a theory a delicate balance between rigor and lucidity: enough to spell out carefully what the theory claims, but not too much to become forbidding. It's one of those methodological and rhetorical matters that's strictly speaking not part of one's theory, but only part of how one *states* it.

1.1.3 Learnability and Universal Grammar
Chomsky's next question is, If linguistic knowledge consists of a mental grammar, how does the mental grammar get into the speaker's mind? Clearly a certain amount of environmental input is necessary, since chil-

dren acquire mental grammars appropriate to their linguistic communities. However, the combinatorial principles of mental grammar cannot be directly perceived in the environmental input: they must be generalizations constructed (unconsciously) in response to perception of the input. Therefore the language learner must come to the task of acquisition equipped with a capacity to construct I-linguistic generalizations on the basis of E-linguistic input. How do we characterize *this* capacity?

The standard lore outside the linguistics community has it that this capacity is simply general-purpose intelligence of a very simple sort. This lore is remarkably persuasive and persistent, and over and over it finds its way into psychological theories of language. Chomsky's (1959) response to Skinner (1957) and Pinker and Prince's (1988) to Rumelhart and McClelland (1986) are detailed attempts to dispel it, nearly thirty years apart. As linguistic theory has demonstrated, the complexities of language are such that general-purpose problem solving would seem not enough. I like to put the problem as the "Paradox of Language Acquisition": If general-purpose intelligence were sufficient to extract the principles of mental grammar, linguists (or psychologists or computer scientists), at least some of whom have more than adequate general intelligence, would have discovered the principles long ago. The fact that we are all still searching and arguing, while every normal child manages to extract the principles unaided, suggests that the normal child is using something other than general-purpose intelligence.

Following standard practice in linguistics, let's call this extra something *Universal Grammar* (UG). What does UG consist of? Acquiring a mental grammar requires (1) a way to generate a search space of candidate mental grammars and (2) a way to determine which candidate best corresponds to the environmental input (i.e., a learning procedure). In principle, then, UG could involve either a specified, constrained search space or a specialized, enriched learning procedure, or both.

Standard practice in linguistics has usually presumed that UG creates the search space: without considerable initial delimitation, it is unlikely that any general-purpose learning procedure, no matter how sophisticated, could reliably converge on such curious notions as long-distance reflexives, reduplicative infixation, and quantifier scope. Even less is it likely that any learning procedure could converge on the correct choice among Government-Binding Theory (GB), Lexical-Functional Grammar (LFG), Head-Driven Phrase Structure Grammar (HPSG), Cognitive Grammar, Arc-Pair Grammar, and Tagmemics (not to mention the as yet undiscovered correct alternative). Rather, the usual assumption among linguists is that the correct theory and the repertoire of choices it presents must be available to the child in advance. Standard practice is somewhat less explicit on whether, given the search space, the learning procedure for I-language is thought of as anything different from ordinary learning. In any event, it is unclear whether there is such a thing as "ordinary learning" that encompasses the learning of social mores, jokes, tennis serves, the faces at a party, an appreciation of fine wines, and tomorrow's luncheon date, not to mention language.

There is a trade-off between these two factors in acquisition: the more constrained the search space is, the less strain it puts on the learning procedure. The general emphasis in linguistic theory, especially since the advent of the principles-and-parameters approach (Chomsky 1980), has been on constraining the search space of possible grammars, so that the complexity of the learning procedure can be minimized. Although I am in sympathy with this general tack, it is certainly not the only possibility. In particular, the more powerful general-purpose learning proves to be, the fewer burdens are placed on the prespecification of a search space for I-language. (One of the threads of Lakoff's (1987) argument is that linguistic principles share more with general cognitive principles than generative grammarians have noticed. Though he may be right, I don't think *all* aspects of linguistic principles can be so reduced.)[1]

1.1.4 Innateness

The next step in Chomsky's argument is to ask how the child gets UG. Since UG provides the basis for learning, it cannot itself be learned. It therefore must be present in the brain prior to language acquisition. The only way it can get into the brain, then, is by virtue of genetic inheritance. That is, UG is innate. At a gross level, we can imagine the human genome specifying the structure of the brain in such a way that UG comes "preinstalled," the way an operating system comes preinstalled on a computer. But of course we don't "install software" in the brain: the brain just grows a certain way. So we might be slightly more sophisticated and say that the human genome specifies the growth of the brain in such a way that UG is an emergent functional property of the neural wiring.

This is not the place to go into the details. Suffice it to say that, more than anything else, the claim of innateness is what in the 1960s brought linguistics to the attention of philosophers, psychologists, biologists—and the general public. And it is this claim that leads to the potential integration of linguistics with biology, and to the strongest implications of linguistics for fields such as education, medicine, and social policy. It is also the one that has been the focus of the most violent dispute. If we wish to situate linguistics in a larger intellectual context, then, it behooves us to keep our claims about innateness in the forefront of discourse, to formulate them in such a way that they make contact with available evidence in other disciplines, and, reciprocally, to keep an eye on what other disciplines have to offer.

1.1.5 Relation of Grammar to Processing

Let us look more explicitly at how linguistic theory might be connected with nearby domains of inquiry. Let us begin with the relation of the mental grammar—something resident in the brain over the long term—to the processes of speech perception and production. There are at least three possible positions one could take.

The weakest and (to me) least interesting possibility is that there is no necessary relation at all between the combinatorial principles of mental grammar and the principles of processing. (One version of this is to say that what linguists write as mental grammars are simply one possible way of formally describing emergent regularities in linguistic behavior, and that the processor operates quite differently.) To adopt this as one's working hypothesis has the effect of insulating claims of linguistic theory from psycholinguistic disconfirmation.

But why should one desire such insulation, if the ultimate goal is an integrated theory of brain and mental functions? To be sure, psycholinguistic results have sometimes been overinterpreted, for example when many took the demise of the derivational theory of complexity in sentence processing (Slobin 1966; Fodor, Bever, and Garrett 1974) to imply the demise of transformational grammar. But surely there are ways to avoid such conclusions other than denying any relation between competence and processing. The relation may have to be rethought, but it is worth pursuing.

A second position one could take is that the rules of mental grammar are explicitly stored in memory and that the language processor "consults" them or "invokes" them in the course of sentence processing. (One could think of the grammar as "declarative" in the computer science sense.) This does not necessarily mean that following rules of grammar need be anything like following rules of tennis, in particular because rules of grammar are neither consciously accessible nor consciously taught.

A third possibility is that the rules of mental grammar are "embodied" by the processor—that is, that they are themselves instructions for constructing and comprehending sentences. (This corresponds to the computer science notion of "procedural" memory.) Back in the 1960s, we were firmly taught not to think of rules of grammar this way. As the story went, speakers don't produce a sentence by first generating the symbol *S*; then elaborating it into *NP + VP*, and so on, until eventually they put in words; and finally "semantically interpreting" the resulting structure, so in the end they find out what they wanted to say. That is, the natural interpretation of the Standard Theory was not conducive to a procedural interpretation of the rules. On the other hand, Berwick and Weinberg (1984) develop an alternative interpretation of transformational grammar that they do embody in a parser. Moreover, other architectures and technologies might lend themselves better to an "embodied" interpretation (as argued by Bresnan and Kaplan (1982) for LFG, for instance).

This is not the place to decide between the two latter possibilities or to find others—or to argue that in the end they are indistinguishable psycholinguistically. The next chapter will propose an architecture for grammar in which at least some components must have relatively direct processing counterparts, so (like Bresnan and Kaplan) I want to be able to take psycholinguistic evidence seriously where available.

One rather coarse psycholinguistic criterion will play an interesting role in what is to follow. In a theory of performance, it is crucial to distinguish those linguistic structures that are stored in long-term memory from those that are composed "on line" in working memory. For example, it is obvious that the word *dog* is stored and the sentence *Your dog just threw up on my carpet* is composed. However, the status of in-between cases such as *dogs* is less obvious. Chapters 5–7 will suggest that attention to this distinction has some useful impact on how the theory of competence is to be formulated.

1.1.6 Relation of Grammar to Brain

Unless we choose to be Cartesian dualists, the mentalist stance entails that knowledge and use of language are somehow instantiated in the brain. The importance of this claim depends on one's stance on the relation of mental grammar to processing, since it is processing that the brain must accomplish. But if one thinks that the rules of mental grammar have something to do with processing, then neuroscience immediately becomes relevant. Conversely, if one considers studies of aphasia to be relevant to linguistic theory, then one is implicitly accepting that the grammar is neurally instantiated to some degree.

Can we do better than the formal approach espoused by linguistic theory, and explain language really in terms of the neurons? Searle (1992) and Edelman (1992), among others, have strongly criticized formal/computational approaches to brain function, arguing that only in an account of the neurons is an acceptable theory to be found. I agree that eventually the neuronal basis of mental functioning is a necessary part of a complete theory. But current neuroscience, exciting as it is, is far from being able to tackle the question of how mental grammar is neurally instantiated. For instance:

1. Through animal research, brain-imaging techniques, and studies of brain damage, we know what many areas of the brain do as a whole. But with the exception of certain lower-level visual areas, we have little idea *how* those areas do what they do. (It is like knowing what parts of a television set carry out what functions, without knowing really how those parts work.)

2. We know how certain neurotransmitters affect brain function in a global way, which may explain certain overall effects or biases such as Parkinson's disease or depression. But this doesn't inform us about the fine-scale articulation of brain function, say how the brain stores and retrieves individual words.

3. We know a lot about how individual neurons and some small systems of neurons work, but again little is known about how neurons encode words, or even speech sounds—though we know they must do it somehow.

For the moment, then, the formal/computational approach is among the best tools we have for understanding the brain at the level of functioning relevant to language, and over the years it has proven a pragmatically useful perspective.[2] Moreover, it's highly unlikely that the details of neural instantiation of language will be worked out in our lifetime. Still, this doesn't mean we shouldn't continue to try to interpret evidence of brain localization from aphasia and more recently from PET scans (Jaeger et al. 1996) in terms of overall grammatical architecture.

In addition, as more comes to be known about the nature of neural computation in general, there may well be conclusions to be drawn about what kinds of computations one might find natural in rules of grammar. For example, we should be able to take for granted by now that no theory

of processing that depends on strict digital von Neumann–style computation can be correct (Churchland and Sejnowski 1992; Crick 1994); and
this no doubt has ramifications for the theory of competence, if we only
keep our eyes open for them. And of course, conversely: one would hope
that neuroscientists would examine the constraints that the complexity of
language places on theories of neural computation.

1.1.7 Evolutionary Issues

If language is a specialized mental capacity, it *might* in principle be different from every other cognitive capacity. Under such a conception, linguistic theory is isolated from the rest of cognitive psychology. Again, I
find a less exclusionary stance of more interest. The claim that language is
a specialized mental capacity does not preclude the possibility that it is in
part a specialization of preexisting brain mechanisms. That's characteristic of evolutionary engineering. For example, many mental phenomena,
such as the organization of the visual field, music, and motor control,
involve hierarchical part-whole relations (or constituent structure); so it
should be no surprise that language does too. Similarly, temporal pat-
terning involving some sort of metrical organization appears in music
(Lerdahl and Jackendoff 1983) and probably motor control, as well as in
language. This does not mean language is *derived* or "built metaphorically" from any of these other capacities (as one might infer from works
such as Calvin 1990 and Corballis 1991, for instance). Rather, like fingers
and toes, their commonalities may be distinct specializations of a common evolutionary ancestor.

Pushing Chomsky's conception of language as a "mental organ" a little
further, think about how we study the physical organs. The heart, the
thumb, the kidney, and the brain are distinct physical organs with their
own particular structures and functions. At the same time, they are all
built out of cells that have similar metabolic functions, and they all
develop subject to the constraints of genetics and embryology. Moreover,
they have all evolved subject to the constraints of natural selection. Hence
a unified biology studies them both for their particularities at the organ
level and for their commonalities at the cellular, metabolic, and evolutionary level.

I think the same can be said for "mental organs." Language, vision,
proprioception, and motor control can be differentiated by function and
in many cases by brain area as well. Moreover, they each have their own
very particular properties: only language has phonological segments and

nouns, only music has regulated harmonic dissonance, only vision has (literal) color. But they all are instantiated in neurons of basically similar design (Crick 1994; Rosenzweig and Leiman 1989); their particular areas in the brain have to grow under similar embryological conditions; and they have to have evolved from less highly differentiated ancestral structures. It is therefore reasonable to look for reflections of such "cellular-level" constraints on learning and behavior in general.

Such a conclusion doesn't take away any of the uniqueness of language. Whatever is special about it remains special, just like bat sonar or the elephant's trunk (and the brain specializations necessary to use them!). However, to the extent that the hypothesis of UG bids us to seek a unified psychological and biological theory, it makes sense to reduce the distance in "design space" that evolution had to cover in order to get to UG from our nonlinguistic ancestors. At the same time, the Paradox of Language Acquisition, with all its grammatical, psychological, developmental, and neurological ramifications, argues that the evolutionary innovation is more than a simple enlargement of the primate brain (as for instance Gould (1980) seems to believe).

1.2   Necessities and Assumptions

So far I have just been setting the context for investigating the design of mental grammar. Now let us turn to particular elements of its organization. A useful starting point is Chomsky's initial exposition of the Minimalist Program (Chomsky 1993, 1995), an attempt to reconstruct linguistic theory around a bare minimum of assumptions.

Chomsky identifies three components of grammar as "(virtual) conceptual necessities":

Conceptual necessity 1
The computational system must have an interface with the articulatory-perceptual system (A-P). That is, language must somehow come to be heard and spoken.

Conceptual necessity 2
The computational system must have an interface with the conceptual-intentional system (C-I). That is, language must somehow come to express thought.

Conceptual necessity 3
The computational system must have an interface with the lexicon. That is, words somehow have to be incorporated into sentences.

This much is unexceptionable, and most of the present study will be devoted to exploring the implications.

However, Chomsky also makes a number of assumptions that are not conceptually necessary. Here are some that are particularly relevant for the purposes of the present study.

Assumption 1 (Derivations)
"The computational system takes representations of a given form and modifies them" (Chomsky 1993, 6). That is, the computational system performs *derivations*, rather than, for example, imposing multiple simultaneous constraints.

To be slightly more specific, a derivational approach constructs well-formed structures in a sequence of steps, where each step adds something to a previous structure, deletes something from it, or otherwise alters it (say by moving pieces around). Each step is discrete; it has an input, which is the output of the previous step, and an output, which becomes the input to the next step. Steps in the middle of a derivation may or may not be well formed on their own; it is the output that matters. By contrast, a constraint-based approach states a set of conditions that a well-formed structure must satisfy, without specifying any alterations performed on the structure to achieve that well-formedness, and without any necessary order in which the constraints apply.

Derivations and constraints are of course not mutually exclusive. In particular, such important parts of grammar as binding theory are usually conceived of as constraints on some level of syntactic derivation—though they are clearly parts of the computational system (see chapter 3). In addition, as was noted by Chomsky (1972), it is possible to construe a derivation simply as a series of constrained relations among a succession of phrase markers (e.g. leading from D-Structure to S-Structure). What distinguishes a derivation (even in this latter construal) from the sort of alternative I have in mind is that a derivation involves a *sequence* of related phrase markers, of potentially indefinite length. In more strictly constraint-based theories of grammar (e.g. LFG, HPSG, Generalized Phrase Structure Grammar (GPSG), Categorial Grammar, Construction Grammar, Optimality Theory), constraints determine the form of a single level or a small, theory-determined number of distinct levels. Much earlier in the history of generative grammar, McCawley (1968a) proposed that phrase structure rules be thought of as constraints on well-formed trees rather than as a production system that derives trees.

Chomsky (1993, 10; 1995, 223–224) defends the derivational conception, though he is careful to point out (1995, 380, note 3) that "the ordering of operations is abstract, expressing postulated properties of the language faculty of the brain, with no temporal interpretation implied." That is, derivational order has nothing to do with processing: "the terms *output* and *input* have a metaphorical flavor...." We will return to Chomsky's defense of derivations here and there in the next three chapters.

The next assumption is, as far as I can tell, only implicit.

Assumption 2 (Substitution)
The fundamental operation of the computational system is *substitution* of one string or structural complex for another in a phrase marker. The Minimalist Program adds the operations "Select" and "Merge," meant to take the place of phrase structure expansion in previous Chomskian theories.

Notably excluded from the repertoire of operations is any variety of *unification* (Shieber 1986), in which features contributed by different constituents can be combined (or superimposed) within a single node. Unification plays a major role in all the constraint-based approaches mentioned above.

The next assumption concerns the nature of the lexical interface.

Assumption 3 (Initial lexical insertion)
The lexical interface is located at the initial point in the syntactic derivation. This assumption takes two forms.
a. From *Aspects* (Chomsky 1965) through GB, the interface is mediated by a rule of *lexical insertion*, which projects lexical entries into X-bar phrase structures at the level of D(eep)-Structure.
b. In the Minimalist Program, lexical items are combined with each other by the operation Merge, building up phrase structure recursively. (This approach resembles the conception of Tree-Adjoining Grammar (Joshi 1987; Kroch 1987).)

Excluded are a number of other possibilities. One is the idea of "late lexical insertion," which crops up from time to time in the literature— starting with Generative Semantics (McCawley 1968b) and continuing through Distributed Morphology (Halle and Marantz 1993). In this alternative, syntactic structures are built up and movement rules take place *before* lexical items (or, in some variants, phonological features of lexical items) are inserted into them. We will explore a more radical alternative in chapter 4.

Another aspect of the standard conception of the lexical interface concerns what lexical insertion inserts.

Assumption 4 (X^0 lexical insertion)
Lexical insertion/Merge enters words (the X^0 categories N, V, A, P) into phrase structure.

Traditionally excluded is the possibility of inserting lexical entries that are larger than words, for instance lexical VPs. This leads to difficulties in the treatment of idioms such as *kick the bucket*, which superficially look like VPs. Also excluded is the possibility of inserting lexical entries smaller than words, for instance causative affixes or agreement markers; these categories must head their own X-bar projections. I will examine the consequences of assumption 4 in chapters 5–7 and formulate an alternative.

The next assumption is stated very explicitly by Chomsky (1993, 2).

Assumption 5 (Nonredundancy)
"A working hypothesis in generative grammar has been that ... the language faculty is nonredundant, in that particular phenomena are not 'overdetermined' by principles of language."

Chomsky observes that this feature is "unexpected" in "complex biological systems, more like what one expects to find ... in the study of the inorganic world." He immediately defends this distancing of generative grammar from interaction with related domains: "The approach has, nevertheless, proven to be a successful one, suggesting that [it is] more than just an artifact reflecting a mode of inquiry."

One might question, though, how successful the approach actually has proven when applied to the lexicon, as Chomsky advocates elsewhere (1995, 235–236).

I understand the lexicon in a rather traditional sense: as a list of "exceptions," whatever does not follow from general principles.... Assume further that the lexicon provides an "optimal coding" of such idiosyncrasies.... For the word *book*, it seems the optimal coding should include a phonological matrix of the familiar kind expressing exactly what is not predictable....

As Aronoff (1994) points out, this conception goes back at least to Bloomfield (1933), who asserts, "The lexicon is really an appendix of the grammar, a list of basic irregularities" (p. 274).

However, there is a difference between assuming that *all* irregularities are encoded in the lexicon and assuming that *only* irregularities are encoded in the lexicon, the latter apparently what Chomsky means by "optimal coding." Chapters 5–7 will evaluate this latter assumption, suggesting that a certain amount of redundancy is inevitable. (As a hint of what is to come, consider how one might code the word *bookend*, so as to express "exactly what is not predictable" given the existence of the words *book* and *end*.)

Although perhaps formally not so elegant, a linguistic theory that incorporates redundancy may in fact prove empirically more adequate as a theory of competence, and it may also make better contact with a theory of processing. As a side benefit, the presence of redundancy may bring language more in line with other psychological systems, to my way of thinking a desideratum. For instance, depth perception is the product of a number of parallel systems such as eye convergence, lens focus, stereopsis, occlusion, and texture gradients. In many cases more than one system comes up with the same result, but in other cases (such as viewing two-dimensional pictures or random-dot stereograms) the specialized abilities of one system come to the fore. Why couldn't language be like that?

1.3   Syntactocentrism and Perfection

Next comes an important assumption that lies behind all versions of Chomskian generative grammar from the beginning, a view of the language faculty that I will dub *syntactocentrism*.

Assumption 6 (Syntactocentrism)
The fundamental generative component of the computational system is the syntactic component; the phonological and semantic components are "interpretive."

This assumption derives some of its intuitive appeal from the conception of a grammar as an algorithm that generates grammatical sentences. Particularly in the early days of generative grammar, serial (von Neumann–style) algorithms were the common currency, and it made sense to generate sentences recursively in a sequence of ordered steps (assumption 1). Nowadays, there is better understanding of the possibilities of parallel algorithms—and of their plausibility as models of mental function. Hence it is important to divorce syntactocentrism from considerations of efficient computation, especially if one wishes to integrate linguistics with the other cognitive sciences.

Chomsky, of course, has always been careful to characterize a generative grammar not as a method to construct sentences but as a formal way to describe the infinite set of possible sentences. Still, I suspect that his syntactocentrism in the early days was partly an artifact of the formal techniques then available.

Another possible reason for syntactocentrism is the desire for nonredundancy (assumption 5). According to the syntactocentric view, the discrete infinity of language, which Chomsky takes to be one of its essential and unique characteristics, arises from exactly one component of the grammar: the recursive phrase structure rules (or in the Minimalist Program, the application of Select and Merge). Whatever recursive properties phonology and semantics have, they are a reflection of interpreting the underlying recursion in syntactic phrases.

But is a *unique* source of discrete infinity necessary (not to mention conceptually necessary)?

As an alternative to syntactocentrism, chapter 2 will develop an architecture for language in which there are three independent sources of discrete infinity: phonology, syntax, and semantics. Each of these components is a generative grammar in the formal sense, and the structural description of a sentence arises from establishing a correspondence among structures from each of the three components. Thus the grammar as a whole is to be thought of as a parallel algorithm. There is nothing especially new in this conception, but it is worth making it explicit.

Is there anything in principle objectionable about such a conception? Recalling Chomsky's injunction against construing the grammar as the way we actually produce sentences, we should have no *formal* problem with it; it is just a different way of characterizing an infinite set. Does it introduce unwanted redundancy? I will argue that the three generative components describe orthogonal dimensions of a sentence, so that it is not in principle redundant. On the other hand, as we will see, redundancies are in practice present, and probably necessary for learnability of the grammar. Is that bad? This remains to be seen.

From the point of view of psychology and neuroscience, of course, redundancy is expected. Moreover, so are multiple sources of infinite variability, each with hierarchical structure. One can understand an unlimited number of hierarchically organized visual scenes and conjure up an unlimited number of visual images; one can plan and carry out an action in an unlimited number of hierarchically organized ways; one can appreciate an unlimited number of hierarchically organized tunes. Each of these, then, requires a generative capacity in a nonlinguistic modality. Moreover, animal behavior is now understood to be far more complex and structured than used to be believed; its variety, especially in higher mammals, calls for a generative capacity that can interpret and act upon an unlimited number of different situations. So language is hardly the only source of generativity in the brain. Why, then, is there any prima facie advantage in claiming that language is itself generated by a *single* source?[3]

If we wish to explain eventually how language could have arisen through natural selection, it is also of interest to consider an evolutionary perspective on syntactocentrism. An obvious question in the evolution of language is, What are the cognitive antecedents of the modern language capacity? Bickerton (1990) offers an intriguing and (to me at least) plausible scenario. He asks, How much could be communicated by organisms that could perceive articulated sounds and establish sound-to-meaning associations (i.e. words), but that had no (or very rudimentary) capacity for syntax? His answer is, Quite a lot, as we can see from the speakers of pidgin languages, from children at the two-word stage, and from agrammatic aphasics. Moreover, if the claims are to be believed, the apes that have been taught a form of sign language do manage to communicate fairly successfully, despite (according to Terrace 1979) lacking any appreciable syntactic organization.[4] Bickerton proposes, therefore, that along the evolutionary pathway to language lay a stage he calls *protolanguage*, which had meaningful words but lacked (most) syntax. Bickerton claims that the ability for protolanguage can still manifest itself in humans when full language is unavailable, for example in the cases mentioned above.

Let us suppose something like Bickerton's story: that earlier hominids had a capacity to take vocal productions as conventional symbols for something else—a rudimentary sound-meaning mapping.[5] Now of course, simply stringing together a sequence of conventionalized symbols leaves it up to the hearer to construct, on grounds of pragmatic plausibility, how the speaker intends the concepts expressed to be related to one another. That is, protolanguage is essentially words plus pragmatics. As Pinker and Bloom (1990) argue, one can see the selective advantage in adding grammatical devices that make overt the intended relationships among words— things like word order and case marking. Having syntax takes much of the burden of composing sentence meanings off of pure pragmatics.

If one accepts some version of this scenario (and I don't see any alternatives other than "unsolved/unsolvable mystery" waiting in the wings), then syntax is the last part of the language faculty to have evolved. Not that the evolution of syntax is inevitable, either: Bickerton thinks that hominids had protolanguage for a million years or more, but that language appeared only with *Homo sapiens*, 200,000 years ago or less. (See Bickerton 1990 for the reasons behind this claim; also see Pinker 1992 for a skeptical appraisal.)

On this view, the function of syntax is to regiment protolanguage; it serves as a scaffolding to help relate strings of linearly ordered words (one kind of discrete infinity) more reliably to the multidimensional and relational modality of thought (another kind of discrete infinity). Syntax, then, does not embody the primary generative power of language. It does indeed lie "between" sound and meaning, as in the syntactocentric view, but more as a facilitator or a refinement than as a creative force.

I am the first to acknowledge that such an argument is only suggestive—though I think it does have the right sort of flavor. It does not force us to explain all properties of syntax in evolutionary terms, for instance the existence of adverbs or the particular properties of reflexives—any more than the claim that the human hand evolved forces us to explain the selective advantage of exactly five fingers on each hand. The solutions that natural selection finds are often matters of historical contingency; they have only to be better than what was around before in order to confer a selective advantage. In this sense, the design of language may well be an accretion of lucky accidents.[6]

Chomsky, as is well known, has expressed skepticism (or at least agnosticism) about arguments from natural selection, one of his more extreme statements being, "We might reinterpret [the Cartesians' 'creative principle,' specific to the human species] by speculating that rather sudden and dramatic mutations might have led to qualities of intelligence that are, so far as we know, unique to man, possession of language in the human sense being the most distinctive index of these qualities" (1973, 396). Chomsky might of course be right: especially in the principled absence of fossil vowels and verbs, we have no way of knowing exactly what happened to language a million years ago. Evolutionary arguments, especially those concerning language, cannot usually be as rigorous as syntactic arguments: one cannot, for example, imagine trusting an evolutionary argument that adverbs couldn't evolve, and thereupon modifying one's syntactic theory.

However, *there is no linguistic argument for syntactocentrism.* To be sure, syntactocentrism has successfully guided research for a long time—but it is still just an assumption that itself was partly a product of historical accident. If syntactic results can be rigorously reinterpreted so as to harmonize with psychological and evolutionary plausibility, I think we should be delighted, not dismissive.

In Chomsky's recent work (especially Chomsky 1995), a new theme has surfaced that bears mention in this context.

Assumption 7 (Perfection)
Language approximates a "perfect" system.

It is not entirely clear what is intended by the term *perfect*, but hints come from this passage (Chomsky 1995, 221):

> If humans could communicate by telepathy, there would be no need for a phonological component, at least for the purposes of communication.... These requirements for language to accommodate to the sensory and motor apparatus] might turn out to be critical factors in determining the inner nature of C_{HL} [the computational system] in some deep sense, or they might turn out to be "extraneous" to it, inducing departures from "perfection" that are satisfied in an optimal way. The latter possibility is not to be discounted.

In other words, language could be perfect if only we didn't have to talk. Moreover, Chomsky speculates that language might be the only such "perfect" mental organ: "The language faculty might be unique among cognitive systems, or even in the organic world, in that it satisfies minimalist assumptions.... [T]he computational system C_{HL} [could be] biologically isolated" (1995, 221). This view, of course, comports well with his skepticism about the evolutionary perspective.

I personally find this passage puzzling. My own inclination would be to say that if we could communicate by telepathy, we wouldn't need *language.* What might Chomsky have in mind? An anecdote that I find revealing comes from Dennett's (1995, 387) recounting of a debate at Tufts University in March 1978.

> There were only two interesting possibilities, in Chomsky's mind: psychology could turn out to be "like physics"—its regularities explainable as the consequences of a few deep, elegant, inexorable laws—or psychology could turn out to be utterly lacking in laws—in which case the only way to study or expound psychology would be the novelist's way.... Marvin Minsky [offered a] "third 'interesting' possibility: psychology could turn out to be like engineering".... Chomsky ... would have no truck with engineering. It was somehow beneath the dignity of the mind to be a gadget or a collection of gadgets.

But of course it is characteristic of evolution to invent or discover "gadgets"—kludgy ways to make old machinery over to suit new purposes. The result is not "perfection," as witness the fallibility of the human back. If we were designing a back for an upright walker on optimal physical principles, we would likely not come up with the human design, so susceptible to strain and pain. But if we had to make it over from a mammalian back, this might be about the best we could come up with. If we were designing reproduction from scratch, would we come up with sex as we practice it?

Similarly, I would expect the design of language to involve a lot of Good Tricks (to use Dennett's term) that make language more or less good enough, and that get along well enough with each other and the preexisting systems. But nonredundant perfection? I doubt it. Just as the visual system has overlapping systems for depth perception, language has overlapping systems for regulating θ-roles, among them word order, case, and agreement, as well as overlapping systems for marking topic such as stress, intonation, case, and position. Conversely, many systems of language serve multiple purposes. For instance, the same system of case morphology is often used in a single language for structural case (signaling grammatical function), semantic case (argument or adjunct semantic function) and quirky case (who knows what function). The very same Romance reflexive morphology can signal the binding of an argument, an impersonal subject, the elimination of an argument (decausativization), or nothing in particular (with inherently reflexive verbs).

This is not to say we shouldn't aim for rigor and elegance in linguistic analysis. Admitting that language isn't "perfect" is not license to give up attempts at explanation. In particular, we still have to satisfy the demands of learnability. It is just that we may have to reorient our sense of what "feels like a right answer," away from Chomsky's sense of "perfection" toward something more psychologically and biologically realistic. It may then turn out that what looked like "imperfections" in language—such as the examples just mentioned—are not reason to look for more "perfect" abstract analyses, as Chomsky and his colleagues often have done; rather, they are just about what one should expect.

These issues may seem quite distant from day-to-day linguistic research. Nevertheless, I find it important to work through them, in an effort to uncover some of the biases that form the background for empirical analysis. Much of what is to follow here depends on laying these biases bare and questioning them.

Chapter 2

Interfaces; Representational Modularity

Let us look more closely at the first two "conceptual necessities" of the previous chapter: the interfaces between language and the "articulatory-perceptual" system on one hand and between language and the "conceptual-intentional" system on the other. A curious gap in Chomsky's exposition of the Minimalist Program is the absence of any independent characterization of these interfaces, which now become all-important in constraining the theory of syntax. This chapter will dig the foundations a little deeper and ask what these interfaces must be like.

We will begin with the better understood of the two interfaces, that of language with the "articulatory-perceptual" system. We will then briefly consider the nature of the more controversial "conceptional-intentional" interface, continuing with it in more detail in chapter 3. The present chapter will conclude by discussing a more general conception of mental organization, Representational Modularity, in terms of which these interfaces emerge as natural components. Chapter 4 will take up Chomsky's third interface, between the combinatorial system and the lexicon.

2.1 The "Articulatory-Perceptual" Interfaces

Consider speech production. In order to produce speech, the brain must, on the basis of linguistic representations, develop a set of motor instructions to the vocal tract. These instructions are not part of linguistic representations. Rather, the usual claim is that phonetic representations are the "end" of linguistic representation—they are the strictly linguistic representations that most closely mirror articulation—and that there is a nontrivial process of conversion from phonetic form to motor instructions.[1]

Similarly for speech perception: the process of phonetic perception is a nontrivial conversion from some sort of frequency analysis to phonetic form (if it were trivial, Haskins Laboratories would have been out of business years ago!). That is, the auditory system per se is not a direct source of linguistic representations.

Moreover, the signals coming from the auditory system are not, strictly speaking, compatible with those going to the motor system. If an evil neurosurgeon somehow wired your auditory nerve up directly to the motor strip, you would surely not end up helplessly shadowing all speech you heard. (Who knows what you would do?) It is only at the abstract level of phonetic representation, distinct from both auditory and motor signals, that the two can be brought into correspondence to constitute a unified "articulatory-perceptual" representation.

We must also not forget the counterpart of phonetic representation for signed languages: it must represent the details of articulation and perception in a fashion that is neutral between gestural articulation and visual perception. It must therefore likewise be an abstraction from both.

In fact, phonetic representation (spoken or signed) is not in one-to-one correspondence with either perceptual or motor representations. Consider the relation of auditory representation to phonetic representation. Certain auditory distinctions correspond to phonetic distinctions; but others, such as the speaker's voice quality, tone of voice, and speed of articulation, do not. Likewise, certain phonetic distinctions correspond to auditory distinctions; but others, such as division into discrete phonetic segments, analysis into distinctive features, and the systematic presence of word boundaries, do not.

Similarly for speech production. In particular, phonetic representation does not uniquely encode motor movements. For example, the motor movements involved in speech can be modulated by concurrent nonlinguistic tasks such as holding a pipe in one's mouth—without changing the intended phonetics.

I spoke above of a "conversion" of phonetic representations into motor instructions during speech production. Given just the elementary observations so far, we see that such a conversion cannot be conceived of as a derivation in the standard sense of generative grammar. It is not like, for instance, moving syntactic elements around in a tree, or like inserting or changing phonological features—that is, a series of operations on a formal structure that converts it into another formal structure built out of similar elements. Rather, phonetic representations are formally composed out of one alphabet of elements and motor instructions out of another. Thus the conversion from one to the other is best viewed formally as a set of principles of the general form (1).

(1) *General form of phonetic-to-motor correspondence rules*
    Configuration X in phonetic representation
    corresponds to
    configuration Y in motor instructions.

That is, these principles have two structural descriptions, one in each of the relevant domains.

Two important points. First, the principles (1) applying to a phonetic representation underdetermine the motor instructions: recall the example of speaking with a pipe in one's mouth. Moreover, many aspects of coarticulation between speech sounds are none of the business of phonetic representation—they are determined by constraints within motor instructions themselves.

Second, some of the principles (1) may be "permissive" in force. For example, a pause for breath (a motor function, not a linguistic function) is much more likely to occur at a word boundary than within a word or especially within a syllable, but a pause is hardly necessary at any particular word boundary. In other words, the presence of breath intake in motor output is influenced by, but not determined by, word boundaries in phonetic representations. To accommodate such circumstances, the general form (1) must be amplified to (2), where the choice of modality in the rule specifies whether it is a determinative rule (*must*), a "permissive" rule (*may*), or a default rule (*preferably does*).[2]

(2) *General form of phonetic-to-motor correspondence rules*
    Configuration X in phonetic representation
    {must/may/preferably does} correspond to
    configuration Y in motor instructions.

Parallel examples can easily be constructed for the relation of auditory perception to phonetic representation and for perception and production of signed languages.

Thus the phonetic-motor interface formally requires three components:

(3) a. A set of phonetic representations available for motor interpretation (the motor interface level of phonology/phonetics)
    b. A set of motor representations into which phonetic representations are mapped (the phonetic interface level of motor representation)
    c. A set of phonetic-motor correspondence rules of the general form (2), which create the correlation between the levels (3a) and (3b)

This prescription can be generalized to the structure of any interface between two distinct forms of representation.

(4) *Components of an interface between system A and system B (an* A-B interface*)*

    a. A set of representations in system A to which the interface has access (the *system B interface level(s) of system A* or BIL_A)

    b. A set of representations in system B to which the interface has access (the *system A interface level(s) of system B* or AIL_B)

    c. A set of *A-to-B correspondence rules*, of the general form illustrated in (5), which create the correlation between BIL_A and AIL_B.

(5) *General form of correspondence rules*
Configuration X in BIL_A
{must/may/preferably does} correspond to
configuration Y in AIL_B.

Crucially, the correspondence rules do not perform derivations in the standard sense of mapping a structure within a given format into another structure within the same format: they map between one format of representation and another. Furthermore, they are not "translations" or one-to-one mappings from A to B; a given representation in BIL_A constrains, but does not uniquely determine, the choice of representation in AIL_B.

Thus, when Chomsky (1993, 2) speaks of the "interface level A-P" as "providing the instructions for the articulatory-perceptual ... system[s]," this is an oversimplification. Phonetic representation is only indirectly a set of instructions to the motor system; and it is not at all a set of instructions to the auditory system, but rather an indirect consequence of input to the auditory system.

In fact, it is clear that there cannot be a single interface of language with the articulatory-perceptual system. The principles placing language in correspondence with articulation are by necessity quite different from those placing language in correspondence with auditory perception. Thus Chomsky's assertion of the "virtual conceptual necessity" of *an* articulatory-perceptual interface must be broken into two parts: language must have an articulatory interface and a perceptual interface.

However, it is a conceptual possibility that one component of these two interfaces is shared—that the articulatory interface level of language is the same as the perceptual interface level. The broadly accepted assumption, of course, is that there is such a shared level: phonetic representation. This is the force of Chomsky's assertion that there is "an" interface, which he calls PF (phonetic form). But the existence of such a shared representation is (at least in part) an empirical matter.[3]

One further point bears mention. Chomsky asserts the importance of a principle he calls Full Interpretation.

> We might ... [say] that there is a principle of full interpretation (FI) that requires that every element of PF and LF ... must receive an appropriate interpretation. ... None can simply be disregarded. At the level of PF, each phonetic element must be licensed by some physical interpretation. The word *book*, for example, has the phonetic representation [buk]. It could not be represented [fburk], where we simply disregard [f] and [r]; that would be possible only if there were particular rules or general principles deleting these elements. (1986, 98)

There is an important ambiguity in this statement. On the one hand, it is surely correct that every element of PF that *can* be related to auditory and motor representations *must* be so related. We clearly do not want a theory of PF in which the correspondence rules can arbitrarily disregard particular segments.[4] On the other hand, there may be aspects of PF that are present for the purpose of level-internal coherence but that are invisible to the correspondence rules. For example, as noted earlier, word boundaries are not consistently interpretable in auditory or motor terms; nevertheless they are present in PF so that the phonetic string can be related to the lexicon and ultimately to syntax and meaning. Nor do phonetic features necessarily correspond perfectly consistently to motor representation (much less to "physical interpretation"). Thus the principle FI needs a certain amount of modulation to be accurate with respect to its role in PF.

This would not be so important, were it not for the fact that Chomsky uses FI at the PF interface to motivate an analogous principle at the LF interface with more crucial consequences, to which we return in chapter 4.

2.2 The Phonology-Syntax Interface

In this section we will look more closely within the "computational system." First, though, a terminological point. The term *syntax* can be used generically to denote the structural principles of any formal system, from human language as a whole to computer languages, logical languages, and music. Alternatively, it can be used more narrowly to denote the structural principles that determine the organization of NPs, VPs, and so on. In the present study I will use the term only in the latter, narrow sense, often calling it *(narrow) syntax* as a reminder; I will use the term *formal system* or *generative system* for the general sense.

With this clarification of the terminology, let us ask, Is PF part of (narrow) syntax? The general consensus seems to be that it is not. The basic intuition is that, for example, *noun*, an element of (narrow) syntax, and +*voice*, an element of PF, should not belong to the same component of grammar. PF is of course a level of *phonological structure*. Now it used to be thought (Chomsky 1965, 1980, 143; Chomsky and Halle 1968) that phonological structure is simply a low (or late) level of syntactic structure, derived by erasing syntactic boundaries, so that all that is visible to phonological rules is the string of words. Hence phonological structure (and therefore PF) could be thought of as derived essentially by a continuation of (narrow) syntactic derivation. But the revolution in phonological theory starting in the mid-1970s (e.g. Liberman and Prince 1977; Goldsmith 1976) has altered that view irrevocably.

On current views, which are as far as I know nearly universally accepted among phonologists, the units of phonological structure are such entities as segments, syllables, and intonational phrases, which do not correspond one to one with the standard units of syntax. For instance, syllabification and foot structure (phonological entities) often cut across morpheme boundaries (lexical/syntactic entities).

(6) a. Phonological: [or+ga+ni] [za+tion]
    b. Morphological: [[[organ]iz]ation]

English articles form a phonological unit with the next word (i.e. they cliticize), whether or not they form a syntactic constituent with it.

(7) a. Phonological: [abig] [house], [avery] [big] [house]
    b. Syntactic: [[a] [[big] [house]]], [[a] [[[very]big] [house]]]

And intonational phrasing cuts across syntactic phrase boundaries.

(8) a. Phonological: [this is the cat] [that ate the rat] [that ate the cheese]
    b. Syntactic: [this is [the cat [that [ate [the rat [that [ate [the cheese]]]]]]]]

Consequently, the constituent structure of PS cannot be produced by simply erasing syntactic boundaries.

To make this point clearer, consider the unit [*abig*] in (7a). There seems little sense in trying to identify its *syntactic* category, in trying to decide whether it is a determiner or an adjective, since as a unit it has no identifiable syntactic properties. Nor can it be produced by any standardly sanctioned syntactic operation, since the determiner can't lower to the adjective position and the adjective can't undergo head-to-head movement to the determiner (or if it can, the adverb in *a very big house* can't). Rather, [*abig*] is just a phonological word, a nonsyntactic unit.

Similarly, intonational phrases such as those in (8a) cannot always be identified with syntactic units such as NP, VP, or CP. Although it is true that intonational phrasing may affect the interpretation of focus (which is often taken to be syntactic), such phrasing may cut across syntactic constituency. For example, the italicized intonational phrases in (9) are not complete syntactic constituents (capitals indicate focal stress).

(9) What did Bill think of those DOGS?
   [Well], [*he very much LIKED*] [the collie and the SPANiel], [*but he didn't much CARE*] [for the boxer and the GREYhound].

Consider also the sentence in (10), marked with two different intonational phrasings (both of which are attested on television). Not only are there constituents here that are not syntactic constituents, there is no detectable semantic difference between the two versions.

(10) a. [*Sesame Street* is a production of] [the Children's Television Workshop].
    b. [*Sesame Street*] [is a production] [of the Children's Television Workshop].

Still, intonational phrasing is not entirely arbitrary with respect to syntax; an intonation break cannot be felicitously added after *Children's* in (10b), for instance.

The upshot is that intonational structure is *constrained by* syntactic structure but not *derived from* it; some of its aspects are characterized by autonomous phonological principles whose structural descriptions make no reference to syntax, for instance a general preference for the intonational phrases of a sentence to be approximately equal in length (see, among others, Gee and Grosjean 1983; Selkirk 1984; Jackendoff 1987a, appendix A; Hirst 1993).

More generally, there appears to be some consensus that phonological rules cannot refer directly to syntactic categories or syntactic constituency. Rather, they refer to prosodic constituency, which, as we have just seen, is only partially determined by syntactic structure. (See, for instance, Zwicky and Pullum 1983 and the papers in Inkelas and Zec 1990.) Conversely, syntactic rules do not refer to phonological domains or to the phonological content of words.[5]

Stepping back from the details, what have we got? It appears that phonological structure and syntactic structure are independent formal systems, each of which provides an exhaustive analysis of sentences in its own terms.

1. The generative system for syntactic structure (SS) contains such primitives as the syntactic categories N, V, A, P (or their feature decomposi-
tions) and functional categories (or features) such as Number, Gender,
Person, Case, and Tense. The principles of syntactic combination include
the principles of phrase structure (X-bar theory or Bare Phrase Structure
or some equivalent), the principles of long-distance dependencies, the
principles of agreement and case marking, and so forth.

2. The generative system for phonological structure (PS) contains such
primitives as phonological distinctive features, the notions of syllable,
word, and phonological and intonational phrase, the notions of stress,
tone, and intonation contour. The principles of phonological combination
include rules of syllable structure, stress assignment, vowel harmony, and
so forth.

Each of these requires a generative grammar, a source of "discrete infinity," neither of which can be reduced to the other.

   Given the coexistence of these two independent analyses of sentences, it
is a conceptual necessity, in precisely Chomsky's sense, that the grammar
contain a set of correspondence rules that mediate between syntactic and
phonological units. Such rules must be of the general form given in (11),
pairing a structural description in syntactic terms with one in phonological terms.

(11) *General form for phonological-syntactic correspondence rules
     (PS-SS rules)*
     Syntactic structure X
     {must/may/preferably does} correspond to
     phonological structure Y.

Two simple examples of such rules are given in (12).

(12) a. A syntactic X^0 constituent preferably corresponds to a
        phonological word.
     b. If syntactic constituent X_1 corresponds to phonological
        constituent Y_1,
        and syntactic constituent X_2 corresponds to phonological
        constituent Y_2,
        then the linear order of X_1 and X_2 preferably corresponds to the
        linear order of Y_1 and Y_2.

These rules contain the modality "preferably" because they are subject to
exception. (12a), which asserts the (approximate) correspondence of syn-

tactic to phonological words, has exceptions in both directions. Clitics such as *a* in (7) are syntactic words that are not phonological words and so must adjoin to adjacent phonological words. Conversely, compounds such as *throttle handle* are syntactic words—X^0 categories that act as single syntactic units but that consist of more than one phonological word.

(12b), which asserts the correspondence of linear order in phonological and syntactic structure, is normally taken to be an absolute rather than a default principle; that is why earlier versions of syntax were able to assume that phonological structure results from syntactic bracket erasure, preserving order.[6] However, there prove to be certain advantages in allowing (12b) to have exceptions forced by other principles. I have in mind clitic placement in those dialects of Serbo-Croatian where the clitic cluster can follow the first phonological constituent, as in (13) (from Halpern 1995, 4).

(13) Taj je   čovek svirao klavir.
     that AUX man   played piano

Here the auxiliary appears in PF between the determiner and the head noun of the subject, syntactically an absurd position. Halpern (1995) and Anderson (1995) suggest that such clitics are syntactically initial but require phonological adjunction to a host on their left; the resulting placement in PF is the optimal compromise possible between their syntactic position and rule (12b).

This overall conception of the phonology-syntax interface leads to the following methodology: whenever we find a phonological phenomenon in which syntax is implicated (or vice versa), a PS-SS correspondence rule of the form (11) must be invoked. In principle, of course, PS-SS correspondence rules might relate anything phonological to anything syntactic—but in fact they do not. For example, syntactic rules never depend on whether a word has two versus three syllables (as stress rules do); and phonological rules never depend on whether one phrase is c-commanded by another (as syntactic rules do). That is, many aspects of phonological structure are invisible to syntax and vice versa. The empirical problem, then, is to find the most constrained possible set of PS-SS rules that both properly describes the facts and is learnable. That is, UG must delimit the PS-SS correspondence rules, in addition to the rules of phonology proper and the rules of syntax proper. Such considerations are essentially what we see going on in discussions of the phonology-syntax interface such as those cited above—though they are rarely couched in the present terms.

Returning to the initial question of this section, we conclude that PF, the articulatory-perceptual interface level of language, is part of phonological structure, and therefore it is not a level of (narrow) syntactic structure. In fact, (narrow) syntax, the organization of NPs and VPs, has *no* direct interface with the articulatory-perceptual system; rather, it interfaces with phonological structure, which in turn interfaces with articulation and perception. In trying to formulate a theory of (narrow) syntax, then, we may ask what point in the derivation of syntactic structure is accessible to the PS-SS correspondence rules. Leaving the question open until chapter 4, I will use the term *Phonological Interface Level* of syntax (PIL_{SS}) for this level of syntax. (This presumes there is only a single syntactic level that interfaces with phonology; chapter 4 will show why it is unlikely that there is more than one.)

Likewise, there has to be a particular level of phonological structure that is available to the PS-SS correspondence rules. Let us call this the *Syntactic Interface Level* of phonology (SIL_{PS}). The full phonology-syntax interface, then, consists of PIL_{SS}, SIL_{PS}, and the PS-SS correspondence rules.

In Chomsky's exposition of the Minimalist Program, the closest counterpart of this interface is the operation *Spell-Out*. The idea is that "before" Spell-Out (i.e. on the (narrow) syntactic side of a derivation, or what Chomsky calls the *overt syntax*), phonological features are unavailable to rules of grammar. Spell-Out strips off the features of phonological relevance and delivers them to "the module Morphology, which constructs wordlike units that are then subjected to further phonological processes ... and which eliminates features no longer relevant to the computation" (Chomsky 1995, 229); "in particular, the mapping to PF ... eliminates formal [i.e. syntactic] and semantic features" (Chomsky 1995, 230). In other words, phonological features are accessible only to phonology-morphology, which in turn cannot access syntactic and semantic features; and Spell-Out, the analogue of the PS-SS correspondence rules in the present proposal, accomplishes the transition.

From the present perspective, the main trouble with Spell-Out—beyond its vagueness—is that it fails to address the independent generative capacity of phonological structure: the principles of syllable and foot structure, the existence and correlation of multiple tiers, and the recursion of phonological constituency that is in part orthogonal to syntactic constituency, as seen in (6)–(10). When the phonological component is invested with an independent generative capacity, this problem drops away immediately.

2.3   The "Conceptual-Intentional" Interface

Next let us consider the "conceptual-intentional" system. I take it that Chomsky intends by this term a system of mental representations, not part of language per se, in terms of which reasoning, planning, and the forming of intentions takes place. Most everyone assumes that there is some such system of mind, and that it is also responsible for the understanding of sentences in context, incorporating pragmatic considerations and "encyclopedic" or "world" knowledge. Let us provisionally call this system of representations *conceptual structure* (CS); further differentiation will develop in section 2.6.

Whatever we know about this system, we know it is not built out of nouns and verbs and adjectives; I will suppose, following earlier work (Jackendoff 1983, 1990), that its units are such entities as conceptualized physical objects, events, properties, times, quantities, and intentions. These entities (or their counterparts in other semantic theories) are always assumed to interact in a formal system that mirrors in certain respects the hierarchical structure of (narrow) syntax. For example, where (narrow) syntax has structural relations such as head-to-complement, head-to-specifier, and head-to-adjunct, conceptual structure has structural relations such as predicate-to-argument, category-to-modifier, and quantifier-to-bound variable. Thus, although conceptual structure undoubtedly constitutes a syntax in the generic sense, its units are not NPs, VPs, etc., and its principles of combination are not those used to combine NPs, VPs, etc.; hence it is not syntax in the narrow sense. In particular, unlike syntactic and phonological structures, conceptual structures are (assumed to be) purely relational, in the sense that linear order plays no role.[7]

Conceptual structure must provide a formal basis for rules of inference and the interaction of language with world knowledge; I think it safe to say that anyone who has thought seriously about the problem realizes that these functions cannot be defined using structures built out of standard syntactic units. In fact, one of the most famous of Chomsky's observations is that sentence (14) is perfect in terms of (narrow) syntax and that its unacceptability lies in the domain of conceptualization.

(14) Colorless green ideas sleep furiously.

Similarly, the validity of the inferences expressed in (15) and the invalidity of those in (16) is not a consequence of their syntactic structures, which are parallel; it must be a consequence of their meaning.

(15) a. Fritz is a cat. Therefore, Fritz is an animal.
   b. Bill forced John to go. Therefore, John went.

(16) a. Fritz is a doll. #Therefore, Fritz is an animal.
   b. Bill encouraged John to go. #Therefore, John went.

If conceptual structure, the form of mental representation in which contextualized interpretations of sentences are couched, is not made out of syntactic units, it is a conceptual necessity that the theory of language contain rules that mediate between syntactic and conceptual units. These rules, the *SS-CS correspondence rules*, mediate the interface between syntax and the conceptual-intentional system. Their general form can be sketched as in (17).[8]

(17) *General form of SS-CS correspondence rules*
   Syntactic structure X
   {must/may/preferably does} correspond to
   conceptual structure Y.

The theory of the SS-CS interface must also designate one or more levels of syntactic structure as the *Conceptual Interface Level(s)* or CIL_{SS}, and one or more levels of conceptual structure as the *Syntactic Interface Level(s)* or SIL_{CS}. Early versions of the Extended Standard Theory such as Chomsky 1972 and Jackendoff 1972 proposed multiple CILs in the syntax. However, a simpler hypothesis is that there is a *single* point in the derivation of syntactic structure that serves as the interface level with conceptual structure. This is essentially Chomsky's (1993) assumption, and I will adopt it here, subject to disconfirming evidence.

   Chomsky identifies the level of language that interfaces with the conceptual-intentional system as *Logical Form* (LF), a level built up out of syntactic units such as NPs and VPs. Thus, in our more detailed exposition of the interface, LF plays the role of the CIL_{SS}. In his earlier work at least, Chomsky explicitly dissociates LF from inference, making clear that it is a level of (narrow) syntax and not conceptual structure itself: "Determination of the elements of LF is an empirical matter not to be settled by a priori reasoning or some extraneous concern, for example codification of inference" (Chomsky 1980, 143; an almost identical passage occurs in Chomsky 1986, 205). In part, Chomsky is trying to distance himself here from certain traditional concerns of logic and formal semantics, an impulse I share (Jackendoff 1983, chapters 3, 4, 11, for instance). Still, there has to be *some* level of mental representation at which inference is codified; I take this to be conceptual structure, a level that is *not* encoded in (narrow) syntactic terms. (Incidentally, contra one way of reading this quotation from Chomsky, it is clear that speaker intuitions about inference are as "empirical" as intuitions about grammaticality; consequently theories of a level that codifies inference are potentially as empirically based as theories of a level that codifies grammaticality.)

I agree with Chomsky that, although conceptual structure is what language *expresses*, it is not strictly speaking a part of the language faculty; it is language independent and can be expressed in a variety of ways, partly depending on the syntax of the language in question. I take conceptual structure to be a central cognitive level of representation, interacting richly with other central cognitive capacities (of which more in section 2.6 and chapter 8). Language is not necessary for the use of conceptual structure: it is possible to imagine nonlinguistic organisms such as primates and babies using conceptual structures as part of their encoding of their understanding of the world. On the other hand, the SS-CS correspondence rules *are* part of language: if there were no language, such rules would have no point—it would be like ending a bridge in midair over a chasm.

There has been constant pressure within linguistic theory to minimize the complexity of the SS-CS interface. For example, Generative Semantics sought to encode aspects of lexical meaning in terms of syntactic combination (deriving *kill* from the same underlying syntactic structure as *cause to become not alive*, to cite the most famous example (McCawley 1968b)). Montague Grammar (and more generally, Categorial Grammar) seeks to establish a one-to-one relation between principles of syntactic and semantic combination. More recently, GB often appeals to Baker's (1988) Uniformity of Theta Assignment Hypothesis (UTAH), which proposes a one-to-one relation between syntactic configurations and thematic roles (where a thematic role is a conceptual notion: an Agent, for instance, is a character playing a role in an event); and the field is witnessing a revival of the syntacticization of lexical semantics (e.g. Hale and Keyser 1993), a topic to which we return in chapter 5.

In my opinion, the evidence is mounting that the SS-CS interface has many of the same "sloppy" characteristics as the PS-SS interface. First of all, it is widely accepted that syntactic categories do not correspond one to one with conceptual categories. All physical object concepts are expressed by nouns, but not all nouns express physical object concepts (consider *earthquake, concert, place, redness, laughter, justice*). All verbs express

event or state concepts, but not all event or state concepts are expressed
by verbs (*earthquake* and *concert* again). Prepositional phrases can express
places (*in the cup*), times (*in an hour*), or properties (*in the pink*). Adverbs
can express manners (*quickly*), attitudes (*fortunately*), or modalities
(*probably*). Thus the mapping from conceptual category to syntactic category is many-to-many, though with interesting skewings that probably
enhance learnability. (18) schematizes some of the possibilities (see Jackendoff 1983, chapters 3 and 4, for justification of this ontology in conceptual structure).

(18) N: Object (*dog*), Situation (*concert*), Place (*region*), Time (*Tuesday*),
        etc.
     V: Situation (Events and States)
     A: Property
     P: Place (*in the house*), Time (*on Tuesday*), Property (*in luck*)
     Adv: Manner (*quickly*), Attitude (*fortunately*), Modality (*probably*)

Second, other than argument structure, much of the conceptual material
bundled up inside a lexical item is invisible to syntax, just as phonological
features are. As far as syntax can see, *cat* and *dog* are indistinguishable
singular count nouns, and *eat* and *drink* are indistinguishable verbs that
take an optional object. That is, the syntactic reflexes of lexical meaning
differences are relatively coarse. (See Pinker 1989 for much data and
elaboration.)

Third, some syntactic distinctions are related only sporadically to conceptual distinctions. Consider grammatical gender. In the familiar Euro-
pean languages, grammatical gender classes are a hodgepodge of semantic
classes, phonological classes, and brute force memorization. But from the
point of view of syntax, we want to be able to say that, no matter for what
crazy reason a noun happens to be feminine gender, it triggers the very
same agreement phenomena in its modifiers and predicates.[9]

Fourth, a wide range of conceptual distinctions can be expressed in
terms of apparently identical syntactic structure. For instance, the syntactic position of direct object can express the thematic roles Theme,
Goal, Source, Beneficiary, or Experiencer, depending on the verb (Jackendoff 1990, chapter 11); some of these NPs double as Patient as well.

(19) a. Emily threw the ball.   (object = Theme/Patient)
     b. Joe entered the room.   (object = Goal)
     c. Emma emptied the sink.   (object = Source/Patient)
     d. George helped the boys.   (object = Beneficiary)

    e. The story annoyed Harry.   (object = Experiencer)

    f. The audience applauded the clown.   (object = ??)

To claim dogmatically that these surface direct objects must all have different underlying syntactic relations to the verb, as required by UTAH, necessarily results in increasing unnaturalness of underlying structures and derivations. We return to this issue in the next section.

Fifth, a wide range of syntactic distinctions can signal the very same conceptual relation. For instance, as is well known (Verkuyl 1972; Dowty 1979; Declerck 1979; Hinrichs 1985; Krifka 1992; Tenny 1994; Jackendoff 1991, 1996e), the telic/atelic distinction (also called the temporally delimited/nondelimited distinction) can be syntactically differentiated through choice of verb (20a), choice of preposition (20b), choice of adverbial (20c), and choice of determiner in subject (20d), object (20e), or prepositional object (20f).

(20) a. John destroyed the cart (in/*for an hour).   (telic)
        John pushed the cart (for/*in an hour).   (atelic)
    b. John ran to the station (in/*for an hour).   (telic)
        John ran toward the station (for/*in an hour).   (atelic)
    c. The light flashed once (in/*for an hour).   (telic)
        The light flashed constantly (for/*in an hour).   (atelic)
    d. Four people died (in/*for two days).   (telic)
        People died (for/*in two days).   (atelic)
    e. John ate lots of peanuts (in/*for an hour).   (telic)
        John ate peanuts (for/*in an hour).   (atelic)
    f. John crashed into three walls (in/*for an hour).   (telic)
        John crashed into walls (for/*in an hour).   (atelic)

So far as I know, there have been no successful attempts to find a uniform underlying syntactic form that yields this bewildering variety of surface forms; rather, it is nearly always assumed that this phenomenon involves a somewhat complex mapping between syntactic expression and semantic interpretation.[10]

In short, the mapping between syntactic structure and conceptual structure is a many-to-many relation between structures made up of different sets of primitive elements. Therefore it cannot be characterized derivationally, that is, by a multistep mapping, each step of which converts one syntactic structure into another. As in the case of the PS-SS interface, then, the empirical problem is to juggle the content of syntactic structure, conceptual structure, and the correspondence rules between them, in such a way as to properly describe the interaction of syntax and semantics and at the same time make the entire system learnable.

2.4 Embedding Mismatches between Syntactic Structure and Conceptual Structure

Let me illustrate the way expressive power can be juggled between syntax and the SS-CS interface. Perhaps the most basic principle of the SS-CS correspondence is the approximate preservation of embedding relations among maximal syntactic phrases. This may be stated as (21).

(21) If syntactic maximal phrase X_1 corresponds to conceptual constituent Z_1,
and syntactic maximal phrase X_2 corresponds to conceptual constituent Z_2,
then, iff X_1 contains X_2, Z_1 preferably contains Z_2.

A subcase of (21) is the standard assumption that semantic arguments of a proposition normally appear as syntactic arguments (complements or specifier) of the clause expressing that proposition. This leaves open which semantic argument corresponds to which syntactic position. Do Agents always appear in the same syntactic position? Do Patients? Do Goals?

UTAH and the Universal Alignment Hypothesis of Relational Grammar (Rosen 1984; Perlmutter and Postal 1984) propose that this mapping is biunique, permitting the SS-CS connection to be absolutely straightforward. On the other hand, the consequence is that the sentences in (19) must be syntactically differentiated at some underlying level in order to account for their semantic differences. Their superficial syntactic uniformity, then, requires complexity in the syntactic derivation.

Various less restrictive views of argument linking, including those of Carter (1976), Anderson (1977), Ostler (1979), Marantz (1984), Foley and Van Valin (1984), Carrier-Duncan (1985), Grimshaw (1990), Bresnan and Kanerva (1989), Jackendoff (1990, chapter 11), and Dowty (1991), appeal to some sort of hierarchy of semantic argument types that is matched with a syntactic hierarchy such as subject–direct object–indirect object. On this view, there need be no syntactic distinction among the sentences in (19), despite the semantic differences; the matching of hierarchies is a function of the SS-CS rules. Hence syntax is kept simple and the complexity is localized in the correspondence rules.[11]

The mapping of argument structure is not the only place where there is a trade-off between complexity in the syntax and complexity in the correspondence rules. Traditional generative grammar has assumed that (21) is not a default rule but a rigid categorical rule (i.e. *preferably* is omitted). Much of the tradition developed in response to apparent counterexamples. Let us briefly consider a few progressively more problematic examples.

First, a standard argument—part of the canon—is that (22a) must be derived from an underlying syntactic structure something like (22b), so that *Bill* can appear within the subordinate clause in consonance with its role as an argument of the subordinate proposition.

(22) a. [Bill seems [to be a nice fellow]].
     b. [e seems [Bill to be a nice fellow]]

However, (21) as stated is also consistent with the sort of analysis adopted within the LFG and HPSG traditions: *Bill* simply appears syntactically outside the clause expressing the embedded proposition, and it is associated with the embedded proposition by a principle that overrules (21). The traditional solution indeed simplifies the SS-CS interface, but at the cost of adding complexity to syntax (namely the application of a raising rule). The alternative instead simplifies the syntax by "base-generating" (22a); the cost is an additional principle in the correspondence rules. At the moment I am not advocating one of these views over the other: the point is only that they are both reasonable alternatives.

Similarly, traditional generative grammar has held that the final relative clause in (23a) is extraposed from an underlying structure like (23b), in consonance with its being a modifier of *man*.

(23) a. A man walked in who was from Philadelphia.
     b. [A man who was from Philadelphia] walked in.

Alternatively, (23a) could be "base-generated," and the relative clause could be associated with the subject by a further correspondence rule that overrides the default case (21). (See Culicover and Rochemont 1990 for one version of this.) That the latter view has some merit is suggested by the following example, of a type pointed out as long ago as Perlmutter and Ross 1970:

(24) A man walked in and a woman walked out who happened to look sort of alike.

Here the relative clause cannot plausibly be hosted in underlying structure by either of the noun phrases to which it pertains (*a man* and *a woman*), because it contains a predicate that necessarily applies to both jointly.

(22a) and (23a) are cases where a syntactic constituent is "higher" than it should be for its semantic role. (25a,b) are cases where the italicized syntactic constituent is "lower" than it should be.

(25) a. Norbert is, *I think*, a genius.
        ($\cong$ I think Norbert is a genius.)
    b. An *occasional* sailor walked by.
        ($\cong$ Occasionally a sailor walked by.)

Earlier work in transformational grammar (e.g. Ross 1967) did not hesitate to derive these by lowering the italicized phrase into its surface position from the position dictated by its sense. More recent traditions, in which lowering is anathema, have been largely silent on such examples. Again, it is possible to imagine a correspondence rule that accounts for the semantics without any syntactic movement, but that overrides (21).

This is not the point at which these alternatives can be settled. I present them only as illustrations of how the balance of expressiveness can be shifted between the syntax proper and the correspondence rules. The point in each case is that some mismatch between meaning and surface syntax exists, and that the content of this mismatch must be encoded *somewhere* in the grammar, either in syntactic movement or in the SS-CS correspondence. Many more such situations will emerge in chapter 3.

2.5   The Tripartite Parallel Architecture

Let us now integrate the four previous sections. The traditional hypothesis of the autonomy of syntax amounts to the claim that syntactic rules have no access to nonsyntactic features except via an interface. Given the distinctness of auditory, motor, phonological, syntactic, and conceptual information, we can expand this claim, and see phonology and conceptual structure as equally autonomous generative systems.

We can regard a full grammatical derivation, then, as three independent and parallel derivations, one in each component, with the derivations imposing mutual constraints through the interfaces. The grammatical structure of a sentence can be regarded as a triple, $\langle$PS, SS, CS$\rangle$. Following Chomsky (1993), we can think of a (narrow) syntactic derivation as "converging" if it can be mapped through the interfaces into a well-

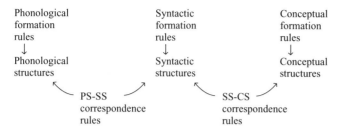

Figure 2.1
The tripartite parallel architecture

formed phonological structure and conceptual structure; it "crashes" if no such mapping can be achieved. Figure 2.1 sketches the layout of such a grammar. In addition, phonological structure is connected through other sets of correspondence rules with auditory and motor information, as we will see shortly.

A similar conception of parallel, mutually constraining derivations is found in Autolexical Syntax (Sadock 1991), though it deals primarily only with the phonology-syntax interface. Shieber and Schabes (1991) likewise set up parallel derivations in a Tree-Adjoining Grammar formalism, but they deal only with the syntax-semantics interface.[12] What I think is relatively novel here is looking at both interfaces at once, observing that (1) they have similar structure, and (2) as will be seen in chapter 4, we must also invoke what is in effect a direct interface from phonology to semantics.[13]

As promised in chapter 1, this conception abandons Chomsky's syntactocentric assumption (assumption 6), in that phonology and semantics are treated as generative completely on a par with syntax. The syntactocentric architecture can be seen as a special case of figure 2.1, one in which phonological and conceptual structures have no properties of their own—in which all their properties are derivable from syntax. On such a view, the phonological and conceptual formation rules in figure 2.1 are in effect vacuous, and the correspondence rules are the only source of properties of phonological and conceptual structure. However, we have seen in sections 2.2 and 2.3 that phonological and conceptual structures *do* have properties of their own, not predictable from syntax, so we must abandon the syntactocentric picture.

For fun, suppose instead that syntactic structures had no properties of their own, and that all *their* properties were derivable from phonology and conceptual structure. Then the *syntactic* formation rules in figure 2.1 would be in effect vacuous, and we would have a maximally minimalist syntax—the sort of syntax that the Minimalist Program claims to envision. However, there are certainly properties of syntactic structure that cannot be reduced to phonology or semantics: syntactic categories such as N and V; language-specific word order, case marking, and agreement properties; the presence or absence in a language of *wh*-movement and other long-distance dependencies; and so on. So syntactic formation rules are empirically necessary as well, and the parallel tripartite model indeed seems justified.

We have also abandoned the assumption (assumption 1) that the relation among phonology, syntax, and semantics can be characterized as derivational. There may well be derivations in the formation rules for each of these components, but between the components lie correspondence rules, which are of a different formal nature.

The notion of correspondence rules has led some colleagues to object to the tripartite model: "Correspondence rules are too unconstrained; they can do anything." What we have seen here, though, is that correspondence rules are *conceptually necessary* in order to mediate between phonology, syntax, and meaning. It is an unwarranted assumption that they are to be minimized and that all expressive power lies in the generative components. Rather, as we have seen, the issue that constantly arises is one of balance of power among components. Since the correspondence rules are part of the grammar of the language, they must be acquired by the child, and therefore they fall under all the arguments for UG. In other words, correspondence rules, like syntactic and phonological rules, must be constrained so as to be learnable. Thus their presence in the architecture does not change the basic nature of the theoretical enterprise. (For those who wish to see correspondence rules in action, much of Jackendoff 1990 is an extended exposition of the SS-CS correspondence rules under my theory of conceptual structure.)

Other colleagues have found it difficult to envision how a tripartite parallel model could serve in a processing theory. However, this should be no reason to favor the syntactocentric model, which, as stressed in chapter 1, is recognized *not* to be a model of processing: imagine starting to think of what to say by generating a syntactic structure. In section 4.5, after I have built the lexicon into the architecture, I will sketch how the tripartite architecture might serve in processing.

Finally, some people simply see no reason to abandon syntactocentrism despite nearly two decades of evidence for the (relative) autonomy of phonology (I leave semantics aside, on the grounds that I have a personal interest). I urge readers with such inclinations to consider again the possibility that the syntactocentric model is just a habit dating back to the 1960s.

2.6. Representational Modularity

This way of looking at the organization of grammar fits naturally into a larger hypothesis of the architecture of mind that might be called *Representational Modularity* (Jackendoff 1987a, chapter 12; 1992a, chapter 1). The overall idea is that the mind/brain encodes information in some finite number of distinct representational formats or "languages of the mind." Each of these "languages" is a formal system with its own proprietary set of primitives and principles of combination, so that it defines an infinite set of expressions along familiar generative lines. For each of these formats, there is a module of mind/brain responsible for it. For example, phonological structure and syntactic structure are distinct representational formats, with distinct and only partly commensurate primitives and principles of combination. Representational Modularity therefore posits that the architecture of the mind/brain devotes separate modules to these two encodings. Each of these modules is domain specific (phonology and syntax respectively); and (with certain caveats to follow shortly) each is informationally encapsulated in Fodor's (1983) sense.

Representational modules differ from Fodorian modules in that they are individuated by the representations they process rather than by their function as faculties for input or output; that is, they are at the scale of individual levels of representation, rather than being an entire faculty such as language perception. The generative grammar for each "language of the mind," then, is a formal description of the repertoire of structures available to the corresponding representational module.

A conceptual difficulty with Fodor's account of modularity is that it fails to address how modules communicate with each other and how they communicate with Fodor's central, nonmodular cognitive core. In particular, Fodor claims that the language perception module derives "shallow representations"—some form of syntactic structure—and that the central faculty of "belief fixation" operates in terms of the "language of thought," a nonlinguistic encoding. But Fodor does not say how "shallow representations" are converted to the "language of thought," as they must be if linguistic communication is to affect belief fixation. In effect, the language module is so domain specific and informationally encapsulated that nothing can get out of it to serve cognitive purposes.[14]

The theory of Representational Modularity addresses this difficulty by positing, in addition to the *representation modules* proposed above, a system of *interface modules*. An interface module communicates between two levels of encoding, say L_1 and L_2, by carrying out a partial translation of information in L_1 form into information in L_2 form (or, better, imposing a partial homomorphism between L_1 and L_2 information).[15] In the formal grammar, then, the correspondence rule component that links L_1 and L_2 can be taken as a formal description of the repertoire of partial translations accomplished by the L_1-L_2 interface module. A faculty such as the language faculty can then be built up from the interaction of a number of representational modules and interface modules. The tripartite architecture in figure 2.1 represents each module as a rule component.

An interface module, like a Fodorian module, is domain specific: the phonology-to-syntax interface module, for instance, knows only about phonology and syntax, not about visual perception or general-purpose audition. Such a module is also informationally encapsulated: the phonology-to-syntax module dumbly takes whatever phonological inputs are available in the phonology representation module, maps the appropriate parts of them into syntactic structures, and delivers them to the syntax representation module, with no help or interference from, say, beliefs about the social context. More generally, interface modules communicate information from one form of representation only to the next form up- or downstream. In short, the communication among languages of the mind, like the languages themselves, is mediated by modular processes.[16]

The language faculty is embedded in a larger system with the same overall architecture. Consider the phonological end of language. Phonetic information is not the only information derived from auditory perception. Rather, the speech signal seems to be delivered simultaneously to four or more independent interfaces: in addition to phonetic perception (the audition-to-phonology interface), it is used for voice recognition, affect (tone-of-voice) perception, and general-purpose auditory perception (birds, thunder, bells, etc.). Each of these processes converges on a different representational "language"—a different space of distinctions; and each is subject to independent dissociation in cases of brain damage. At the same time, phonological structure (of which phonetic representation is one

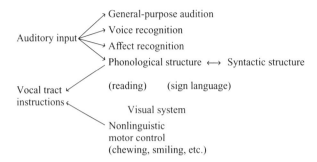

Figure 2.2
Some modules that interact with auditory input, vocal tract instructions, and phonology

aspect) takes inputs not only from the auditory interface, but also from a number of different interfaces with the visual system, including at least those involved in reading and sign language.[17] Moreover, phonological structure is not the only faculty feeding motor control of the vocal tract, since vocal tract musculature is also involved in eating, in facial expression, and in actions like grasping a pipe in the mouth. Figure 2.2 sketches these interactions; each arrow stands for an interface module.

There is some evidence for the same sorts of multiple interactions at the cognitive end of language as well. Consider the question of how we talk about what we see, posed by Macnamara (1978). Macnamara argues that the only possible answer is that the brain maps information from a visual/spatial format into the propositional format here called conceptual structure. Barbara Landau and I have elaborated Macnamara's position (Jackendoff 1987b, 1996a; Landau and Jackendoff 1993). We observe that certain types of conceptual information (such as the type-token distinction and type taxonomies) cannot be represented visually/spatially; conversely, certain types of visual/spatial information (such as details of shape) cannot be represented propositionally/linguistically. Consequently visual/spatial representation must be encoded in one or more modules distinct from conceptual structure, and the connection from vision to language must be mediated by one or more interface modules that establish a partial relation between visual and conceptual formats, parallel to the interfaces interior to the language faculty.

For the same reason, conceptual structure must be linked to all the other sensory modalities of which we can speak. In Jackendoff 1983 I hypothesize that conceptual structure is the link among multimodal

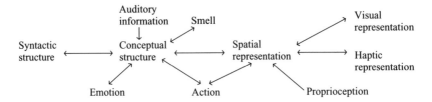

Figure 2.3
Some modules that interact with conceptual structure

perceptual representations, for example enabling us to identify the sound of a bell with its appearance. However (in contradiction to Jackendoff 1983), there is reason to believe that some multimodal information is integrated elsewhere in the system. For instance, the visual system is supposed to derive information about object shape and location from visual inputs. Landau and Gleitman (1985) make the obvious point that the haptic system (sense of touch) also can derive shape and location information; and we can be surprised if vision and touch fail to provide us with the expected correlation. Also, body senses such as proprioception can give us information about location of body parts; and an integrated picture of how one's body is located in the environment is used to guide actions such as reaching and navigation. Landau and I therefore suggest that the upper end of the visual system is not strictly visual, but is rather a multimodal *spatial representation* that integrates all information about shape and location (Landau and Jackendoff 1993). Figure 2.3 shows all this organization.[18]

Within the visual system itself, there is abundant evidence for similar organization, deriving more from neuropsychology than from a theory of visual information structure (though Marr (1982) offers a distinguished example of the latter). Numerous areas in the brain are now known to encode different sorts of visual information (such as shape, color, and location), and they communicate with each other through distinct pathways. For the most part there is no straight "derivation" from one visual level to another; rather, the information encoded by any one area is influenced by its interfaces with numerous others (see Crick 1994 for an accessible survey).

The idea behind the tripartite architecture emerged in my own thinking from research on musical grammar (Lerdahl and Jackendoff 1983; Jackendoff 1987a, chapter 11). In trying to write a grammar that accounted for the musical intuitions of an educated listener, Lerdahl and I found it

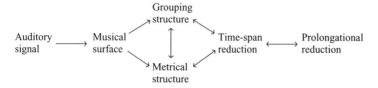

Figure 2.4
Modules of musical grammar

impossible to write an algorithm parallel to a transformational grammar that would generate all and only the possible pieces of tonal music with correct structures. For example, the rhythmic organization of music consists of a counterpoint between two independent structures, grouping structure and metrical structure, each of which has its own primitives and principles of combination. In the optimal case, the two structures are in phase with each other, so that grouping boundaries coincide with strong metrical beats. But music contains many situations, the simplest of which is an ordinary upbeat, in which the two structures are out of phase. Consequently, Lerdahl and I found it necessary to posit separate generative systems for these structures (as well as for two others) and to express the structural coherence of music in terms of the optimal fit of these structures to the musical surface (or sequence of notes) and to each other.[19] Figure 2.4 sketches the organization of the musical grammar in terms of representation and interface modules.

Following the approach of Representational Modularity, one can envision a theory of "gross mental anatomy" that enumerates the various "languages of the mind" and specifies which ones interface most directly with which others. Combining figures 2.1–2.4 results in a rough sketch of part of such a theory. A "fine-scale mental anatomy" then details the internal workings of individual "languages" and interfaces. Linguistic theory, for example, is a "fine-scale anatomy" of the language representation modules and the interface modules that connect them with each other and with other representations. Ideally, one would hope that "mental anatomy" and brain anatomy will someday prove to be in an interesting relationship.

Representational Modularity is by no means a "virtual conceptual necessity." It is a hypothesis about the overall architecture of the mind, to be verified in terms of not only the language faculty but other faculties as well.[20] I therefore do not wish to claim for it any degree of inevitability.

Nevertheless it appears to be a plausible way of looking at how the mind is put together, with preliminary support from many different quarters.

Returning to the issue with which this chapter began, the syntactocentric architecture of the Minimalist Program is envisioned within a view of language that leaves tacit the nature of interfaces and isolates language from the rest of the mind: recall Chomsky's remark that language might well be unique among biological systems. Here, by asking how interfaces work, we have arrived at an alternative architecture for grammar, the tripartite parallel model. This model proves to integrate nicely into a view of the architecture of the mind at large. I take this to be a virtue.

Chapter 3

More on the Syntax-Semantics Interface

3.1 Enriched Composition

Let us next focus further on the Conceptual Interface Level (CIL) of (narrow) syntax. As observed in chapter 2, GB identifies this level as Logical Form (LF). It is worth taking a moment to examine the basic conception of LF. According to one of the earliest works making detailed use of LF, May 1985, it is supposed to encode "whatever properties of syntactic form are relevant to semantic interpretation—those aspects of semantic structure that are expressed syntactically. Succinctly, the contribution of grammar to meaning" (May 1985, 2). This definition is essentially compatible with the definition of CIL: it is the level of syntax that encodes whatever syntactic distinctions are available to (or conversely, expressed by) conceptual distinctions.

Chomsky (1979, 145) says, "I use the expression *logical form* really in a manner different from its standard sense, in order to contrast it with *semantic representation*[,] ... to designate a level of linguistic representation incorporating all semantic properties that are strictly determined by linguistic rules." Chomsky emphasizes here that LF, unlike the underlying structures of Generative Semantics, is not supposed to encode *meaning* per se: other aspects of meaning are left to cognitive, nonlinguistic systems (such as conceptual structure). Crucially, LF does not purport to encode those aspects of meaning internal to lexical items. For example, although it does encode quantifier scope, it does not encode the lexical meaning differences among quantifiers such as *all* and *some*, or *three* and *four*. These differences appear only in conceptual structure.

In later statements Chomsky is less guarded: "PF and LF constitute the 'interface' between language and other cognitive systems, yielding direct representations of sound on the one hand and meaning on the other ..."

(Chomsky 1986, 68). Here LF seems to be identified directly with conceptual structure, and the differences between syntactic elements and truly conceptual elements (discussed here in section 2.3) have been elided. In fact, looking back to the earlier quotation, we find some signs of the same elision in the phrase "a level of linguistic representation incorporating ... semantic properties." If semantic properties are incorporated in a linguistic level, but if conceptual structure, the locus of semantic properties, is not a linguistic level, then in terms of what primitives are the semantic properties of LF to be encoded? Given that LF is supposed to be a *syntactic* level, the assumption has to be that some semantic properties are encoded in syntactic terms—in terms of configurations of NPs and VPs. However, this assumption cannot be strictly true, given that semantic properties do not involve configurations of NPs and VPs at all; rather, they involve whatever units conceptual structures are built out of. So in what sense can we understand Chomsky's statement?

It appears that Chomsky, along with many others in the field, is working under a standard (and usually unspoken) hypothesis that I will call *syntactically transparent semantic composition* (or *simple composition* for short).[1]

(1) *Syntactically transparent semantic composition*
   a. All elements of content in the meaning of a sentence are found in the lexical conceptual structures (LCSs) of the lexical items composing the sentence.
   b. The way the LCSs are combined is a function only of the way the lexical items are combined in syntactic structure (including argument structure). In particular,
      i. the internal structure of individual LCSs plays no role in determining how the LCSs are combined;
      ii. pragmatics plays no role in determining how LCSs are combined.

Under this set of assumptions, LCSs themselves have no effect on how they compose with each other; composition is guided entirely by syntactic structure. Hence one can conceive of syntactic structure as directly mirrored by a coarse semantic structure, one that idealizes away from the internal structure of LCSs. From the point of view of this coarse semantic structure, an LCS can be regarded as an opaque monad. One effect is that the SS-CS interface can be maximally simple, since there are no interactions in conceptual structure among syntactic, lexical, and pragmatic effects. Under such a conception, we can speak elliptically of syntax "incorporating semantic properties," meaning that syntax precisely mirrors coarse semantic configurations. I suggest that Chomsky's characterization of LF should be thought of as elliptical in precisely this way.

Note, incidentally, that most work in formal semantics shares Chomsky's assumptions on this issue. In particular, because lexical items are for the most part regarded as semantically undecomposable entities, there can be no interaction between their internal structure and phrasal composition. Moreover, the standard treatment of compositionality requires a disambiguated syntax; hence no aspects of a sentence's interpretation can arise from outside the sentence itself. (See Partee 1995 for a summary of these issues in formal semantics.)

The hypothesis of syntactically transparent semantic composition has the virtue of theoretical elegance and constraint. Its effect is to enable researchers to isolate the language capacity—including its contribution to semantics—from the rest of the mind, as befits a modular conception. It can therefore be seen as a potentially positive contribution to psychological theory.

However, it *is* only a hypothesis. This chapter will suggest that, whatever its a priori attractiveness, it cannot be sustained. Rather, a more appropriate hypothesis treats simple composition as a default in a wider range of options that I will call *enriched composition*. (Much of this hypothesis and many of the examples to follow are derived from Pustejovsky 1991a, 1995.)

(2) *Enriched composition*

    a. The conceptual structure of a sentence may contain, in addition to the conceptual content of its LCSs, other material that is not expressed lexically, but that must be present in conceptual structure either (i) in order to achieve well-formedness in the composition of the LCSs into conceptual structure (*coercion*, to use Pustejovsky's term) or (ii) in order to satisfy the pragmatics of the discourse or extralinguistic context.

    b. The way the LCSs are combined into conceptual structure is determined in part by the syntactic arrangement of the lexical items and in part by the internal structure of the LCSs themselves (Pustejovsky's *cocomposition*).

According to (2), the internal structure of LCSs is not opaque to the principles that compose LCSs into the meaning of the sentence; rather, composition proceeds through an interaction between syntactic structure and the meanings of the words themselves. If this is so, it is impossible to isolate a coarse semantic structure that idealizes away from the details of LCSs and that thus mirrors precisely the contribution of syntax to meaning. One therefore cannot construe LF as a syntactic level that essentially encodes semantic distinctions directly. Rather, the SS-CS interface is more complex: the effect of syntactic structure on conceptual structure interleaves intimately with the effects of word meanings and pragmatics.

A theory of enriched composition represents a dropping of constraints long entrenched in linguistic theory; syntactically transparent composition is clearly simpler. However, a more constrained theory is only as good as the empirical evidence for it. If elevated to the level of dogma (or reduced to the level of presupposition), so that no empirical evidence can be brought to bear on it, then it is not being treated scientifically. I am proposing here to treat it as a hypothesis like any other, and to see what other, possibly more valuable, generalizations will be lost if we insist on it.[2]

In sections 3.2–3.6 we will briefly look at several cases of enriched composition. Any one of them alone might be dismissed as a "problem case" to be put off for later. However, the number and variety of different cases that can be attested suggest a larger pattern inconsistent with syntactically transparent composition.

After looking at these cases, we will see how enriched composition bears on problems of binding and quantification. One of the important functions of LF—in fact the original reason it was introduced—is to encode quantifier scope relations. In addition, since the theory of quantifier scope includes the binding of variables by quantifiers, anaphoric binding in general also falls under the theory of LF. In sections 3.7 and 3.8 we will see that certain instances of anaphora and quantification depend on enriched composition, drawing on the internal structure of LCSs and even on semantic material not present in LCSs at all. This means that *the phenomena of binding and quantification that LF is supposed to account for cannot be described in their full generality by means of a syntactic level of representation; rather, they can only be most generally encoded at conceptual structure, a nonsyntactic level.* In turn, if the full range of relevant facts is to be encoded in conceptual structure, it misses a generalization to encode a subset of them in syntax as well, as the standard conception of LF does. The conclusion will be that it serves no purpose to complicate (narrow) syntax by including a syntactic level of LF distinct from S-Structure.

3.2 Aspectual Coercion

3.2.1 Verbal Coercions

A case of enriched composition that has been widely studied (see, e.g., Pustejovsky 1991b; Jackendoff 1991; Talmy 1978; Hinrichs 1985; Verkuyl 1993) concerns sentences like those in (3).

(3) a. The light flashed until dawn.
    b. Bill kept crossing the street.

(3a) carries a sense of repeated flashing not to be found in any of its lexical items. (One might propose that *flash* is vague with respect to whether or not it denotes a single flash; I would deny this, on the grounds that *The light flashed* does not seem vague on this point.) (3b) is ambiguous with respect to whether Bill crossed the street repeatedly or continued in his effort to cross once. This ambiguity does not appear to arise through any lexical ambiguity in the words of the sentence: *cross* is not ambiguous between crossing repeatedly and crossing partially, and, since *Bill kept sleeping* is not ambiguous, it seems odd to localize the ambiguity in *keep* or *-ing*. Rather, these readings arise through the interactions of the lexical meanings with each other.

In the analysis of (3a) offered by most authors cited above, *until* semantically sets a temporal bound on an ongoing process. However, *flash* does not itself denote an ongoing process. Therefore the sentence is interpreted so as to involve a *sequence* of flashes, which forms a suitable process for *until* to bound. The semantic content "sequence" is an *aspectual coercion*, added by a general principle that is capable of creating aspectual compatibility among the parts of a sentence.

(3b) presents a parallel story. The verb *keep* requires its argument to be an ongoing process; but *cross the street* is not an ongoing process, because it has a specified endpoint. There are two ways it can be reinterpreted as a process. The first is to construe it as repeated action, like (3a). The other is to conceptually "zoom in" on the action, so that the endpoint disappears from view—one sees only the ongoing process of Bill moving in the direction of the other side of the street. Such a process appears in the second reading of (3b); the sentence asserts that this process has continued over some period of time. Such a "zooming in" is a consequence of enriched composition, which makes the accomplishment *cross the street* aspectually compatible with *keep*.

Such aspectual coercions do not depend on particular lexical items. Rather, similar repetition with *until* appears with any point-action verb phrase, such as *slap Bill*, *clap*, or *cross the border*; and it is produced not just with *until*, but by other "bounding" phrases as well, for instance *in an hour*. The choice between repetition and partial completion occurs with any gerundive complement to *keep* that expresses an accomplishment, such as *walk to school* (but not *walk toward school*) or *eat an apple* (but not plain *eat*); and this choice appears not just in complements of *keep* but also with *stop, continue,* and *for an hour*.

As these examples show, the need for aspectual coercion can be determined only after the composition of the VP has taken place. It depends, for example, on whether there is a delimited object or completed path (*to*) that renders the entire VP a completed action; or alternatively, whether there is no object, an unbounded object (*eat custard*), or an incomplete path (*toward*) that renders the VP an atelic action. Hence the aspectual ambiguity after *keep* cannot be localized in lexical polysemy.

Aspectual coercions therefore are most generally treated as the introduction of an extra specialized function, interpolated in the course of semantic composition in order to ensure semantic well-formedness, along the lines of (4).

(4) a. *Repetition*
       Interpret VP as [REPETITION OF VP].
    b. *Accomplishment-to-process*
       Interpret VP as [PROCESSUAL SUBEVENT OF VP].

The idea behind (4) is as follows: when the reading of VP is composed with that of its context, the interpretation of VP alone is not inserted into the appropriate argument position of the context, as would occur in simple composition. Rather, VP is treated as the argument of the special functions REPETITION OF X or PROCESSUAL SUBEVENT OF X, and the result is inserted into the argument position of the context.

More schematically, simple composition would produce a function-argument structure F(X), where F is the function expressed by the syntactic head and X is the argument expressed by the syntactic complement. However, in cases such as (3), X does not serve as a suitable argument for F. Hence the process of composition interpolates a "coercing function" G to create instead the structure $F(G(X))$, where X is a suitable argument for G, and $G(X)$ is a suitable argument for F.

3.2.2 Mass-Count Coercions

Many sources point out a formal parallelism between the process-accomplishment distinction in sentences and the mass-count distinction in noun phrases. And of course, the idea of a sequence of events can be conveyed in noun phrases by pluralizing a noun that expresses an event, as in *many flashes of light*. Given such parallelisms, one might expect a counterpart of aspectual coercion in NPs, and indeed many are well known, for instance (5).

(5) a. I'll have a coffee/three coffees, please.
    b. We're having rabbit for dinner.

(5a) is a case where count syntax is attached to a normally mass noun, and the interpretation is inevitably 'portion(s) of coffee'. (5b) is a case where an animal name is used with mass syntax and understood to mean 'meat of animal'.

Although these coercions are often taken to be perfectly general principles (under the rubrics "Universal Packager" and "Universal Grinder" respectively), I suspect that they are somewhat specialized. For instance, the (5a) frame applies generally to food and drink, but it is hard to imagine applying it to specified portions of cement (*He poured three cements today*) or to the amount of water it takes to fill a radiator (*It takes more than three waters to fill that heating system*). That is, the coerced reading actually means something roughly as specific as 'portion of food or drink suitable for one person'.[3] Similarly, the coercion in (5b) can apply to novel animals (*We're having eland for dinner*), but it cannot easily apply to denote the substance out of which, say, vitamin pills are made (*There's some vitamin pill on the counter for you*). So it appears that, although these cases include as part of their meaning a mass-to-count or count-to-mass coercing function, one's knowledge of English goes beyond this to stipulate rather narrow selectional restrictions on when such coercion is possible and what it might mean. At the same time, the fact that the phenomenon is general within these rather narrow categories (for instance *eland*) suggests that lexical polysemy is not the right solution. Rather, these appear to be specialized coercions in which the source reference is mass and the shifted reference is count (5a) or vice versa (5b), but further content is present in the coercing function as well.

The general conclusion, therefore, is that the correspondence rules in the SS-CS interface permit conceptual structure to contain these specialized bits of content that are unexpressed in syntax. Like the verbal coercions in section 3.2.1, such a possibility violates condition (1a), the claim that semantic content is exhausted by the LCSs of the lexical items in the sentence. Rather, this condition must be replaced with condition (2a), the premise of enriched composition.

3.3 Reference Transfer Functions

A superficially different case of enriched interpretation turns out to share certain formal properties with the cases just discussed: the case of reference transfer, first made famous in the "counterpart" theory of McCawley and Lakoff (see Morgan 1971), then explored more systematically by others (see, e.g., Nunberg 1979; Fauconnier 1985; Jackendoff 1992b). The classic case is Nunberg's, in which one waitress says to another something like (6).

(6) The ham sandwich in the corner wants some more coffee.

The subject of (6) refers to a customer who has ordered or who is eating a ham sandwich. It would be absurd to claim that the lexical entry of *ham sandwich* is polysemous between a ham sandwich and a customer. The alternative is that the interpretation of (6) in context must involve a principle that Nunberg calls *reference transfer*, which allows one to interpret *ham sandwich* (the "source reading") to mean something roughly like 'person contextually associated with ham sandwich' (the "shifted reading").

An advocate of syntactically transparent composition will take one of two tacks on reference transfer: either (1) it is a rule of pragmatics and takes place "after" semantic composition; or (2) the subject of (6) contains some phonologically null syntactic elements that have the interpretation 'person contextually associated with'. In Jackendoff 1992b I argue that neither of these accounts will suffice.

Consider first the possibility that a reference transfer is "mere pragmatics." A principle similar to that involved in (6) is involved in (7). Imagine Richard Nixon has attended a performance of the opera *Nixon in China*, in which the character of Nixon was sung by James Maddalena.

(7) Nixon was horrified to watch himself sing a foolish aria to Chou En-lai.

Here, *himself* has a shifted reading: it refers not to Nixon himself but to the character onstage. That is, a reference transfer makes *Nixon* and the anaphor *himself* noncoreferential. On the other hand, such noncoreference is not always possible.

(8) *After singing his aria to Chou En-lai, Nixon was horrified to see himself get up and leave the opera house.

That is, the shifted reading cannot serve as antecedent for anaphora that refers to the real Nixon. No matter how one accounts for the contrast between (7) and (8), it cannot be determined until "after" the shifted reading is differentiated from the original reading. Thus, under the standard assumption that binding is a grammatical principle, the reference transfer cannot be relegated to "late principles of pragmatics"; it must be fully integrated into the composition of the sentence. In addition, looking ahead to the discussion of binding in section 3.7, we see that, if reference transfer is a matter of pragmatics, the contrast between (7) and (8) poses an insuperable problem for a syntactic account of binding.

Note, by the way, that I agree that reference transfer *is* a matter of pragmatics—that it is most commonly evoked when context demands a nonsimple reference (though see section 3.5.3). I am arguing, though, that it is nevertheless part of the principles of semantic composition for a sentence—in other words, that one cannot "do semantic composition first and pragmatics later."

However, one might claim that reference transfer has a syntactic reflex, thereby preserving syntactically transparent composition. For instance, *ham sandwich* in (6) and *himself* in (7) might have the syntactic structures (9a) and (9b) respectively under one possible theory and (10a) and (10b) under another. Such an account would have the virtue of making the distinction between (7) and (8) present in syntax as well as semantics, so that binding theory could be preserved in syntax.

(9) a. person with a [ham sandwich]
    b. person portraying [himself]

(10) a. [$_{NP}$ e [ham sandwich]]
     b. [$_{NP}$ e [himself]]

The trouble with the structures in (9) is that they are too explicit: one would need principles to delete specified nouns and relationships—principles of a sort that for 25 years have been agreed not to exist in generative grammar (not to mention that (9b) on the face of it has the wrong reading). So (9) can be rejected immediately. What of the second possibility, in which a null element in syntax is to be interpreted by general convention as having the requisite reading? The difficulty is that even a general convention relies on enriched composition: *e* has no interpretation of its own, so a special rule of composition must supply one. Moreover, as shown in Jackendoff 1992b, reference transfers are not homogeneous and general, so several special rules are necessary. Let us briefly review three cases here.

3.3.1 Pictures, Statues, and Actors
The use of *Nixon* to denote an actor portraying Nixon, or to denote the character in the opera representing Nixon, falls under a more general principle that applies also to pictures and statues.

(11) Look! There's King Ogpu hanging on the wall/standing on top of the parliament building.

But this principle does not apply to *stories* about people.

(12) Harry gave us a description/an account of Ringo. ≠ *Harry gave us Ringo.

Furthermore, the nouns *picture* and *sketch* can be used to denote either a physical object containing a visual representation or a brief description. Only on the former reading can they be the target of a reference transfer.

(13) a. Bill was doing charcoal sketches of the Beatles, and to my delight he gave me Ringo.
     b. *Bill was giving us quick (verbal) sketches of the new employees, and to my surprise he gave us Harry.

That is, the reference transfer responsible for (7) is not perfectly general; it occurs only with a semantically restricted class.

3.3.2 Cars and Other Vehicles
Another frequently cited reference transfer involves using one's name to denote one's car, as in (14a). (14b) shows that reflexivization is available for such shifted expressions. However, (14c–e) show that the shift is available only in describing an event during the time one is in control of the car.

(14) a. A truck hit Bill in the fender when he was momentarily distracted by a motorcycle.

b. Bill squeezed himself [i.e. the car he was driving] between two buses.

c. ? A truck hit Ringo in the fender while he was recording *Abbey Road*. (OK only if he drove to the studio!)

d. *A truck hit Bill in the fender two days after he died.

e. *Bill repainted himself [i.e. his car].

Moreover, this shift applies to cars and perhaps bicycles, but definitely not to horses.[4]

(15) Ringo suffered smashed spokes/handlebars/*hooves in the accident. (where it's Ringo's bike/horse)

Unlike the shifted referent in the statue/actor/picture case (16a), the shifted referent in the vehicle case cannot comfortably be the target of a discourse pronoun (16b).

(16) a. Hey, that's Ringo hanging over there [*pointing to portrait of Ringo*]! Isn't he/it beautifully painted!

b. Hey, that's Ringo parked over there [*pointing to Ringo's car*]! Isn't *he/??it beautifully painted!

3.3.3 Ham Sandwiches

The *ham sandwich* cases require as *source* of the transfer some salient property.

(17) The ham sandwich/The big hat/The foreign accent over there in the corner wants some more coffee.

But it cannot be something that independently would do as the subject of the sentence.

(18) #The blonde lady/The little dog over there in the corner wants a hamburger. (i.e. the man with the blonde lady/little dog)

Unlike in the previous two cases, there is no possibility of using a shifted pronoun or reflexive whose antecedent is the original referent.

(19) a. *I gave the ham sandwich to itself [i.e. to the person who ordered it].

b. *The ham sandwich pleased itself.

Nor can a pronoun or reflexive referring to the source have the shifted noun as antecedent.

(20) *The ham sandwich [i.e. the person who ordered it] put it(self) in his pocket.

In short, each of these reference transfers has its own peculiar properties. Evidently, a speaker of the language must have acquired something in order to use them properly and to have the intuitions evoked above. My sense therefore is that a speaker's knowledge includes a principle of enriched composition, along the lines of the specialized mass/count coercions in section 3.2.2. The three cases sketched here have roughly the forms in (21).

(21) a. Interpret an NP as [VISUAL REPRESENTATION OF NP].[5]
  b. Interpret an NP as [VEHICLE CONTROLLED BY NP].
  c. Interpret an NP as [PERSON CONTEXTUALLY ASSOCIATED WITH NP].

Notice the similarity of these principles to those in (4): they involve pasting a coercing function around an NP's simple compositional reading X to form an enriched reading G(X), in violation of the condition of exhaustive lexical content.

3.4 Argument Structure Alternations

Let us next consider two cases of argument structure alternations in which a theory of enriched composition offers the potential of better capturing generalizations.

3.4.1 Interpolated Function Specified by General Principle
Consider these argument structure alternations ((22) from Grimshaw 1979; see also Dor 1996; (23) from Jackendoff 1996c). The subscripts on the verbs discriminate between argument structure/subcategorization frames.

(22) a. Bill asked$_a$ who came/what happened.
  b. Bill asked$_b$ the time/her name.

(23) a. Bill intended$_a$ to come/to bring a cake.
  b. Bill intended$_b$ that Sue come/that Sue bring a cake.

A paraphrase reveals the semantic relationship between the frames.

(24) a. Bill asked$_b$ the time. = Bill asked$_a$ *what* the time *was*.
  b. Bill intended$_b$ that Sue come. = Bill intended$_a$ *to bring about* that Sue come. (or ... *to have* Sue come)

These alternations can easily be treated as lexical polysemy. However, consider *ask*. Grimshaw (1979) observes that whenever a verb takes an indirect question complement in alternation with a direct object (e.g. *tell*, *know*), it also permits certain direct objects to be interpreted in the manner shown in (24a), as part of an elliptical indirect question *what NP is/ was*. The NPs that can be so interpreted are limited to a class including such phrases as *the time, the outcome, NP's name, NP's height*. Most NPs are not subject to such an interpretation: *ask a question* ≠ *ask what a question is*; *tell the story* ≠ *tell what the story is*; *know his wife* ≠ *know who his wife is*; and so on.

As Grimshaw observes, this distribution suggests that the (b)-type interpretation is not a lexical property of *ask*, but rather follows from the fact that *ask* takes an indirect question complement alternating with a direct object, plus a general principle of interpretation, which applies to all verbs like *ask*, *tell*, and *know*.

A similar result obtains with *intend*, which alternates between a controlled VP complement denoting a volitional action (23a) and a *that*-subjunctive complement (23b). Verbs with the same syntactic alternation and the same interpretation of the complement as a volitional action show the same relationship between the readings.

(25) Bill agreed/arranged that Sue bring a cake. = Bill agreed/arranged *to have/bring about that* Sue bring a cake.

This interpretation however does not appear with verbs such as *prefer* and *desire*, which satisfy the same syntactic conditions as *intend*, but whose VP complements need not denote volitional actions. Again, it would be possible to treat these alternations as lexical polysemy. However, the character of the alternation suggests a more general principle of interpretation that supplies the interpolated content italicized in (24b) and (25).

I wish to argue, therefore, that *ask* and *intend* (as well as the families of verbs to which they belong) are not lexically polysemous; rather, the readings in the (b) frames are in part the product of special SS-CS correspondence rules, stated informally in (26).

(26) a. Interpret an NP such as *the time, the outcome, NP's name*, as
        [Indirect question WHAT NP BE].[6]
     b. Interpret *that* [s ... subjunctive ...] as
        [Voluntary action BRING ABOUT THAT S].

Just in case a verb takes an NP syntactically and an indirect question semantically, (26a) allows the NP to be interpreted as an indirect question and thereby to satisfy the verb's indirect question argument. Similarly, just in case a verb takes a *that*-subjunctive syntactically and a voluntary action semantically, (26b) allows the *that*-subjunctive to satisfy the voluntary action argument.

This solution reduces lexical polysemy: the (b) frames are no longer lexically specialized readings. The price is the specialized correspondence rules—rules that go beyond syntactically transparent composition to allow implicit interpolated functions. Notice again that the effect of these special rules is to paste a coercing function around the reading of the complement, in this case to make it conceptually compatible with the argument structure of the verb (i.e. to make the resulting composition well formed). Again we are faced with a violation of the condition of exhaustive lexical content, (1a).

3.4.2 Interpolated Function Specified by Qualia of Complement
Another type of argument structure alternation, discussed by Pustejovsky (1991a, 1995) and Briscoe et al. (1990), appears with verbs such as *begin* and *enjoy*.

(27) a. Mary began$_a$ to drink the beer.
     b. Mary began$_b$ the beer.

(28) a. Mary enjoyed$_a$ reading the novel.
     b. Mary enjoyed$_b$ the novel.

As in the previous cases, it is possible to find a paraphrase relationship between the two frames. However, there is a crucial difference. In the previous cases, the appropriate material to interpolate in the (b) frame was a constant, independent of the choice of complement. In these cases, though, the choice of appropriate material to interpolate varies wildly with the choice of complement.

(29) a. Mary began$_b$ the novel. = Mary began$_a$ to read/to write/*to drink/*to appreciate the novel.
     b. Mary began$_b$ the beer. = Mary began$_a$ to drink/?to bottle/*to read/*to appreciate the beer.
     c. Mary enjoyed$_b$ the novel. = Mary enjoyed$_a$ reading/writing/ *drinking/*appreciating the novel.
     d. Mary enjoyed$_b$ the beer. = Mary enjoyed$_a$ drinking/??bottling/ *reading/*appreciating the beer.

A general solution to these alternations, then, cannot invoke lexical polysemy: each verb would have to have indefinitely many different readings. Rather, the generalization is as follows: these verbs select semantically for an activity. When their complement directly expresses an activity (i.e. the (a) frame or an NP such as *the dance*), simple composition suffices. However, if the complement does not express an activity (e.g. *the novel*), then two steps take place. First, a rule not unlike those in (4), (21), and (26) interpolates a general function that permits the NP to satisfy the activity variable of the verb.

(30) Interpret NP as [$_{\text{Activity}}$ F (NP)]. (i.e. an unspecified activity involving NP, "doing something with NP")

However, (30) leaves open what the activity in question is.

Pustejovsky (1991a, 1995) claims that the second step of interpretation specifies the activity by examining the internal semantic structure of the complement. He posits that part of the LCS of a noun naming an object is a complex called its *qualia structure*, a repertoire of specifications including the object's appearance, how it comes into being, how it is used, and others. For example, the qualia of *book* include its physical form, including its parts (pages, covers, spine); its role as an information-bearing object; something about its (normally) being printed; something specifying that its proper function is for people to read it. Within its role as an information-bearing object, there will be further specification of how the information comes into being, including the role of author as creator.

The acceptable interpolated predicates in (29) stipulate either a characteristic activity one performs with an object or the activity one performs in creating these objects. Hence the desired activity predicates can be found in the qualia structures of the direct objects. However, this requires violating condition (1b), the idea that the content of an LCS plays no role in how it combines with other items. Rather, we must accept condition (2b): the conceptual function of which the direct object of *begin* or *enjoy* is an argument is determined by looking *inside* the semantic content of the object. Only the general *kind* of function (here, activity) is determined by the verb *begin* or *enjoy* itself. This is a case of what Pustejovsky calls *cocomposition*.[7] This approach systematically eliminates another class of lexical polysemies, this time a class that would be impossible to specify completely.

It might be claimed that qualia structure is really "world knowledge" and does not belong in linguistic theory. To be sure, the fact that books are read *is* part of one's "world knowledge." But it is also surely part of one's knowledge of *English* that one can use the sentence *Mary began the novel* to express the proposition that Mary began to read the novel. To me, examples like this show that world knowledge necessarily interacts with the SS-CS correspondence rules to some degree: the correspondence rules permit certain aspects of a proposition to be systematically elided if reconstructible from the context—which includes world knowledge encoded within an LCS.

3.5   Adjective-Noun Modification

3.5.1   Adjectives That Invoke the Qualia Structure of the Noun

The modification of nouns by adjectives is usually considered to be formally a predicate conjunction; a *red house* is something that is a house and that is red. Pustejovsky (1991a, 1995) demonstrates a wide range of cases (some previously well known) where such an analysis fails. (31)–(33) present some examples.

(31) a. a fast typist = someone who types fast
        ≠ someone who is a typist and who is fast
     b. a fast car = a car that travels fast
        ? = something that is a car and that is fast
     c. a fast road = a road on which one travels fast
        ≠ something that is a road and that is fast

(32) a. a sad woman = a woman experiencing sadness
        ? = someone who is a woman and who is sad
     b. a sad event = an event that makes its participants experience sadness
        ? = something that is an event and that is sad
     c. a sad movie = a movie that makes its viewers experience sadness
        ? = something that is a movie and that is sad

(33) a. a good knife = a knife that is good for cutting
        ≠ something that is a knife and that is good
     b. a good road = a road that is good for traveling on
        ≠ something that is a road and that is good
     c. a good typist = someone who is good at typing
        ≠ someone who is a typist and who is good

In each case, the (likely) meaning of the adjective-noun combination is richer than a simple conjunction of the adjective and noun as predicates. It would miss the point to respond by proposing that the adjectives are multiply polysemous, for then they would need different readings for practically every noun they modify. A better solution is to make the adjectives closer to monosemous, but to adopt a richer notion of adjective-noun modification. For example, suppose *fast* simply pertains to the rate of a process (relative to some standard for that process). If it modifies a noun that denotes a process, such as *waltz*, then it can be composed with it by simple composition. But as it stands, it cannot pertain to a typist (a person, not a process) or a road (an object, not a process). The principles of composition must therefore find a process for *fast* to modify, and they will look for such a process within the qualia structure of the host noun. The qualia structure of *typist* specifies most prominently that such a person types; hence this is the most prominent activity to which *fast* can pertain. Similarly, the qualia structure of *road* specifies that it is an object over which one travels; thus traveling becomes the activity to which *fast* pertains.

Similarly, *sad* pertains to a person's emotional experience. It therefore can modify *woman* by simple composition, but not *event* or *movie*. Rather, it must pertain to the emotional experience of characters found in the qualia structure of *event* and *movie*, as reflected in the paraphrases in (32). *Good* evaluates an object in its capacity to serve some function; in the absence of a specified function (e.g. *This is a good knife for throwing*), the default function is chosen from the specification of proper function in the qualia structure of the noun. (Katz (1966) analyzes (33) similarly, without drawing the general conclusion about adjective modification pursued here.)

This use of qualia structure differs from that in section 3.4.2. There, a characteristic activity was copied from qualia structure to serve as a coercion function in argument structure; one *enjoys reading the book*, for instance. In this case, an element of qualia structure is instead used as host for the content of the adjective. The fact that similar elements of the noun emerge in both cases, for instance characteristic activities, suggests that qualia structure has an independently motivated existence.

One can imagine two alternatives to admitting enriched composition in these examples. As mentioned above, one would be to claim that each of these adjectives is polysemous. The difficulty with this (as pointed out by Katz (1966)) is that an adjective such as *good* would need as many different readings as there are functions for objects. The other alternative would be simply to deny the phenomenon, to claim that a *fast road* simply is 'a road that is fast', and to further claim that the speed is attributed to travel on the road as a matter of pragmatics—"world knowledge of roads" or the like. I take the latter position to be an assertion that pragmatics is unconstrained and autonomous from linguistic semantics. Yet the fact that similar bits of "world knowledge" play various roles in understanding various constructions suggests that something systematic and constrained is going on. I wish the theory of conceptual structure and of conceptual composition to be able to characterize this systematicity instead of ignoring it.

3.5.2 Adjectives That Semantically Subordinate The Nouns

As seen in (34), a well-known class of adjectives fails altogether to make sense in paraphrases of the sort in (31)–(33). More appropriate paraphrases look like those in (35).[8]

(34) a. a fake gun ≠ something that is a gun and that is fake
     b. an alleged killer ≠ someone who is a killer and who is alleged
     c. a toy horse ≠ something that is a horse and that is a toy

(35) a. a fake gun = something that is intended to make people think it is a gun
     b. an alleged killer = someone who is alleged to be a killer
     c. a toy horse = something whose function in play is to simulate a horse

The details of the paraphrases in (35) are not crucial. What is important is that the noun does not appear in the usual frame 'something that is an N and ...', but rather inside a clause whose content is determined by the adjective (e.g. *fake* N = 'something that is intended to make people think it is N'). Thus these adjectives compose with nouns in an unusual way: syntactically they are adjuncts, but semantically they are heads, and the N functions as an argument. In other words, we have two quite different principles of composition for the very same syntactic configuration.

When faced with two distinct ways of composing A-N combinations, someone who advocates (or, more often, presupposes) simple composition will conclude that two distinct syntactic structures give rise to these interpretations. In particular, one might want to claim that in the latter form of composition, the adjective is actually the syntactic head as well. However, I see no evidence internal to syntax to substantiate such a claim: it is driven only by the assumption that transparent composition of the purest sort is the only possible realization of the syntax-semantics relationship. In the present approach, the choice of means of combination is driven by the LCS of the adjective: if it is a normal attributive adjective, it will integrate with the qualia structure of the noun; if it is a *fake*-type adjective, it will take the noun as an argument. Such LCS-driven choice is in line with hypothesis (2b).

Interestingly, the adjective *good* is polysemous (as are other evaluative adjectives such as *excellent, terrific, lousy*). One reading, shown in (33), was already discussed in section 3.5.1. However, as pointed out by Aronoff (1980), another reading emerges in sentences like *This stump makes a good chair*. The presupposition is that the stump is not a chair, but it is being used as one. That is, *makes a good N* means something like 'adequately fulfills the normal function of an N (even though it isn't one)'. This form of composition thus parallels the *fake*-type adjectives. Notice that the criteria placed on a good knife that *is* a knife (composition as in (33)) are considerably more stringent than those on a screwdriver that *makes* a good knife—and a knife can't *make* a good knife. This shows that the two readings are distinct, though related. (The verb *makes*, although it forces this reading, is not necessary: *This stump is a good chair* is perfectly acceptable as well.)

Notice that this type of composition also invokes the qualia structure of the noun. The qualities that the stump has that make it a good chair depend on the proper function of *chair*. Hence, as in the other reading of *good*, the proper function of the noun must be pulled out of its qualia structure.

3.5.3 Modification That Coerces the Reading of the Head Noun
Consider modification by the adjective *wooden*. If applied to some physical object X, it undergoes simple composition to create a reading 'X made of wood' (*wooden spoon* = 'spoon made of wood'). However, suppose we have a combination like *wooden turtle*. Turtles are not made of wood, they are made of flesh and blood. So simple composition of this phrase yields an anomaly, just like, say, **wooden chalk*. However, *wooden turtle* turns out to be acceptable because we understand *turtle* to denote not a real turtle but a statue or replica of a turtle. Notice that *wooden* itself does not provide the information that the object is a statue or replica; otherwise *wooden spoon* would have the same interpretation, which of course it does not. And **wooden chalk* is bad presumably because we don't normally conjure up the idea of models of pieces of chalk. (Perhaps in the context of a dollhouse it would be appropriate.)[9]

The possibility of understanding *turtle* to mean 'replica of a turtle', of course, is now not just a matter of "convention" or pragmatics; rather, it is provided explicitly by the reference transfer function (21a). (21a) was proposed as a principle to make linguistic expression compatible with contextual understanding, including nonlinguistic context. However, here it is invoked to provide a well-formed interpretation of an otherwise anomalous phrase. Moreover, the extra material provided by (21a) provides the host for modification by the adjective, so it cannot be "added later," "after" simple composition takes place. This coercion of the reading of the head noun is yet another example where a theory of enriched interpretation is necessary, where not all semantic information in an interpretation comes from the LCSs of the constituent words.

3.6 Summary

We have surveyed a considerable number of situations that appear to call for enriched principles of composition. Others will emerge in sections 7.7 and 7.8. Across these situations a number of commonalities emerge, summarized in table 3.1.

Table 3.1
Summary of instances of enriched composition

	a	b	c	d
Aspectual coercions	x			x
Mass-count coercions	x			x
Pictures	x		x	x
Cars	x		x	x
Ham sandwiches	x		x	x
Ask-/intend-type alternations	x			x
Begin-/enjoy-type alternations		x		x
Fast		x		
Fake		x		
Wooden	x			x

a = Not all semantic information comes from lexical entries
b = Composition guided by internal structure of LCSs
c = Pragmatics invoked in composition
d = Composition involves adding interpolated coercion function

Questions raised by these cases include:

1. What is the overall typology of rules of enriched composition? Can they insert arbitrary material in arbitrary arrangements, or are there constraints? Do the similarities among many of these cases suggest the flavor of tentative constraints?
2. Are these rules subject to linguistic variation?
3. In the discussion above, I have frequently used paraphrase relations to argue for enriched composition. How valid is this methodology in general? To what extent can a paraphrase employing simple composition reliably reveal material concealed by enriched composition?
4. In designing a logical language, it would be bizarre to sprinkle it so liberally with special-purpose devices. What is it about the design of natural language that allows us to leave so many idiosyncratic bits of structure unexpressed, using, as it were, conventionalized abbreviations?

Keeping in mind the pervasive nature of enriched composition and its implications for the complexity of the SS-CS interface, let us now turn to the two major phenomena for which LF is supposed to be responsible: binding and quantification.

3.7 Anaphora

This section will briefly consider several cases where the criteria for binding cannot be expressed in syntactic structure. However, they can be expressed in conceptual structure, either because of the internal structure of LCSs, or because of material supplied by principles of enriched composition, or because of other semantic distinctions that cannot be reduced to syntactic distinctions. Thus, I will claim, binding is fundamentally a relation between conceptual constituents, not between syntactic constituents.

What does this claim mean? The idea is that the traditional notation for binding, (36a), is not the correct formalization. Rather, (36a) should be regarded as an abbreviation for the three-part relation (36b).

(37) a. NP_i binds $[NP, anaphor]_i$

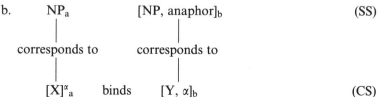

b. $\quad NP_a \qquad\qquad [NP, anaphor]_b \qquad\qquad$ (SS)

$\qquad$ corresponds to $\quad$ corresponds to

$\qquad [X]^\alpha_a \quad$ binds $\quad [Y, \alpha]_b \qquad\qquad$ (CS)

That is, the antecedent NP expresses a conceptual structure X, the anaphor NP expresses a conceptual structure Y, and the actual binding relation obtains between X and Y. The binding is notated by the Greek letters: a superscripted Greek letter indicates a binder, and the corresponding Greek letter within brackets indicates a bindee.

Under this conception of binding, what should the counterpart of GB binding theory look like? If the relation between syntactic anaphors and their antecedents is mediated by both syntax and conceptual structure, as shown in (36b), we might expect a "mixed" binding theory that involves conditions over both structures. More specifically, when the anaphor and the antecedent are syntactically explicit (as in standard binding examples), we might expect both syntactic and conceptual conditions to be invoked. On the other hand, (36b) presents the possibility of anaphoric relations that are not expressed directly in the syntax, but only implicitly, in the meaning of the sentence. Under such conditions, we might expect only conceptual structure conditions to apply. It is conceivable that *all* apparent syntactic conditions on binding can be replaced by conceptual structure conditions (as advocated by Kuno (1987) and Van Hoek (1995), among others), but I will not explore this stronger hypothesis here.

In order to show that (36b) rather than (36a) is the proper way to conceive of binding, then, it is necessary to find cases in which syntactic mechanisms are insufficient to characterize the relation between anaphors and their antecedents. Here are some.

3.7.1 Binding Inside Lexical Items
What distinguishes the verb *buy* from the verb *obtain*? Although there is no noticeable syntactic difference, *X buys Y from Z* carries an inference not shared by *X obtains Y from Z*, namely that X pays money to Z. This difference has to come from the LCS of the verb: whereas the LCS of both verbs contains the information in (37a), *buy* also contains (37b), plus further information that does not concern us here. (The argument does not depend on formalism, so I characterize this information totally informally.)

(37) a. Y changes possession from Z to X
     b. money changes possession from X to Z

Thus the LCS of *buy* has to assign two distinct semantic roles (θ-roles) to the subject and to the object of *from*.

Notice that these θ-roles are present, implicitly, even when the relevant argument is not expressed syntactically, as in (38).

(38) a. X bought Y.

  b. Y was bought from Z.

In (38a) we still understand that there is someone (or something such as a vending machine) from whom Y was obtained, and that this person received money from X; in (38b) we still understand that there is someone who obtained Y, and that this person gave money to Z. One could potentially say that (38a) has a null PP whose object receives these θ-roles, but accounting syntactically for the absence of *from* proves tricky. Similarly, one could potentially say that (38b) has a null underlying subject, but it is now widely accepted that passives do not have underlying syntactic subjects. So there are technical difficulties associated with claiming that such "understood" or "implicit" θ-roles are expressed by null arguments in syntax (see Jackendoff 1993b for more detailed discussion of Emonds's (1991) version of this claim).

This leaves us with the problem of how implicit characters are understood as having multiple θ-roles. In Jackendoff 1990 I proposed that the LCS of *buy* encodes the subevents in the way shown in (39). (I omit the larger relation that unifies these subevents into a transaction rather than just two random transfers of possession.)

(39) Y changes possession from Z^α to X^β

  money changes possession from β to α

The Greek letters in the second line function as variables, bound to the superscripts in the first line. Consequently, whoever turns over Y receives money, and whoever turns over money receives Y—regardless of whether these characters are mentioned in syntax.

Such binding of variables in LCS has precisely the effects desired for standard bound anaphora. For example, *Bill bought a book from each student* has the reading 'For each student x, a book changed possession from x to Bill and money changed possession from Bill to x'. The problem is that the two occurrences of the variable x are inside the LCS of *buy* and never appear as separate syntactic constituents. Thus there is no way to express their binding at LF, the syntactic level at which binding relations are supposed to be made explicit. LF thus misses an important semantic generalization about bound anaphora. On the other hand, at the level of conceptual structure, these bound variables are explicit, and their relation looks just like the conceptual structure associated with bound anaphora—a necessary coreference between two characters with different θ-roles. Hence conceptual structure, the lower level of (36b), is the proper level at which to encode the properties of bound anaphora most generally.

3.7.2   Control Determined by LCS

One of the earliest cited types of evidence that enriched composition is involved in binding concerns the control of complement subjects, obviously a case that falls within the general account of binding. In Jackendoff 1972, 1974 I presented evidence that many cases of complement subject control are governed by the thematic roles of the verb that takes the complement—where thematic roles are argued to be structural positions in the verb's LCS. Similar arguments have since been adduced by Cattell (1984), Williams (1985), Chierchia (1988), Farkas (1988), and Sag and Pollard (1991).

The original arguments turn on examples like these (where I use traditional subscripting to indicate coreference):

(40) a. John$_i$ got [PRO$_i$ to leave].
     b. Bill got John$_i$ [PRO$_i$ to leave].

(41) a. John$_i$ promised [PRO$_i$ to leave].
     b. John$_i$ promised Bill [PRO$_i$ to leave].

When *get* switches from intransitive to transitive, control switches from object to subject; but when *promise* switches from intransitive to transitive, control does not shift. In Jackendoff 1972 I observed that the switch in control with *get* parallels the switch in the Recipient role in (42), whereas the lack of switch with *promise* parallels that with a verb such as *sell*.

(42) a. John got a book.   (John is Recipient)
     b. Bill got John a book.   (John is Recipient)

(43) a. John sold a book.   (John is Source)
     b. John sold Bill a book.   (John is Source)

The proposal therefore is that the controller of *get* is identified with its Goal role, which switches position depending on transitivity; the controller of *promise* is identified with its Source role, which does not switch position. (The subject is also Agent, of course. I choose Source as the determining role for reasons to emerge in a moment.)

Verbs that behave like *promise* are rare in English, including *vow* and a couple of others. However, in nominalized form there are some more that have not been previously pointed out in the literature.

(44) a. John$_i$'s promise/vow/offer/guarantee/obligation to Bill [PRO$_i$ to leave]
     b. John$_i$'s agreement/contract with Bill [PRO$_i$ to leave]

Other than *promise* and *vow*, these nominals do not correspond to verbs that have a transitive syntactic frame, so they have not been recognized as posing the same problem. In contrast, note that in the syntactically identical (45), control goes with the object of *to*, the thematic Goal.

(45) John's order/instructions/encouragement/reminder to Bill$_i$ [PRO$_i$ to leave]

The need for thematic control is made more evident by the use of these nominals with light verbs.[10]

(46) a. John$_i$ gave Bill a promise [PRO$_i$ to leave].
     b. John got from Bill$_i$ a promise [PRO$_i$ to leave].
     c. John gave Bill$_i$ an order [PRO$_i$ to leave].
     d. John$_i$ got from Bill an order [PRO$_i$ to leave].

Here control switches if either the light verb or the nominal is changed. The principle involved matches thematic roles between light verb and nominal. In (46a) the subject of *give* is Source; therefore the Source of the promise is the subject of *give*. Since the Source of *promise* controls the complement subject, the controller is *John*. If the light verb is changed to *get*, whose Source is in the object of *from*, control changes accordingly, as in (46b). If instead the nominal is changed to *order*, whose Goal is controller, then control switches over to the Goal of the verb: the indirect object of *give* (46c) and the subject of *get* (46d).

There are exceptions to the thematic generalization with *promise*, the best-known of which is (47).

(47) Bill$_i$ was promised [PRO$_i$ to be allowed to leave].

Here control goes with the Goal of *promise*. However, this case takes us only deeper into enriched composition, since it occurs only with a passive complement in which the controller receives permission or the like.

(48) Bill$_i$ was promised [PRO$_i$ $\left\{ \begin{array}{l} \text{to be permitted to leave} \\ \text{*to permit Harry to leave} \\ \text{*to get permission to leave} \\ \text{*to leave the room} \\ \text{*to be hit on the head} \end{array} \right\}$].

In other words, control cannot be determined without first composing the relevant conceptual structure of the complement, which cannot be localized in a single lexical item or structural position.

More complex cases along similar lines arise with verbs such as *ask* and *beg*.

(49) a. Bill asked/begged Harry$_i$ [PRO$_i$ to leave].
     b. Bill$_i$ asked/begged Harry [PRO$_i$ to be permitted to leave].

One might first guess that the difference in control has to do simply with the change from active to passive in the subordinate clause. But the facts are more complex. Here are two further examples with passive subordinate clauses, syntactically parallel to (49b):

(50) a. Bill asked Harry$_i$ [PRO$_i$ to be examined by the doctor].
     b. *Bill$_i$ asked Harry$_j$ [PRO$_{i/j}$ to be forced to leave].

In (50a) PRO proves to be *Harry*, not *Bill*; (50b) proves to be ungrammatical, on grounds that seem to be rooted in the semantics of the complement clause. It appears, then, that the interpretation of PRO is a complex function of the semantics of the main verb and the subordinate clause.

It so happens that all the verbs and nominals cited in this subsection have a semantic requirement that their complements denote a volitional action, much like the *intend*-type verbs cited in section 3.4.1. It is therefore interesting to speculate that part of the solution to the switches of control in (47)–(50) is that a rule of coercion is operating in the interpretation of these clauses, parallel to rule (26b). For example, (47) has an approximate paraphrase, 'Someone promised Bill to *bring it about that* Bill would be allowed to leave', and a similar paraphrase is possible for (49b). These being the two cases in which control is not as it should be, it may be that a more general solution is revealed more clearly once the presence of the coerced material is acknowledged. (This is essentially the spirit of Sag and Pollard's (1991) solution.)

In short, control theory, which is part of binding theory, cannot be stated without access to the interior structure of lexical entries and to the composed conceptual structure of subordinate clauses, possibly even including material contributed by coercion. Under the assumption of syntactic binding theory (at S-Structure or LF) and the hypothesis of syntactically transparent semantic composition, this is impossible. A proper solution requires a binding theory of the general form (36b), where LCSs are available to binding conditions, and a theory of enriched composition, where not all semantic information is reflected in syntactic structure.

3.7.3 Ringo Sentences

Section 3.3 has already alluded to a class of examples involving the interaction of binding with reference transfer. Here is another example.

Suppose I am walking through the wax museum with Ringo Starr, and we come to the statues of the Beatles, and to my surprise,

(51) Ringo starts undressing himself.

This has a possible reading in which Ringo is undressing the statue. In other words, under special circumstances, binding theory can apply even to noncoreferential NPs.

However, as observed above, there is an interesting constraint on this use. Suppose Ringo stumbles and falls on one of the statues, in fact

(52) Ringo falls on himself.

The intended reading of (52) is perhaps a little hard to get, and some speakers reject it altogether. But suppose instead that *I* stumble and bump against a couple of the statues, knocking them over, so that John falls on the floor and

(53) *Ringo falls on himself.

This way of arranging binding is totally impossible—far worse than in (52). But the two are syntactically and even phonologically identical. How do we account for the difference?

In Jackendoff 1992b I construct an extended argument to show that there is no reasonable way to create a syntactic difference between (52) and (53), either at S-Structure or at LF. In particular, severe syntactic difficulties arise if one supposes that the interpretation of *Ringo* that denotes his statue has the syntactic structure [NP *statue of* [Ringo]] or even [NP *e* [Ringo]]. Rather, the difference relevant to binding appears only at the level of conceptual structure, where the reference transfer for naming statues has inserted the semantic material that differentiates them. In other words, certain aspects of the binding conditions must be stated over conceptual structure (the lower relation in (36b)), not syntactic structure; binding depends on enriched composition.

As it happens, though, the difference in conceptual structure between (52) and (53) proves to be identical to that between (54a) and (54b). (55a,b) show the two forms.

(54) a.   Ringo fell on the statue of himself.
     b. *The statue of Ringo fell on himself.

(55) a.   [FALL ([RINGO]$^\alpha$, [ON [VISUAL-REPRESENTATION [α]]])]
     b.   [FALL ([VISUAL-REPRESENTATION [RINGO]$^\alpha$], [ON [α]])]

The syntactic difference between (52)–(53) and (54) is that in the latter case, the function VISUAL-REPRESENTATION is expressed by the word *statue*, whereas in the former case it arises through a reference transfer coercion.

Given that both pairs have (in relevant respects) the same conceptual structure, the conceptual structure binding condition that differentiates (52) and (53) (one version of which is proposed in Jackendoff 1992b) can also predict the difference between these. However, in standard accounts, (54a) and (54b) are differentiated by syntactic binding conditions. Clearly a generalization is being missed: two sets of conditions are accounting for the same phenomenon. Because the syntactic conditions cannot generalize to (52)–(53), they are the ones that must be eliminated. In short, LF, the level over which binding conditions are to be stated, is not doing the work it is supposed to.

To the extent that there *are* syntactic conditions on anaphora, in the proposed approach they are stated as part of the correspondence rules that map anaphoric morphemes into conceptual structure variables. That is, syntactic conditions on binding appear in rules of the form (56).

(56) If NP$_1$ maps into conceptual structure constituent X$^\alpha$, then
     [NP$_2$, +anaphor] can map into conceptual structure constituent [α]
     (i.e. NP$_1$ can bind NP$_2$) only if the following conditions obtain:
     a.   Conditions on syntactic relation of NP$_1$ and NP$_2$: . . .
     b.   Conditions on structural relation of X$^\alpha$ and α in conceptual
          structure: . . .

In other words, syntactic conditions on binding are not altogether excluded; it is just that they are part of the interface component rather than the syntax.

3.7.4 Bound Pronouns in Sloppy Identity

The next case, presented more fully in Culicover and Jackendoff 1995, concerns the binding of pronouns in "sloppy identity" contexts. Consider (57).

(57) John took his kids to dinner, but
    a. Bill didn't.
    b. Bill would never do so.
    c. nobody else did.
    d. nobody else would ever do so.

These are all subject to the well-known strict versus sloppy identity ambiguity, whereby (57a), for example, can be interpreted as either 'Bill didn't take John's kids to dinner' or 'Bill didn't take his own kids to dinner'. In order to account for this difference, the interpretation of the null VP must contain some variable or pointer that can be bound either to *John* or to *Bill*. Moreover, this variable behaves like a bound variable, in that it is bound in the standard way by the quantifier *nobody else* in (57c,d). That much is "conceptually necessary."

The question is at what level of representation this binding is represented. It is not at the phonological interface level, since the relevant pronouns are not present in the overt utterance. Usually (e.g. Fiengo and May 1994) some process of "reconstruction" is suggested, whereby the null VP in (57a,c) and *do so* in (57b,d) are replaced by *take his kids to dinner* at LF. Then *his* is bound by normal mechanisms of binding.

Chomsky (1993) suggests instead that there is no reconstruction. Rather, the null VP in (57a), for instance, is to be produced by a deletion of unstressed *take his kids to dinner* in the PF component (i.e. in the course of Spell-Out), but this phrase is present throughout the rest of the derivation. However, Chomsky's proposal does not address how to deal with the replacement of *take his kids to dinner* by *do so* (or other VP anaphors like *do it* and *do likewise*). Thus the invocation of the PF component here is ill advised, and we can discard it immediately.

The problem with the reconstruction solution has to do with how the grammar in general determines the antecedent of "reconstruction." Consider sentences such as (58a–c), a type discussed by Akmajian (1973).

(58) a. John patted the dog, but Sam did it to the cat.
    b. Mary put the food in the fridge, then Susan did the same thing with the beer.
    c. John kissed Mary, and then it happened to Sue too.

There is no ready syntactic expression of the ellipted material. (59) presents some possibilities, all miserable failures.

(59) a. *John patted the dog, but Sam patted (the dog/it) to the cat.
   b. Mary put the food in the fridge, then Susan put the food/it in the fridge with the beer. (wrong meaning)
   c. *John kissed Mary, and then John kissed (Mary/her) happened to Sue too.

Akmajian shows that the interpretation of such examples depends on extracting contrasting foci (and *paired* contrasting foci such as *John/the dog* and *Sam/the cat* in (58a)), then reconstructing the ellipted material from the presupposition of the first clause (in (58a), *x patted y*).

Can this ellipted material be reconstructed at LF? One might suggest, for instance, that focused expressions are lifted out of their S-Structure positions to $\bar{\text{A}}$-positions at LF, parallel to the overt movement of topicalized phrases. Chomsky (1971) anticipates the fundamental difficulty for such an approach: many more kinds of phrases can be focused than can be lifted out of syntactic expressions.[11] (Most of the examples in (60) are adapted from Chomsky 1971; capitals indicate focusing stress.)

(60) a. Was he warned to look out for a RED-shirted ex-con?
       *[red$_i$ [was he warned to look out for a t_i-shirted ex-con]]
   b. Is John certain to WIN the election?
       *[win$_i$ [is John certain to t_i the election]]
   c. Does Bill eat PORK and shellfish?
       *[pork$_i$ [does Bill eat t_i and shellfish]]
   d. John is neither EASY to please nor EAGER to please.
       *[easy$_i$ eager$_j$ [John is neither t_i to please nor t_j to please]]
       (Note: The conjoined VPs here present unusually severe problems of extraction and derived structure.)
   e. John is more concerned with AFfirmation than with CONfirmation.
       *[affirmation$_i$ [confirmation$_j$ [John is more concerned with t_i than with t_j]]]

Suppose one tried to maintain that LF movement is involved in (60a–e). One would have to claim that constraints on extraction are much looser in the derivation from S-Structure to LF than in the derivation from D-Structure to S-Structure. But that would undermine the claim that LF movement is also an instance of Move α, since it is only through common constraints that the two can be identified. In turn, the motivation for LF as a syntactic level in the first place was the extension of Move α to covert cases. (See Koster 1987 and Berman and Hestvik 1991 for parallel arguments for other LF phenomena.) In short, either the differentiation of focus and presupposition is present in conceptual structure but not in LF—or else LF loses all its original motivation, in which case the village has been destroyed in order to save it.

To sum up the argument, then:

1. The strict/sloppy identity ambiguity depends on ambiguity of binding; therefore such ambiguity within ellipsis, as in (57), must be resolved at a level where the elliptic material is explicit.
2. Because of examples like (58a–c), ellipsis in general must be reconstructed at a level of representation where focus and presupposition can be explicitly distinguished.
3. Because of examples like (60a–e), focus and presupposition in general cannot be distinguished in LF, but only in conceptual structure.
4. Therefore the strict/sloppy identity ambiguity cannot be stated in syntax, but only in conceptual structure.

The following example puts all these pieces together and highlights the conclusion:

(61) JOHN wants to ruin his books by smearing PAINT on them, but
     BILL wants to do it with GLUE.

Bill's desire is subject to a strict/sloppy ambiguity: whose books does he have in mind? In order to recover the relevant pronoun, *do it* must be reconstructed. Its reconstruction is something like *ruin his books by smearing y on them*, where *y* is a variable in the presupposition, filled in the second clause by the focus *glue*. However, there is no way to produce *ruin his books by smearing y on them* in the logical form of the first clause, because *paint* cannot be syntactically lifted out of that environment, as we can see from (62).[12]

(62) *It is PAINT$_i$ that John is ruining his books by smearing t_i on them.

In short, there is no way for LF to encode the strict/sloppy ambiguity in complete generality. Therefore LF, which is supposed to be the locus of binding relations, cannot do the job it is supposed to. Rather, the phenomena in question really belong in conceptual structure, a nonsyntactic representation.[13]

We thus have four distinct cases where aspects of binding theory must apply to "hidden" elements. In each case these hidden elements can be expressed only in conceptual structure; they cannot be expressed at a (narrow) syntactic level of LF, no matter how different from S-Structure. We conclude that LF cannot be justified on the basis of its supposed ability to encode syntactic properties relevant to anaphora that are not already present in S-Structure. Rather, such properties turn out not to be syntactic at all; the relation "x binds y" is properly stated over conceptual structure, where the true generalizations can be captured.

3.8 Quantification

The other main function attributed to LF is expressing the structure of quantification. Of course, the structure of quantification is involved in inference (the rules of syllogism, for instance), so it is necessarily represented at conceptual structure, the representation over which rules of inference are formally defined. The question, then, is whether scope of quantification needs to be represented structurally in syntax as well.

3.8.1 Quantification into Elliptic Contexts
The theory of quantification has to account for (at least) two things: how quantifiers bind anaphoric expressions, and how they take scope over other quantifiers. The evidence of section 3.7 shows that the binding of anaphoric expressions by quantifiers cannot in general be expressed in syntax. For instance, (57c) and (57d) contain a quantifier binding a covert anaphor within an elliptic VP, and we have just seen that such anaphors cannot in general be reconstructed in syntactic structure—they appear explicitly only in conceptual structure. To push the point home, we can construct a parallel to (61) that uses a quantifier.

(63) JOHN is ruining his books by smearing PAINT on them, but everyone ELSE is doing it with GLUE.

In general, then, the binding of variables by quantifiers can be expressed only at conceptual structure.

What about the relative scope of multiple quantifiers? It is easy enough to extend the previous argument to examples with multiple quantifiers.

(64) a. Some quantifiers in English always take scope over other quantifiers, but none in Turkish do that.

b. Some boys decided to ruin all their books by smearing PAINT on them, because none of them had succeeded in doing it with GLUE.

In order for (64a) to be interpreted, *do that* must be reconstructed as *always take scope over other quantifiers*, and *none* must take scope over *always*. But we have just seen that reconstruction of *do that* is accomplished in general only at conceptual structure, not at a putative syntactic level of LF. The somewhat baroque but perfectly understandable (64b), which parallels (61) and (63), amplifies this point. Therefore LF cannot express all quantifier scope relations, as it is supposed to.

3.8.2 Quantificational Relations That Depend on Internal Structure of LCS

A more subtle argument concerns the semantic nature of "measuring out" in examples like (65) (Tenny 1987, 1992; Verkuyl 1972, 1993; Dowty 1991; Krifka 1992; Jackendoff 1996e).

(65) Bill pushed the cart down Scrack St. to Fred's house.

In (65) the position of the cart is said to "measure out" the event. If the cart's path has a definite spatial endpoint (*to Fred's house* in (65)), then the event has a definite temporal endpoint; that is, it is telic and passes the standard tests for telicity.

(66) Bill pushed the cart down Scrack St. to Fred's house in/*for an hour.

If, on the other hand, the cart's path has no definite endpoint (delete *to Fred's house* from (65)), the event has no definite temporal endpoint and passes the standard tests for atelicity.

(67) Bill pushed the cart down Scrack St. for/*in an hour.

These facts about telicity have typically been the main focus of discussions of "measuring out." But they follow from a more general relationship observed by most of the authors cited above: for each point in time that the cart is moving down Scrack St. to Fred's house, there is a corresponding position on its trajectory.[14] That is, verbs of motion impose a quantification-like relationship between the temporal course of the event and the path of motion: *X measures out Y* can be analyzed semantically as 'For each part of X there is a corresponding part of Y'.

Exactly which constituents of a sentence stand in a measuring-out relationship depends on the verb.

1. With verbs of motion, the temporal course of the event measures out the path, as we have just seen.

2. With verbs of performance, the temporal course of the event measures out the object being performed. For instance, in *Sue sang an aria*, for each point in time during the event, there is a corresponding part of the aria that Sue was singing, and the beginning and the end of the aria correspond to the beginning and the end of the event respectively.

3. With verbs of extension, a path measures out an object. For instance, in *Highway 95 extends down the East Coast from Maine to Florida*, for each location on the East Coast, there is a corresponding part of Highway 95; and the endpoints of the path, Maine and Florida, contain the endpoints of the road. In this case time is not involved at all. A parallel two-dimensional case is verbs of covering: in *Mud covered the floor*, there is a bit of mud for each point of floor. (Of the works cited above, these cases are discussed only in Jackendoff 1996e.)

4. Finally, there are verbs involving objects, paths, and times in which no measuring out appears at all. For instance, in *Bill slowly pointed the gun toward Harry*, the gun changes position over time, but its successive positions do not correspond to successive locations along a path toward Harry. In particular, *toward Harry* with a verb of motion induces atelicity: *Bill pushed the cart toward the house for/*in ten seconds*. But *Bill slowly pointed the gun toward Harry* may be telic: its endpoint is when the gun is properly oriented. (Again, these cases are discussed only in Jackendoff 1996e.)

In other words, the verb has to say, as part of its meaning, which arguments (plus time) measure out which others; the quantificational relationship involved in measuring out has to be expressed as part of the LCS of the verb.

But this means that there are quantifier scope relationships that are imposed by the LCS of a verb. By hypothesis, LF does not express material interior to the LCS of lexical items. Hence LF does not express all quantifier scope relationships.[15]

An advocate of LF might respond that measuring-out relationships are not standard quantification and so should not be expressed in LF. They are interior to LCS and are therefore not "aspects of semantic structure that are expressed syntactically," to repeat May's (1985) terminology. But such a reply would be too glib. One can only understand which entities are measured out in a sentence by knowing (1) which semantic arguments are marked by the verb as measured out, (2) in what syntactic positions these arguments can be expressed, and (3) what syntactic constituents occupy these positions. That is, the combinatorial system of syntax is deeply implicated in expressing the combinatorial semantics of measuring out.

This argument thus parallels the argument for *buy* with anaphora (section 3.7.1). It shows that differences in quantifier scope, if properly generalized, are also imposed by the LCS of lexical items and therefore cannot be encoded in the most general fashion at any (narrow) syntactic level of LF. Combining this with the argument from ellipsis, we conclude that LF cannot perform the function it was invented to perform, and therefore there is ultimately no justification for such a level.

3.9   Remarks

The present chapter has examined the claim that the Conceptual Interface Level in syntax is LF, distinct from S-Structure and invisible to phonology, which syntactically encodes binding and quantification relationships. This claim has been defused in two ways (to some degree at least).

First, by showing that the relation of syntax to conceptual structure is not as straightforward as standardly presumed, I have shown that it is not so plausible to think of *any* level of syntax as directly "encoding semantic phenomena." Second, by looking at nonstandard examples of binding and quantification, I have shown that no syntactic level can do justice to the full generality of these phenomena. Rather, responsibility for binding and quantification lies with conceptual structure and the correspondence rules linking it with syntactic structure. There therefore appears no advantage in positing an LF component distinct from S-Structure that is "closer" to semantics in its hierarchical organization: it simply cannot get syntax "close" enough to semantics to take over the relevant work.

This is not to say that I have a solution for all the many phenomena for which LF has been invoked in the literature; these clearly remain to be dealt with. However, these phenomena have been discussed almost exclusively in the context of GB, a theory that lacks articulated accounts of conceptual structure and of the interface between syntax and conceptual structure. Without a clear alternative semantic account of binding and quantification, it is natural for an advocate of LF to feel justified in treating them as syntactic. But consider, for instance, the treatment of languages with in situ *wh* (e.g. Huang 1982), which has been taken as a strong argument for LF. The ability of verbs to select for indirect questions does not depend on whether the *wh*-word is at the front of the clause: it depends on the clause's being interpretable as a question, a fact about conceptual structure.[16] In turn, the ability of a *wh*-word to take scope over a clause, rendering the clause a question, is indeed parallel to the ability of a quantifier to take scope over a clause. But if quantifier scope is a property of conceptual structure rather than syntax, then there is no problem with treating *wh*-scope similarly. Hence there is no need for syntactic LF movement to capture the semantic properties of these languages.[17] The challenge that such putative LF phenomena pose to the present approach, then, is how to formulate a rigorous theory of conceptual structure that captures the same insights. But there are many different traditions in semantics that can be drawn upon in approaching this task.[18]

Chapter 4

The Lexical Interface

From a formal point of view, the hypothesis of Representational Modularity claims that the informational architecture of the mind strictly segregates phonological, syntactic, and conceptual representations from each other. Each lives in its own module; there can be no "mixed" representations that are partly phonological and partly syntactic, or partly syntactic and partly semantic. Rather, all coordination among these representations is encoded in correspondence rules.

This chapter explores the consequences of this position for the lexical interface—the means by which lexical entries find their way into sentences. It also proposes a simple formalization of how the tripartite structures are coordinated. In the process, important conclusions will be derived about the PS-SS and SS-CS interfaces as well.

4.1 Lexical Insertion versus Lexical Licensing

A perhaps startling consequence of Representational Modularity is that *there can be no such thing as a rule of lexical insertion*. In order to understand this statement, let us ask, What is lexical insertion supposed to be?

Originally, in Chomsky 1957, lexical items were introduced into syntactic trees by phrase structure rules like (1) that expanded terminal symbols into words.

(1) N → dog, cat, banana, . . .

In Chomsky 1965, for reasons that need not concern us here, this mechanism was replaced with a lexicon and a (set of) rule(s) of lexical insertion. Here is how the process is described in Chomsky 1971, 184:

Let us assume . . . that the grammar contains a lexicon, which we take to be a class of lexical entries each of which specifies the grammatical (i.e. phonological, semantic, and syntactic) properties of some lexical item.... We may think of each lexical entry as incorporating a set of transformations[1] that insert the item in question (that is, the complex of features that constitutes it) in phrase-markers. Thus

[2] a lexical transformation associated with the lexical item I maps a phrase-marker P containing a substructure Q into a phrase-marker P′ formed by replacing Q by I.

Unpacking this, suppose the lexical entry for *cat* is (3a) and we have the phrase marker (3b) (Chomsky's P). Lexical insertion replaces the terminal symbol *N* in (3b) (Chomsky's substructure Q) with (3a), producing the phrase marker (3c) (Chomsky's P′).

(3) a.
$$\begin{bmatrix} /\text{kæt}/ \\ \begin{bmatrix} +\text{N}, -\text{V} \\ \text{singular} \end{bmatrix} \\ [_{\text{Thing}} \text{ CAT, TYPE OF ANIMAL, etc.}] \end{bmatrix} \begin{matrix} \text{PS} \\ \text{SS} \\ \text{CS} \end{matrix}$$

b.
```
          NP
         /    \
      Det      N′
               |
               N
```

c.
```
          NP
         /    \
      Det      N′
               |
```
$$\begin{bmatrix} /\text{kæt}/ \\ \begin{bmatrix} +\text{N}, -\text{V} \\ \text{singular} \end{bmatrix} \\ [_{\text{Thing}} \text{ CAT, TYPE OF ANIMAL, etc.}] \end{bmatrix}$$

This leads to the familar conception of the layout of grammar, in which lexical insertion feeds underlying syntactic form. Let us see how the architecture of Chomsky's theories of syntax, outlined in figure 4.1, develops over the years. (I will drop the subscripts on PIL$_{SS}$ and CIL$_{SS}$, because we are dealing with syntactic structure throughout.)

The constant among all these changes is the position of the lexical interface. Throughout the years, the lexicon has always been viewed as

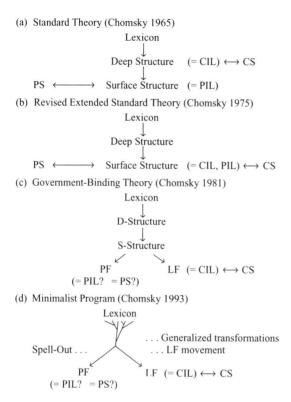

(a) Standard Theory (Chomsky 1965)

(b) Revised Extended Standard Theory (Chomsky 1975)

(c) Government-Binding Theory (Chomsky 1981)

(d) Minimalist Program (Chomsky 1993)

Figure 4.1
The architecture of some of Chomsky's theories

feeding the initial point of the syntactic derivation, and its phonological and semantic information is interpreted "later." It is this assumption (assumption 3 of chapter 1) that I want to examine next.

What is a lexical item? As seen in the above quotation, a lexical item is regarded as a triple of phonological, syntactic, and semantic features (i.e. as a structure ⟨PS, SS, CS⟩), listed in long-term memory.

This view of lexical items raises a uncomfortable situation for any of the layouts of grammar sketched in figure 4.1—one that could have been noticed early on. The operation of lexical insertion is supposed to insert lexical items *in their entirety* into syntactic phrase structures. This means that the phonological and conceptual structures of lexical items are dragged through a syntactic derivation, inertly. They become available only once the derivation crosses the appropriate interface into phonetic or semantic form.

Alternatively, in the Minimalist Program, a lexical item in its entirety is said to *project* initial syntactic structures (through the operation of Merge). For present purposes this amounts to the same thing as traditional lexical insertion, for, as mentioned in chapter 2, the operation Spell-Out is what makes lexical phonology available to further rules. This phonological information has to be transmitted through the derivation from the point of lexical insertion; otherwise Spell-Out could not tell, for instance, whether to spell out a particular noun in the (narrow) syntactic structure as /kæt/ or /bæt/. Thus the Minimalist Program too drags the lexical phonology invisibly through the syntax. (Alternatively, people sometimes advocate a strategy of "going back to the lexicon" at Spell-Out to retrieve phonological information. See section 4.2 for discussion.)

Such a conception of lexical insertion, however, reduces the much-vaunted autonomy of syntax essentially to the *stipulation* that although lexical, phonological, and semantic information is present in syntactic trees, syntactic rules can't see it. (As Ivan Sag (personal communication) has suggested, it is as if the syntax has to lug around two locked suitcases, one on each shoulder, only to turn them over to other components to be opened.)

Some colleagues have correctly observed that there is nothing *formally* wrong with the traditional view; no empirical difficulties follow. Although I grant their point, I suspect this defense comes from the habits of the syntactocentric view. To bring its artificiality more into focus, let us turn the tables and imagine that lexical items complete with syntax and semantics were inserted into *phonological* structure, only to be "interpreted later" by the syntactic and conceptual components. One could make this work formally too, but would one want to?

Quite a number of people (e.g. Otero 1976, 1983; Den Besten 1976; Fiengo 1980; Koster 1987; Di Sciullo and Williams 1987; Anderson 1992; Halle and Marantz 1993; Büring 1993) have noticed the oddity of traditional lexical insertion and have proposed to remove phonological information (and in some versions, semantic information as well) from initial syntactic structures. On this view, the syntactic derivation carries around only the lexical information that syntactic rules can access: syntactic features such as category, person, number, case-marking properties, the mass/count distinction, and syntactic subcategorization (i.e. the φ-features of Chomsky 1981). Di Sciullo and Williams (1987, 54) characterize this approach as follows:

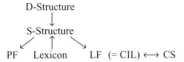

Figure 4.2
The architecture of Government-Binding Theory but with late lexical insertion

[W]hat is syntax about? We could say "sentences" in the usual sense, but another answer could be "sentence forms," where ... syntactic forms are "wordless" phrase markers. "Sentence," then, as ordinarily understood, is not in the purview of syntax, although the syntactic forms that syntax *is* about certainly contribute to the description of "sentences."

Of course, there comes a point in the derivation where the grammar has to know—both phonologically and semantically—whether some noun in the syntactic structure is *cat* or *baì*, whose strictly syntactic features are identical. It therefore eventually becomes necessary to perform some version of lexical insertion. The distinctive characteristic of all these approaches is that they move lexical insertion to some later point in the syntactic derivation. Grafted onto an otherwise unchanged GB theory, they might look in skeleton something like figure 4.2.[2]

Although late lexical insertion keeps phonological and semantic features out of the derivation from D-Structure to S-Structure, it does not keep them out of syntax entirely—they are still present inertly in S-Structure, visible only after the derivation has passed through the relevant interface. However, according to the hypothesis of Representational Modularity, such "mixed" representation should be impossible. Rather, phonological, syntactic, and conceptual representations should be strictly segregated, but coordinated through correspondence rules that constitute the interfaces.[3]

The problem this raises for any standard version of lexical insertion is that a lexical item is by its very nature a "mixed" representation—a ⟨PS, SS, CS⟩ triple. Therefore it cannot be inserted at *any* stage of a syntactic derivation without producing an offending mixed representation.

To put this more graphically, the traditional notation for syntactic trees (4a) is *necessarily* a mixed representation, violating Representational Modularity: *the cat*, at the bottom, is phonological, not syntactic, information. (4a) is traditionally taken as an abbreviation for (4b), where the informal notation *the cat* has been replaced by an explicit encoding of the full lexical entries for these items.

(4) a.

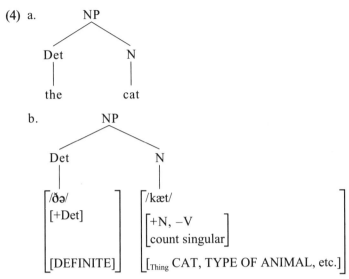

In a conception of grammar that adopts Representational Modularity as an organizing principle, things work out differently: a representation like (4b) is entirely ill formed. Rather, we must replace it with a triple of structures along the lines shown in (5), each of which contains only features from its proper vocabulary. (I utilize conceptual structure formalism in the style of Jackendoff 1990; readers should feel free to substitute their own favorite.)

(5)

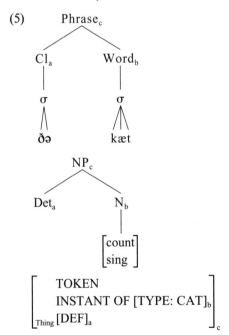

These three structures do not just exist next to one another. They are explicitly linked by subscripted indices. The clitic *the* corresponds to the Det and the definiteness feature, the word *cat* corresponds to the N and the Type-constituent of conceptual structure, and the whole phrase corresponds to the NP and the whole Thing-constituent.[4]

If (5) is the proper way of representing *the cat*, there cannot be a rule that inserts all aspects of a lexical item in syntactic structure. Rather, the only part of the lexical item that appears in syntactic structure is its syntactic features. For example, the word *cat* is represented formally something like (6).

(6)

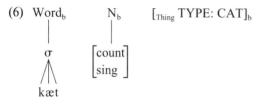

The proper way to regard (6) is as a small-scale correspondence rule. It lists a small chunk of phonology (the *lexical phonological structure* or LPS), a small chunk of syntax (the *lexical syntactic structure* or LSS), and a small chunk of semantics (the *lexical conceptual structure* or LCS), and it shows how to line these chunks up when they are independently generated in the parallel phonological, syntactic, and conceptual derivations. Lexical items, then, are not "inserted" into syntactic derivations; rather, they license the correspondence of certain (near-)terminal symbols of syntactic structure with phonological and conceptual structures.

Lexical correspondence rules are of course not all there is to establishing a correspondence. For instance, the index c in (5) comes from a larger-scale correspondence rule that coordinates maximal syntactic phrases with conceptual constituents. The PS-SS rules (12a,b) and the SS-CS rule (21) in chapter 2 are schemata for more general larger-scale rules; the principles of coercion and cocomposition in chapter 3 are more specific phrasal SS-CS rules; the rules of Argument Fusion and Restrictive Modification in Jackendoff 1990 (chapter 2) and the principles of argument structure linking (chapter 11) are further examples of phrasal SS-CS rules.

In short, *a lexical item is to be regarded as a correspondence rule, and the lexicon as a whole is to be regarded as part of the PS-SS and SS-CS interface modules.* On this view, the formal role of lexical items is not that they are "inserted" into syntactic derivations, but rather that they license the correspondence of certain (near-)terminal symbols of syntactic structure with phonological and conceptual structures.[5] There is no operation of insertion, only the satisfaction of constraints. This means there is no "ordering" of lexical insertion in the syntactic derivation. What it formally means to say that lexical items are "inserted" at some level of S-Structure is that the licensing of syntactic terminal symbols by lexical items is stated over this level of syntax. In turn, what is "carried through" the syntactic derivation, visible to syntactic rules, is not the whole lexical item, but only its syntactic features, in this case [N, count sing] and perhaps its linking subscripts.

This approach, which might be called *lexical licensing*, is meant to replace assumption 3 of chapter 1. Something much like it is found in the formalisms of HPSG, Tree-Adjoining Grammar, and Construction Grammar. Interestingly, the view that syntax carries only syntactic features is also proposed by Halle and Marantz (1993). However, their approach has a rule called Vocabulary Insertion that has the same effect as lexical insertion, except that it applies as part of the mapping between S-Structure and PF in figure 4.2; the idea is that phonological realization of lexical items best awaits the insertion of syntactic inflection.[6] On preliminary examination, it appears that Halle and Marantz's theory can be recast in terms of lexical licensing, in particular reinterpreting their claim of late lexical insertion as a claim that the licensing of the PS-SS correspondence involves the syntactic level of surface structure. (On the other hand, it is not clear to me how semantic interpretation takes place in Halle and Marantz's approach.)

Lexical licensing eliminates an assumption that is tacit in the way conceptual necessity 3 of chapter 1 is stated: the idea that the computational system has a distinct interface with the lexicon. On the present view, there are not three interfaces—a phonological, a semantic, and a lexical one. Rather, the lexical interface is part of the other two. Notice that, although a lexical interface is a "conceptual necessity," nothing requires it to be a *separate* interface!

Why should one consider replacing lexical insertion with lexical licensing? For one thing, it should be recalled that no argument has been given for lexical insertion except that it worked in the *Aspects* framework; it is just a 30-year-old tradition. At the time it was developed, symbol rewriting was the basic operation of formal grammars (assumption 2 of chapter 1), and lexical licensing would not have made formal sense. Now that constraint satisfaction is widely acknowledged as a fundamental operation in grammatical theory, lexical licensing looks much more natural.

At the same time, I see lexical licensing as embodying a more completely worked out version of the autonomy thesis, in that it allows us to strictly segregate information according to levels of representation. Of course, the traditional architecture *in practice* enforces this separation of information (though by stipulation, not on principled grounds). So it is possible to leave syntactic theory otherwise unaltered, at least for a first approximation. (In particular, for many purposes we can continue drawing trees the traditional way, as long as we recognize that the line connecting *N* and *cat* in (4a) is not a domination relation but really an abbreviation for the linking relations shown in (6).)

4.2   PIL = CIL

Next I want to ask what levels of syntax should be identified as the Phonological Interface Level (PIL) and the Conceptual Interface Level (CIL). But I am going to approach the question in a roundabout way, with a different question: Should PIL and CIL be *different* levels of syntax, as is the case in all the diagrams above except (b) of figure 4.1?

I raise the issue this way for an important reason. Lexical items are very finely individuated in phonology and in semantics, but not in syntax. Since syntax can see only syntactic features, all the words in (7a) are syntactically identical, as are those in (7b–d).

(7) a. dog, cat, armadillo
    b. walk, swim, fly
    c. gigantic, slippery, handsome
    d. on, in, near

At the same time, the information that a particular word is *cat* rather than *dog* has to be communicated somehow between phonology and conceptual structure, via the PS-SS and SS-CS interfaces, so that one can say what one means. This is accomplished most simply if these interfaces involve the very same level of syntax, that is, if PIL = CIL. Then it is possible to check a lexical correspondence among all three representations simultaneously, in effect going directly from finely individuated lexical phonological structure /kæt/ to finely individuated lexical conceptual

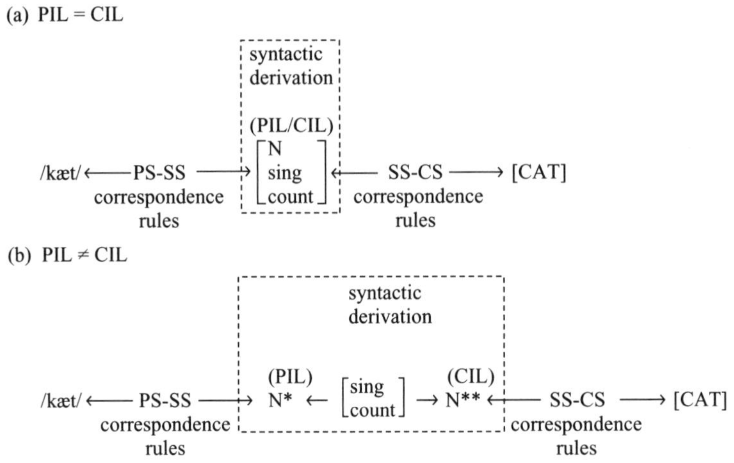

(a) PIL = CIL

(b) PIL ≠ CIL

Figure 4.3
Tracking a lexical item through the syntax (a) if PIL = CIL and (b) if PIL ≠ CIL

structure [CAT], at the same time making sure the syntactic structure is a singular count noun.

What if PIL is not the same level as CIL? Then it is necessary to connect /kæt/ to some noun N* in PIL, connect N* through the syntactic derivation to its counterpart N** in CIL, then connect N** to [CAT]. The problem is that once we are in syntax, we lose track of the fact that N* is connected to /kæt/. Consequently, when we get to its counterpart N**, we have no way of knowing that it should be connected to [CAT] rather than [ARMADILLO]. In other words, if PIL ≠ CIL, some extra means has to be introduced to track lexical items through the syntactic derivation. Figure 4.3 sketches the problem.

Let me outline the two ways I can think of to track lexical items through the syntax. The first way involves giving each lexical item a unique syntactic index that accompanies it through the derivation. Suppose the lexical item *cat* has the index 85. Then /kæt/ maps not just to N at PIL, but to N_{85}. In turn, at CIL, reference back to the lexicon enables N_{85} to map to [CAT] in conceptual structure. This solution works, but the price is the introduction of this lexical index that serves to finely individuate items in syntax—a lexical index that syntactic rules themselves cannot refer to. Since lexical items are already adequately individuated by their phonology and semantics, this lexical index plays no role in the lexicon either. Its only function is to make sure lexical identity is preserved through the syntactic derivation from PIL to CIL. In line with minimalist assumptions (to use Chomsky's turn of phrase), we should try to do without it.

One might suggest that the lexical item's linking index (e.g. the subscripted b in (6)) might serve the purpose of a lexical syntactic index. But the linking index's only proper role is as an interface function: it serves to link syntax to phonology at PIL and to semantics at CIL. If we were also to use it to keep track of lexical items through a syntactic derivation, this would in effect be admitting that all the steps of the derivation between PIL and CIL are also accessible to phonology and semantics: each of these steps can see which phonology and semantics go together. That is, this would indirectly sneak the unwanted richness of mixed representations back into syntax, right after we found a way to eliminate them.

Another way to track lexical items through the derivation is to give an index not to the individual lexical items, but to the lexical nodes in the syntactic tree.[7] For example, the N node of PIL matched with /kæt/ might have the index 68. In turn, this index would be identifiable at CIL. However, it does not uniquely identify *cat*; rather, a well-formedness condition must be imposed on the ⟨PS, SS, CS⟩ triple for a sentence, something like (8).

(8) If the phonological structure of a lexical item W maps to node n at PIL, then the conceptual structure of W must map to node n at CIL.

Again, this would work, but it too invokes a mechanism whose only purpose is to track otherwise unindividuated lexical items through the derivation from PIL to CIL.

Part of the reason for removing lexical phonology and semantics from the syntax is to eliminate all unmotivated syntactic individuation of lexical items. These mechanisms to track items through the derivation are basically tricks to subvert the problems created by such removal. Accordingly, minimalist assumptions demand that we try to do without them.[8]

In short, I will try to work out a theory in which phonology and semantics interface with syntax at the very same level. This way, the PS-SS and SS-CS interfaces can be checked at the same time, and the fine individuation of lexical items can be regarded as passing directly from phonology to semantics without any syntactic intervention.

I can think of three reasons other than simplicity why this is an attractive theory. First, there is a class of lexical items that have no syntactic structure. Some of these have only phonology, for instance *fiddle-de-dee*, *tra-la-la, e-i-e-i-o*, and *ink-a-dink-a-doo*. Others have both phonology and semantics (or pragmatics), for instance *hello, ouch, wow, yippee*, and *dammit.*[9] A syntactician might dismiss these items as "outside language," since they do not participate in the "combinatorial system," except in quotational contexts like (9a), where virtually anything is possible. Note, however, that they do not occur in an environment such as (9b), reserved (in nonteenage dialects) for *non*linguistic expressions.[10] This suggests that they are regarded as linguistic items.

(9) a. "Hello," he said.
     b. Then John went, "[belching noise]"/*"Hello."

In fact, these items are made of standard phonological units, they observe normal syllable structure constraints and stress rules, and they undeniably carry some sort of meaning, albeit nonpropositional. Thus the most appropriate place in the mind to house them would seem to be the natural language lexicon—especially under the assumption of Representational Modularity. They are indeed outside the combinatorial system of (narrow) *syntax*, but not outside *language*. (A more complex case, arguably of the same sort, is expletive infixation, which also has phonology and semantics/pragmatics but no detectable syntax. See chapter 5.)

Now if the use of lexical items involved inserting them in an X^0 position in syntactic structure, then dragging them through a derivation until they could be phonologically and semantically interpreted, we could not use these particular items at all: they could never be inserted, except possibly under a totally vacuous syntactic node *Exclamation*[0] or the like.

Suppose instead that we adopt lexical licensing theory and treat these peculiar words as defective lexical items: *tra-la-la* is of the form $\langle PS, \emptyset, \emptyset \rangle$, and *hello* is of the form $\langle PS, \emptyset, CS \rangle$. They therefore can be unified with contexts in which no syntax is required—for example as exclamations and in syntactic environments such as *the phrase yummy yummy yummy* or *"Ouch," he said* that place no syntactic constraints on the string in question.[11]

Next suppose that the PS-SS interface and the SS-CS interface were to access different levels of syntax, as in (b) of figure 4.3. In this case there would be no way to map the phonology of *hello* into its semantics, since the intermediate levels of syntactic derivation would be absent. By contrast, if PIL = CIL, and all the interface conditions are applied at once, the phonology of *hello* can be mapped into its semantics directly, simply bypassing syntax. That is, on this approach the defective nature of these lexical items follows directly from saying they simply have no syntax; beyond that no extra provision has to be made for them.[12]

This leads directly to a more crucial case. What happens in language acquisition as the child passes from the one-word stage to the development of syntax?[13] Presumably one-word speakers can construct a sound-to-meaning association for their lexical items, but cannot construct syntactic structures with which to combine words meaningfully. (We might think of them as having a "protolanguage" in Bickerton's (1990) sense; see section 1.3.) In a theory where PIL = CIL, we can say that all the words of a one-word speaker behave like *hello*: there is no syntactic structure that imposes further well-formedness conditions on the pairing of sound and meaning, and that offers opportunities for phrasal modification. The development of syntax, then, can be seen just as the gradual growth of a new component of structure within an already existing framework.

By contrast, in a theory where PIL ≠ CIL, the sound-meaning correspondence has to be mediated through a syntactic derivation. We therefore have to suppose that the one-word speaker either (1) really has a syntax but simply cannot use it or (2) does not have a syntax but undertakes a radical restructuring of linguistic organization when syntax develops. Again, both of these options seem to be rhetorical tricks to avoid unpleasant consequences of an assumed architecture of grammar. The most elegant solution, if possible, is to assume only what is "conceptually necessary": the one-word speaker does *not* construct syntactic structure—and the acquisition of syntax does not restructure the architecture of the child's previously existing form-meaning correspondences, but simply adds new constraints and possibilities onto them.

A third argument that PIL = CIL comes from the fact that topic and focus in conceptual structure are often marked phonologically by stress and intonation, with no specifically syntactic effects. If PIL ≠ CIL, either (1) topic and focus must be tracked through the syntax by syntactically inert dummy markers (this is the solution in Jackendoff 1972), or (2) an additional interface must be added that bypasses syntactic structure altogether. However, syntactic constructions such as topicalization, left dislocation, and clefting also mark topic and focus—and these redundantly require the appropriate stress and intonation. This means that the syntax of topic and focus must be correlated with both phonology and semantics. Hence the second possibility is unlikely. On the other hand, if PIL = CIL, all three components can cross-check each other simultaneously when necessary.

We thus conclude, tentatively, that PIL = CIL, that is, that phonology and semantics interface with syntax at the same level. This is a major boundary condition on satisfactory theories of the interfaces, one that, as we can see in figure 4.1, has not been explored in the context of Chomskian varieties of generative grammar. In Chomsky's spirit of minimalism, we will tentatively adopt this hypothesis and see what follows.

The first consequence is a simple theory of lexical insertion/licensing. We can regard lexical insertion/licensing as an operation of *unification* (in the sense of Shieber 1986). However, it differs from standard unification in that an item such as (6) is unified simultaneously with independently generated phonological, syntactic, and conceptual structures, along lines explored by Shieber and Schabes (1991). By virtue of this unification, it contributes its linking indices, which are *not* generated in the independent derivations. It thereby helps establish the correspondence among the three structures.

To illustrate, suppose the three independent sets of formation rules create the structures in (10).

(10)

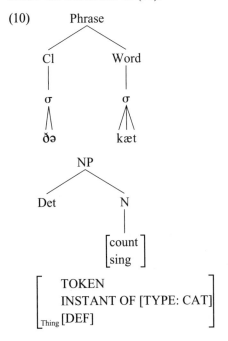

Simultaneous unification of the lexical item *cat* (shown in (6)) with all three structures will have the effect of adding indices to produce (11).

(11)

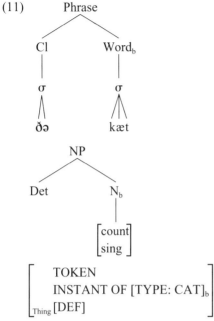

This is on its way to the complete correspondence among these structures shown in (5); other linking indices will come from the lexical item *the* and from larger-scale (phrasal) principles of correspondence. On the other hand, suppose the phonological structure in (10) were instead /bæt/; then *cat* could not unify with it and the derivation would crash for lack of complete correspondence.

The present proposal, then, is an alternative to assumption 2 of chapter 1, the assumption that the fundamental operation of the grammar is sub-stitution of one symbol (or symbol complex) for another, and in particu-lar that lexical insertion is a substitution operation.

Note, incidentally, that the lexically listed phonological structure may lack syllabification and stress, as is generally assumed in the phonological literature. It can still unify with a syllabified and stressed phonological structure; the grammar need not do syllabification and stress "later," "after" lexical insertion. In fact, a monostratal theory of phonology, in which surface output (PF) does not necessarily correspond to lexically listed phonology (such as Optimality Theory; Prince and Smolensky 1993), could be accommodated by relaxing the conditions on unification, so that less than perfect fit is necessary for its satisfaction. We will take this issue up briefly in section 6.2.

Alternatively, the present approach is also consistent with traditional phonological derivations, which account for the disparity between lexical phonological form and PF by successive steps of altering phonological structures. Now, one might think that the argument that PIL = CIL in syntax could be extended to a parallel argument that PF = Syntactic Interface Level in phonology, arguing against traditional derivations. But such would not be the case. The argument that PIL = CIL depends on the need for the lexicon to link phonological structure, syntactic structure, and conceptual structure simultaneously. An analogous argument in phonology would push matters one level of representation toward the periphery: it would depend on a need for the lexicon to link auditory-motor information, phonological structure, and syntactic structure simultaneously. But (as far as I know) this need simply does not exist: the lexicon says nothing whatsoever about auditory and motor information. So there *is* a way that phonology is potentially different from syntax, as Bromberger and Halle (1989) have asserted. Notice, however, that I say "potentially": in fact the architecture proposed here is neutral between derivational and monostratal phonology. (Another alternative is to have two or three discrete levels of phonology related by correspondence rules; this seems to be the spirit of Goldsmith's (1993) "harmonic phonology.")

If indeed PIL = CIL, there are consequences for Chomsky's (1993, 1995) principle of Full Interpretation (FI). As mentioned in chapter 2, the idea behind FI is that the interface levels contain *all and only* elements that are germane to the interface; for example, PIL contains no extraneous phonological segments. However, such a principle is impossible if PIL = CIL, since in general the syntactic information relevant to phonology is not identical with that relevant to semantics. The proper way of stating the principle, then, is that PIL/CIL contains all syntactic elements accessible to PS-SS and SS-CS correspondence rules, and that those rules must take into account all elements that are "visible" to them.

This version of FI does not preclude the existence of syntactic features that are present just for purposes of syntactic well-formedness, for instance meaningless agreement features. A great deal of the machinery in Chomsky 1995 is developed just to eliminate such formal features from LF, in order to satisfy Chomsky's version of FI. In the present light such machinery seems pointless.

4.3   PIL and CIL Are at S-Structure

Having established that PIL and CIL are the same level of syntax, we now return to the question that started the previous section: What level of syntactic structure should be identified as PIL/CIL?

We know that the phonological interface has to be a level at which syntactic rules have already attached case endings, number agreement, and so forth, so that these can be phonologically realized. It also has to be after all movement rules, so that the proper linear order of lexical items is established. PIL therefore has to be at least as late as S-Structure.

Can PIL be any *later* than S-Structure? In GB, the derivation diverges after S-Structure; the "PF component" derives syntactic structures that are accessible to phonological but not semantic interpretation. The PS-SS interface level might therefore be somewhere down inside the PF component (as in Halle and Marantz 1993). However, the present hypothesis denies this possibility: whatever syntactic structure is accessible to the phonological interface must also be simultaneously accessible to the conceptual interface. In other words, PIL can be no later than S-Structure. It therefore must be *precisely* S-Structure.

The immediate consequence is that *there can be no syntactic "PF component"* of the sort assumed in GB—a set of (narrow) syntactic rules that apply after S-Structure and feed the phonological interface. I do not find this a very radical conclusion, given that in a decade and a half of GB research, no rules of the PF component have been established decisively enough to make them part of the general canon. In particular, Newmeyer (1988) points out that so-called minor movement rules and stylistic rules, often assumed to be part of the PF component, all either feed Move α or affect binding conditions, and therefore must precede S-Structure. Chomsky (1993) suggests that certain processes of ellipsis are part of the PF component; section 3.7.4 has shown that they are not.[14]

The more radical conclusion concerns the Conceptual Interface Level, which under the present hypothesis must also be S-Structure. Just as there can be no syntactic structures accessible to phonology that are not accessible to semantics, so there can be no syntactic structures accessible to semantics that are not accessible to phonology. *There therefore can be no syntactic "LF component"* (i.e. no "covert component" in the sense of Chomsky 1995).

Chapter 3 has already discussed many independent reasons why a "covert" syntax cannot get close enough to semantics to capture the

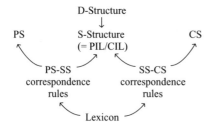

Figure 4.4
The architecture of "neominimalist grammar": the tripartite parallel architecture
with lexical licensing

generalizations attributed to LF. Section 4.4 will take up one further
aspect of the syntax-semantics interface. Here, let me sum up the conclusions of this section by means of a diagram of the architecture of the
grammar, figure 4.4. Notice how similar this is to the Revised Extended
Standard Theory (REST) (part (b) of figure 4.1). The one mistake made
in REST was leaving lexical insertion where it was in the Standard
Theory, instead of moving it to S-Structure along with CIL (though section 4.1 mentioned some researchers who saw this possibility). There is a
historical reason for this oversight, to which I will return in section 4.4.

The hypothesis that PIL = CIL is also consistent with Chomsky's
approach of 1957, which derives surface syntactic structure without using
a distinct level of underlying structure, but instead uses generalized transformations to create complex structures. (A similar approach is found in
Tree-Adjoining Grammar (Joshi 1987; Kroch 1987).) All that is necessary
for phonological and semantic interpretation is that the tree have its complete form at S-Structure. Indeed, this hypothesis also permits "monostratal" theories of syntax such as LFG,[15] GPSG, HPSG, Categorial
Grammar, and Construction Grammar. In such theories, figure 4.4 is
simplified still further by eliminating D-Structure, and "base-generating"
S-Structure instead. In fact, the possibility of base-generating S-Structures
was noticed within the Chomskian paradigm by Koster (1978, 1987) and
Brame (1978) (however, neither of these authors addressed the consequences for lexical insertion). As I said at the outset, I will remain
agnostic here about whether an independent level of D-Structure is necessary; I'll leave it in just in case.

A variant minimalist proposal has recently been offered by Brody
(1995), who claims that the only syntactic level is what he calls Lexico-

Logical Form (LLF). LLF is "base-generated"; it is the level at which lexical insertion takes place; it also functions as CIL in present terms. In Brody's theory, there is no syntactic Move α, overt or covert; Brody argues that the effects of Move α are redundant with constraints on chains. LLF is also the input to Spell-Out, hence in present terms PIL. Thus in many respects his architecture is similar to the present one; it appears that it could readily be adapted to make use of lexical licensing instead of his more traditional lexical insertion.

4.4 Checking Argument Structure

Why has lexical insertion always applied in D-Structure? Since the earliest days of generative grammar, deep structures were postulated in order to explicitly encode the fact that the "surface subject" of a passive is "understood as really the object" and that a *wh*-phrase at the front of a sentence is "understood as" having some other underlying grammatical relation. In turn, it was recognized that the underlying grammatical relation is crucial to deriving the semantic argument structure—who did what to whom. In the Standard Theory, where deep structure was equated with CIL, all this looked very natural.

The discovery that some aspects of semantics such as anaphora and quantifier scope could not be encoded in deep structure led to the early EST, with multiple CILs (Chomsky 1971; Jackendoff 1972). In this theory, deep structure represented those aspects of syntactic structure that encode grammatical relations (i.e. thematic roles), and surface structure represented the rest.[16] Here it still made sense to insert lexical items in deep structures, since this was the proper place to check subcategorization and read off thematic roles.

However, the introduction of trace theory in the mid-1970s provided another possibility: that argument structure conditions can be checked *after* movement, by referring to the traces left behind. In other words, D-Structure checking is now not "conceptually necessary." And in fact GB claims that LF is the sole conceptual interface level, which requires that underlying grammatical relations be recovered via traces.[17]

Traces are not "conceptually necessary," of course, but let us join Chomsky in assuming them. Then it is possible to recover the "understood" grammatical relations of phrases in terms of the chains of traces they leave behind them as they move through the derivation: the bottom of the chain marks the underlying position. The principle can be stated as follows:

(12) *Recovery of Underlying Grammatical Relations* (RUGR)
Given two chains $CH_1 = [\alpha_1, \ldots, \alpha_n]$ and $CH_2 = [\beta_1, \ldots, \beta_m]$, where α_1 and β_1 contain lexical material and all other elements are traces of α_1 and β_1 respectively.
CH_1 subcategorizes/s-selects/θ-marks CH_2 if α_1 lexically subcategorizes/s-selects/θ-marks β_1 in some context C, and α_n and β_m satisfy context C.

RUGR applies at S-Structure to provide all the lexically imposed relations normally assigned to D-Structure. Should it look a little clunky (and therefore unworthy of our minimalist assumptions), it is worth remembering that in GB and the Minimalist Program, where semantic interpretation is interpreted at LF, verbs and their arguments are not in their D-Structure positions either. Thus GB and the Minimalist Program require essentially the same principle in order to integrate the interpretations of heads with their arguments.[18] (RUGR might be thought of as the basis for "reconstruction" effects as well, a possibility I will not explore here.)

If lexical structural relations are imposed on chains at S-Structure rather than on D-Structure, we can immediately eliminate what I find one of the more curious artifacts of GB, the Projection Principle (which Chomsky (1995) also rejects). The Projection Principle stipulates that lexically imposed structural relations (e.g. direct object position for a transitive verb) are present at all levels of syntax, whether filled by lexical material or a trace. The reason the Projection Principle is necessary is to make sure that lexical constraints imposed on D-Structure are recoverable at LF, the semantic interface.

In the present approach, lexical constraints on syntax (e.g. subcategorization and quite possibly "quirky" morphological case marking) are imposed by RUGR at S-Structure, where the lexicon interfaces with syntax. In addition, since the lexicon is part of the SS-CS interface, RUGR also imposes at S-Structure those lexical constraints on semantic combination that involve recovery of grammatical relations (e.g. s-selection, θ-marking). Thus there is no need to preserve throughout the derivation all the lexically imposed structural relations. They need to be invoked only at the single level of S-Structure.

In this light, the Projection Principle reveals itself as a way to drag through the derivation not only the semantic information inserted at D-Structure but also whatever syntactic structure reflects that semantic information, so that semantic interpretation can be performed at LF. The present approach, where the lexical and semantic interfaces are at the very same level of syntax, allows us to dispense with such stipulation.

In fact, in the present theory it doesn't matter whether chains are built by movement, by base-generation of traces in S-Structure (Koster 1978, 1987; Brody 1995), or by a single operation Form Chain (Chomsky 1993, 15). Such constraints as the Empty Category Principle, normally taken to be constraints on movement, then can be treated instead as part of the interpretation or licensing of chains, along lines suggested by Rothstein (1991) (see also Bouchard 1995).[19]

4.5   Remarks on Processing

Ultimately, what does the language processor have to do?[20] In speech perception, it has to map an auditory signal into an intended (contextualized) meaning (i.e. a conceptual structure) in speech production, it has to map an intended meaning into a set of motor instructions. The hypothesis of Representational Modularity suggests that the only way this can be accomplished is via the intermediate levels of representation, namely phonology and syntax. Moreover, the principles by which the processor is constrained to carry out the mapping are precisely the principles expressed in the formal grammar as correspondence rules. In other words, at least this part of the grammar—the part that links auditory and motor signals to phonology, phonology to syntax, and syntax to meaning—should have a fairly direct processing counterpart.

It is less clear how the generative grammars for each individual level of representation are realized in processing. As in the syntactocentric model, we certainly should reject the view that active generation is going on. It makes little sense to think of randomly generating a phonology, a syntax, and a meaning, and then seeing if you can match them up: "Shucks! The derivation crashed! Oh, well, I'll try again...."

Looking to the general case of Representational Modularity (figures 2.2 and 2.3), we see that any single level of representation typically may receive fragmentary input from a number of distinct sources. Its job, then, is to integrate them into a unified form so as to be able to pass a single more complete result on to the next level along the information pathway. So perhaps the best way to view the individual generative grammars is as providing a repertoire for integrating and filling out fragmentary information coming from other representations via correspondence rules.

Let's see, very informally, how this might work out in practice. Let's think of linguistic working memory as containing a number of "blackboards," each of which can be written on in only one form (i.e. one level of representation). Consider the syntax "blackboard." An interface processor whose output is syntax (e.g. the PS-to-SS processor) can be thought of as an agent that writes on the syntax blackboard; an interface processor whose *input* is syntax (e.g. the SS-to-CS processor) can be thought of as an agent that reads whatever happens to be written on the syntax blackboard at the moment. The syntax module proper can be thought of as an integrative agent that does the housekeeping for the syntax blackboard— that tries to make fragments written by other agents into a coherent whole. It is this integrative processor that makes it possible for multiple inputs from different agents (or fragmentary inputs from a single agent) to coalesce into a unified representation. (Similar construals obtain, of course, for the phonology and conceptual blackboards.)[21]

Let's walk through a bit of speech perception, looking at the logic of the situation. Suppose the auditory-to-phonological processor, in response to a speech signal, dumps a string of phonetic information onto the phonology blackboard. The immediate response of the phonology module is to try to break this string into words in order to make it phonologically well formed. It sends a call to the lexicon: "Do you know of any words that sound like this?" The lexicon, by assumption, is dumb and (as Fodor (1983) tellingly points out) must be prepared to deal with the unexpected, so it just sends back all candidates that have phonological structure compatible with the sample structure sent it. (This is consistent with the well-known literature on lexical priming—Swinney 1979; Tanenhaus, Leiman, and Seidenberg 1979.)

But it doesn't just write these candidates on the phonology blackboard. In fact, the syntactic and conceptual parts of words *can't* be written on the phonological blackboard—they're in the wrong format. Rather, the lexicon simultaneously sends the syntactic and conceptual parts of the candidate items to the syntactic and conceptual blackboards respectively, stimulating those modules to get busy. Meanwhile, the phonology-to-syntax interface reads information about the relative order of the words on the phonology blackboard and writes this on the syntax blackboard. At this point the syntax module has the information usually assumed available to a parser—candidate words and their order.

Suppose the phonological string in question is /əperənt/. The lexicon offers the two possibilities in (13).

(13) a. Phonology: [apparent]$_a$ syntax: Adj$_a$
     b. Phonology: [a]$_a$ [parent]$_b$ syntax: Art$_a^N_b$

Suppose the immediately preceding context is the string /ðiy/. The resulting possibilities are (14a,b).

(14) a. Phonology: [the]$_a$ [apparent]$_b$ syntax: Art$_a$^Adj$_b$
     b. Phonology: [the]$_a$ [a]$_b$ [parent]$_c$ syntax: Art$_a$^Art$_b^N_c$

Both of these are phonologically well formed, so the phonology module accepts them. However, (14b) is syntactically ill formed, since it has two articles in a row. It is therefore rejected by the syntax module.

However, for the syntactic parser to reject this analysis is not enough. It must also send information back to the phonology that this analysis has been rejected, so that the phonological segmentation into the words *a parent* and the word boundary between them can also be rejected: one does not *hear* a word boundary here (see chapter 8).

Consider an alternative context for the possibilities in (13a).

(15) a. Phonology: [it] [was] [only] [apparent]$_a$
       Syntax: ... Adj$_a$
     b. Phonology: [it] [was] [only] [a]$_a$ [parent]$_b$
       Syntax: ... Art$_a^N_b$

In this case the syntax can parse both possibilities, so it doesn't send any rejections back to the phonology. But now suppose the following context is (16).

(16) ... not real

The combination of (16) with either possibility in (15) is phonologically and syntactically well formed. However, the integrative processor for conceptual structure will require the phrases following *only* and *not* to form a contrast. Hence the analysis (15a) + (16) will be conceptually well formed and the analysis (15b) + (16) will not. Thus the conceptual processor sends a signal back to the syntax, rejecting the latter analysis after all. In turn, the syntax sends a signal back to the phonology, rejecting the analysis with a word boundary. (If the continuation were ... *not a teacher*, (15a) would be rejected instead.)

It is important to notice that the rejection in this case is fundamentally semantic, not syntactic. That is, acceptance or rejection is not based on whether the original string and the continuation have parallel parts of speech. For instance, the continuations ... *not purple* and ... *not a concert* have grammatical structure parallel to (15a,b) respectively, but make no sense at all. The requirement is for a salient semantic contrast.

Because the rejection of (15b) + (16) requires two successive steps, from conceptual structure to syntax, then from syntax to phonology, we might expect it to take somewhat longer than the rejection of (14b), which takes only one step of feedback. Levelt (1989, 278–281) cites experimental results for a parallel situation in speech production: phonological feedback that causes revision of encoding of conceptual structure into syntax is shown to take longer than syntactic feedback, apparently because the former has to pass through the syntactic level on the way.

The fact that a semantic anomaly may influence syntactic and phonological parsing is no reason to believe that we have to give up the notion of modularity. Strict Fodorian modularity is perhaps threatened, but Fodor's basic notion of specialized, fast, mandatory, domain-specific, and informationally encapsulated processors is not. It is just that we have to conceive of the boundaries and interfaces of modules somewhat differently. In particular, look at the syntactic parser. The only way semantics can affect syntax is by rejecting (or perhaps differentially weighting) a putative syntactic parse in response to the properties of the corresponding conceptual structure. And the only way syntax can affect phonology is by doing the same thing to a putative phonological parse. That is, we are permitting feedback of the sort Fodor rejects, but in a very limited (and as far as I can tell, theoretically and experimentally justified) way. (On the rhetorical issues surrounding "autonomous" versus "interactive" parsers, see Boland and Cutler 1996, where it is argued that the distinction in practice is less sharp than often claimed.)

This story just looks at the bare-bones logic of processing. It still leaves a lot of room for interpretation in terms of implementation. But it seems consistent with my general sense of results in current psycholinguistics, namely that (1) there are discrete stages at which different kinds of representations develop, but (2) different representations can influence each other as soon as requisite information for connecting them is available. So, for example, extralinguistic context cannot influence initial lexical access in speech perception, because there is nothing in the unorganized phonetic input for it to influence. But once lexical access has taken place, lexical conceptual structure *can* interact with context, because it is in compatible form. In turn, depending on the situation, this interaction may take place soon enough to bias later syntactic parsing, as has been found for example by Trueswell and Tanenhaus (1994).

Similarly, evidence is accumulating (Garrett 1975 and especially Levelt 1989) that speech production invokes a number of discrete processes, each with its own time course. These correspond (at least roughly) to selection of lexical items to express intended meaning, construction of a syntactic structure and lexical morphosyntax, construction of a phonological structure with syllabification and stress, and construction of a motor program.[22]

In other words, the architecture proposed here leads to a logic for processing that has attractive interactions with current psycholinguistic research.

4.6   The Lexicon in a More General Mental Ecology

One of the hallmarks of language, of course, is the celebrated "arbitrariness of the sign," the fact that a random sequence of phonemes can refer to almost anything. This implies, of course, that there could not be language without a lexicon, a list of the arbitrary matches between sound and meaning (with syntactic properties thrown in for good measure).

If we look at the rest of the brain, we do not immediately find anything with these same general properties. Thus the lexicon seems like a major evolutionary innovation, coming as if out of nowhere.

I would like to suggest that although the lexicon is perhaps extreme in its arbitrariness, it is not entirely unique as a mental component. Recall again what a word is: a way of associating units from distinct levels of representation. Now consider what it takes to be able to look at a food and know what it tastes like: a learned association between a visual and a gustatory representation. How many of those do we store? A lot, I should think. From a formal point of view these are associations of representations not unlike those between phonological and conceptual structures. And as far as learning goes, they're *almost* as arbitrary as word-meaning associations. Mashed potatoes and French vanilla ice cream don't look that different.

Perhaps a more telling example comes from vision. Recovering 3D information is essential for identifying objects and navigating through the world (Marr 1982). Yet it turns out to be computationally almost impossible to construct reliable 3D spatial representations from 2D (or 2.5D) projections. Some recent work (Cavanagh 1991) has suggested therefore that long-term memory stores matchings of 2D-to-3D structure for familiar objects—in other words, that one has a sort of "visual vocabulary" that one uses to help solve the difficulties of mapping from 2D to

3D on line. In this case, the mapping is not entirely arbitrary, but it is so difficult that the brain stores large numbers of predigested mappings to use as shortcuts.

A parallel might be seen also in motor control. Suppose you learn a complex motor movement, such as a fancy dive or a particular bowing pattern on the violin. We might think of this learning as the construction of a predigested mapping from a large-scale unit on the level of "intended actions" to a complex pattern on the level of motor instructions. Again it's not arbitrary, but processing is speeded up by having preassembled units as shortcuts.

A final example emerges from speech production. Levelt and Wheeldon (1994) present evidence that speakers use a "mental syllabary" in mapping from phonological structure to motor instructions. This is a stored mapping of all the possible phonological syllables of one's language (anywhere from a few hundred to a few thousand, depending on the language) into their motor realizations. This is a special case of the previous one: it is not an arbitrary mapping (except to the extent that it incorporates subphonetic variation that may play a role in regional accent), but it provides a systematic system of shortcuts that enable speech to be executed rapidly. It thus plays a role in the phonetic-to-motor interface somewhat parallel to the lexicon in the PS-SS and SS-CS interfaces.

What do these examples show? The lexicon may be unique in its size and its utter arbitrariness, but it is not unique in its formal character. Like these other cases, it is a collection of stored associations among fragments of disparate representations. And its role in processing is roughly the same: it is part of the interface between the two (or more) representations it connects. Although this may all be obvious, I think it's important to point it out, because it helps put the theory of language in a more general cognitive context.

Chapter 5

Lexical Entries, Lexical Rules

What is in the lexicon and how does it get into sentences? So far we have dealt only with the lexical insertion/licensing of morphologically trivial words like *cat* (chapter 4). Now we turn to morphologically complex elements of various sorts. This chapter will be concerned with sorting out a number of issues in morphology within the present framework, in preparation for subsequent chapters on productive morphology (chapter 6) and on idioms and other fixed expressions (chapter 7).

5.1 Broadening the Conception of the Lexicon

Recall why the lexicon is introduced into the theory. In order to produce the unlimited variety of possible sentences of a language, the language user must have in long-term memory not only the combinatorial rules but also something for them to combine. The lexicon is "conceptually necessary," then, as the long-term memory repository of available pieces of language from which the combinatorial system can build up larger utterances.

In the conception developed in chapter 4, the lexicon is not just a long-term repository of pieces of language. Rather, it is a repository of ⟨PS, SS, CS⟩ triples that enable correspondences to be established between pieces of structure derived by the three independent generative systems.

What are these pieces? The usual assumption, I think, is that we have to look for a standard "size" for lexical items, say words. This emerges as assumption 4 of chapter 1, "Lexical insertion/Merge enters words (the X^0 categories N, V, A, P) into phrase structure," where the standard size is specified in terms of (narrow) syntax. This assumption also appears as a fundamental position in Aronoff 1976, 1994, for instance. Alternatively, the standard size is morphemes—or morphemes and words both (as in Halle 1973, for instance).

But is this realistic? The case of idioms immediately brings us up short, as will be argued in more detail in chapter 7. Though one may be able to convince oneself that *kick the bucket* is a V^0 (a syntactic word), it is hard to imagine extending the same treatment to idioms such as NP_i's got NP_j where pro_i want(s) pro_j or *The cat's got NP's tongue.* Idioms with such complex structure strongly suggest that lexically listed units can be larger than X^0. This chapter and the next will suggest as well that there are lexical units *smaller* than X^0, namely productive derivational and inflectional morphemes. Thus the view to be adopted here is that, although the stereotypical lexical item may be an X^0 such as *cat*, lexical entries in fact come in a variety of sizes.

A similar position is advocated by Di Sciullo and Williams (1987), who call lexical entries *listemes*. They distinguish this notion of "word" from the grammatical (more properly, syntactic) notion of word, which I am here identifying with X^0 constituents; they wish to show that "the listemes of a language correspond to neither the morphological objects nor the syntactic atoms" (p. 1). Although I agree with them that it is of interest for the theory of grammar to distinguish the internal properties of X^0 from the properties of phrases, I do not agree that the theory of listemes is "of no interest to the grammarian" (p. 1). As we have seen, it is important to the grammarian to know how listemes find their way into sentences. If listemes come in sizes other than X^0, then the standard theory of lexical insertion must be reconsidered.[1]

5.2 Morphosyntax versus Morphophonology

There seems to be a recurrent problem about where morphology fits into the theory of grammar—whether it is or is not distinct from syntax and/ or phonology. The tripartite architecture, I think, makes the situation clearer. A lexical item is a triple of phonological, syntactic, and conceptual information that serves as a correspondence rule among the three components. Therefore we expect it to partake of all three. Consequently we should also expect morphological relations, which relate words to words, likewise to partake of all three.

For a simple example, a compound like *doghouse* requires concatenating the phonology of the two constituent words and stressing the first; it also specifies that the result is syntactically a noun formed of two nouns; and finally, it specifies that the result means 'a house for a dog'. Thus in general we must assume that morphology may be divided into morphophonology, morphosyntax, and morphosemantics—plus the correlations among the three.

Just as we expect bracketing mismatches between phonology and syntax at the phrasal level (chapter 2), so we expect bracketing mismatches within words, for example in *atomic scientist*.[2] (I will concentrate here on morphophonology and morphosyntax, omitting morphosemantics for the time being.)

(1) *Morphophonology*   *Morphosyntax*

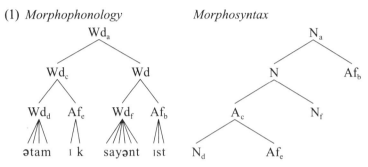

(1) is the closest equivalent in the present notation to Sadock's (1991) "autolexical" approach, which might look something like (2).

(2)   N   "morphological
                                                   structure"

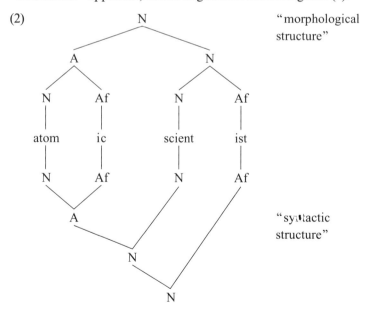

There are two differences between the two notations. The most obvious is that the bracketing that Sadock calls "morphology" is assigned here to morphophonology. There is no reason for it to contain syntactic category labels—and in fact syntactic category labels dominating segmental phonology are outlawed by Representational Modularity. Lieber (1992, chapters 4 and 5) also makes use of a double tree, the lower tree like Sadock's, but the upper tree composed of phonological units such as words, feet, and syllables. This is closer to what is desired here.

The second difference between (1) and (2) is that in (1) no segmental phonology is attached to the morphosyntax (Sadock's "syntax"), again because of Representational Modularity. Here (1) differs also from Lieber's notation. Instead of matching the two representations through a shared segmental phonology, (1) matches them through coindexation of various constituents. The bracketing mismatch is possible because coindexation is not complete.

A more extreme case of mismatch appears in Anderson's (1992) account of Kwakwala, in which articles, which are syntactic left sisters, are treated phonologically as suffixes to the preceding word. (3) is Anderson's auto-lexical representation (p. 20). This looks so strange because it is a massive violation of the overwhelming preference for syntactic words to correspond to phonological words (correspondence rule (12a) of chapter 2).

(3)
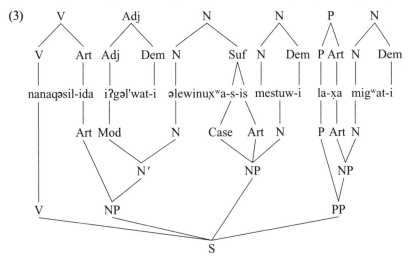

This parallels Sadock's representations in its use of a double tree. However, Anderson's description makes clear that the syntactic labels in the upper bracketing are irrelevant—that the principles governing this bracketing are those of phonological words. Thus on present principles the representation would be more like (4), observing strict Representational Modularity.

(4) *Syntax*

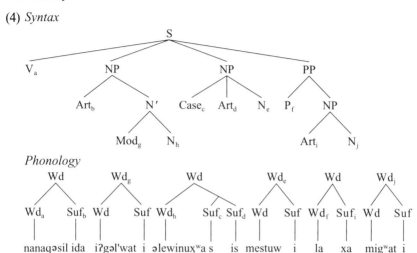

Under this approach, the question of where morphology belongs becomes somewhat more differentiated. Morphosyntax is the syntactic structure of constituents of X^0 nodes in syntax; morphophonology is the phonological structure of constituents of phonological words. The issue of the morphology-syntax interface—that is, the question "Does morphology interact with syntax?"—now becomes "Does morpho*syntax* interact with phrasal syntax?" At the same time, issues such as allomorphy and how affixes affect stress belong to morphophonology.

Table 5.1 shows how phonological structure, syntactic structure, and conceptual structure exist parallel at phrasal and lexical scales (*"lexical"* is in scare quotes because the lexicon does in fact include units larger than X^0).

Table 5.1
Division of lexical and phrasal information among phonological, syntactic, and conceptual structure

	Phonological structure	Syntactic structure	Conceptual structure
Above X^0	Phrasal phonology	Syntax	Phrasal semantics
Below X^0	"Lexical" (morpho)phonology	Morphosyntax	"Lexical" semantics

5.3 Inflectional versus Derivational Morphology

A traditional issue in morphology has been to distinguish inflectional morphology from derivational morphology. Intuitively, affixes like tense, plural, and case are considered inflectional, whereas nominalizing affixes like *-tion* and negative affixes like *un-* are considered derivational. Typically, inflectional affixes fall outside of derivational affixes. Typically, inflection is more regular than derivation. Yet it has proven difficult on grounds of form alone to distinguish the two (Anderson 1982, 1992; Spencer 1991).

Some of the problem comes from a failure to distinguish morphosyntax from morphophonology. The existence of massive phonological irregularity in an inflectional paradigm, for instance, makes it no less inflectional; nor does the phonological regularity of, say, *un-* make it any less derivational. I am essentially going to adopt Anderson's (1982, 1992) characterization of the distinction: inflectional morphology consists of those aspects of word structure (morphosyntax) that interact with phrasal syntax. For example, a sentence, in order to be a sentence, must have a tense marker (or to be an infinitival clause, must lack it); the presence of case markers is determined by phrasal context; and plurality on a noun can condition plurality on its determiner and/or on a verb. Thus it is necessary for purposes of phrasal syntax that nouns appear in both singular and plural and in all case forms, and that verbs appear in all tenses and participial forms and with a full paradigm of agreement markers.

To be sure, derivational morphology affects the syntactic behavior of lexical items. For instance, it can change syntactic category. However, phrasal syntax does not care that *recital* is derived from a verb; in phrasal syntax, *recital* behaves the same way as the underived *concert*. Similarly, derivational morphology certainly can change argument structure, which affects the contexts in which an item can appear in phrasal syntax. For instance, *out*-prefixation drastically changes a verb's argument structure, changing all inputs into transitive verbs (e.g. *outswim* from intransitive *swim*, *outspend* from transitive *spend*, but with a different argument as object). But *every* lexical item presents an argument structure to phrasal syntax. As far as argument structure in phrasal syntax is concerned, *out-V* behaves pretty much like the underived verb *beat* ('win over X in a contest'). That is, the derivational status of *outswim* is not at issue in phrasal syntax.

In other words, derivational morphology can be regarded as essentially invisible to phrasal syntax, whereas inflectional morphology cannot. This is the sense in which Di Sciullo and Williams (1987) can regard the output of derivational morphology as producing "syntactic atoms." This is also the sense intended by the Lexical Integrity Principle of Bresnan and Mchombo (1995), according to which syntactic rules do not have access to the interior of words. Going back further, this is the essential idea behind Chomsky's (1970) lexicalist hypothesis.

A consequence of this position is that inflectional morphology must be syntactically productive: words must be available in all possible inflectional forms in order to satisfy the free combinatorial properties of syntax. This does not mean that all forms are *phonologically* productive, only that they must exist.[3] By contrast, derivational morphology may or may not be productive. For syntactic purposes, it is not necessary to have a consistent output for derivational processes—in fact, phrasal syntax cannot tell whether it is operating with a derivationally complex item or a simple one.

5.4   Productivity versus Semiproductivity

It seems possible to distinguish two different kinds of morphological relationships obtaining among lexical items. One kind is the sort of productive regularity found in, say, the English plural. Given a count noun, the speaker automatically knows that it has a plural form and what that form means. The speaker also has a default value for its pronunciation, which can, however, be blocked by learned irregular cases.

This may be contrasted with a "semiproductive regularity" such as the creation of English denominal verbs like *butter, saddle, shelve,* and *pocket* (see section 5.6). The syntactic regularity is that the output of the process is a transitive verb; semantically, the output may mean roughly 'put N* in/on NP', 'get N* out of/off NP', or 'put NP in/on N*' (where N* is the root noun); phonologically, the output is pronounced (almost) like the noun. This differs from a regular process in two respects. First, we don't know *exactly* what the output of the rule is in a particular case; for instance, *saddle* means more than 'put a saddle on NP', and *shelve* ends with a voiced instead of an unvoiced consonant. Second, we have to know whether the output is actually a word or not. For instance, there *could* be a verb *mustard*, 'to spread mustard on NP', and we could understand it in the appropriate context, but it's not a word in the stored lexicon. That is, semiproductive regularities create potential words, but *actual* words obeying the regularity still have to be acquired one by one.

In other words, the word *bananas* does not have to be listed in the lexicon, but the word *shelve* does. We could say that *bananas* is a word but not a lexical item (or listeme). By contrast, an *ir*regular plural has to be listed; for instance, we have to assume that the existence of *children* blocks the productive formation of *childs*.[4] (I return to the issue of blocking in chapter 6.)

Even if *shelve* is listed, we somehow must also recognize its relation to *shelf*. How is this relation encoded? Since Chomsky's (1970) "Remarks on Nominalization," generative theory has included the notion of a "lexical rule" or a "lexical redundancy rule" that captures regularities among lexical items. For instance, the lexical rule responsible for *shelve* says how it is related to *shelf* phonologically, syntactically, and semantically, and how this fits into a regularity found with many other denominal verbs. The rule either (1) permits the lexicon to list only the nonredundant parts of the word (the "impoverished entry" theory) or (2) reduces the informational cost of listing the word in full (the "full entry" theory). I discuss this choice in section 5.6. By the time the lexical entry is inserted into a sentence, though, it is assumed to be fully filled out. That is, lexical rules are taken to be internal to the lexicon, and invisible to the phrasal part of the grammar.

To sum up so far: On one hand, a word like *shelve* must be listed because the language user has to know that it exists. And it is the word *shelve*, not the word *shelf*, that helps license the sentence *Let's shelve these books*. On the other hand, somewhere in the grammar the relation of *shelve* to the noun *shelf* must be encoded. This is what lexical rules are designed to do.

However, are lexical rules the proper way to encode *productive* regularities? I have in the past taken the position that the regular English past tense is formed by a lexical rule, so that all regular past tenses are listed along with the irregulars (Jackendoff 1975); this is also the position taken by Halle (1973) and the standard position in LFG and HPSG. Wasow (1977), however, argues that one wants to distinguish the properties of lexical rules from those of productive rules (in his framework, transformational relations); he contrasts English adjectival passive participles (lexical and semiproductive) with verbal passives (transformational and productive).

Hankamer (1989) presents a strong argument that productive rules are *not* lexical in the sense defined above, by drawing attention to languages with rich agglutinative morphology such as Turkish or Navajo. In such a language every verb has tens of thousands of possible forms, constructed through productive processes. It makes little sense to claim that each form is individually listed in the lexicon—especially since the forms are immediately available when a Turkish or Navajo speaker acquires a new verb stem. Hankamer calculates in fact that a full listing of the possibilities for Turkish words would likely exceed the information storage limits of the entire brain.

In response to this problem, it is sometimes advocated that lexical rules create a "virtual lexicon," the space of possible derived forms—and that this is distinguished from the "actual lexicon," the list of occurring items. (This is in a sense the position of Lees (1960)—the idea that the lexical rules determine what is *possible* but not what is *actual*. I think it is the position of Di Sciullo and Williams (1987) as well.) There are two difficulties with such a position.

The first is that it fails to distinguish between productive and semi-productive rules. Lexical rules must still fall into two classes: those for which we *know* that an output exists and those for which we must *learn* whether an output exists. Without such a diacritic distinguishing lexical rule types, there is no way of knowing why *shelve* must fall into the actual lexicon but *bananas* need only be in the virtual lexicon.

The second difficulty lies in what is meant by the "virtual lexicon" when it applies to productive rules. *Banana* is part of the actual lexicon, but *bananas* is supposed to be part of the virtual lexicon, something that is available to be inserted into phrase structures even though not listed. Notice the terminological flimflam, though: we could equally well speak of phrasal syntax in the very same terms, saying that the language contains a set of "virtual phrases" that are not listed but are available to be inserted as parts of larger phrases. Such terminology would be very curious indeed. Why should "virtual lexical items" be any different from "virtual phrases"? Seen in this light, the "virtual lexicon" generated by productive rules looks like just the output of another generative system: a combinatorial system that applies *within* X^0 constituents.

Consequently, there seems to me no reason to distinguish productive lexical rules from productive phrasal rules, other than that productive lexical rules apply to constituents smaller than X^0. Under such a construal, all the above issues vanish: *banana* is listed, as are verb stems in

Turkish, say; but *bananas* and all the thousands of Turkish verb forms are not. Rather, they are the product of standard rules of combination that just happen to apply within X^0 constituents.

On such a view, we will treat a productive inflectional ending such as the English plural as its own lexical entry, for a first approximation looking like (5). (Chapter 6 will deal with it in more detail.)

(5)

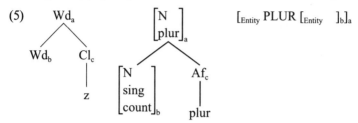

In (5) the left-hand tree encodes the morphophonological structure, a clitic pronounced /z/ that attaches to the ends of words. The middle tree encodes the morphosyntactic structure, an affix that when attached to a singular count noun produces a syntactically plural noun. The right-hand component is the LCS of the plural, a conceptual function whose argument is an entity and whose value is a plural entity (see Jackendoff 1991 for a more detailed analysis in terms of Conceptual Semantics, or substitute your own formalism). These three structures together form a correspondence rule because of the subscripted linking indices. The noun that hosts the plural is subscripted *b* throughout; the resultant Word, plural noun, and plural entity are subscripted *a* throughout; and the clitic/affix is subscripted *c*. (I don't see any need to single out a component of the LCS that corresponds directly to the affix, so the LCS contains no subscript *c*.)

A lexical noun plus (5) will jointly license the correspondence of a plural noun to its semantics and phonology. For instance, (6) will be the phrasal combination for *cats*, where *cat* is as specified in chapter 4.

(6)

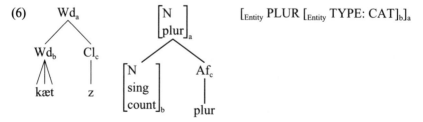

In (6) the linking indices for *cat* have unified with those for the host noun in (5), so that the phonological and semantic content of the host noun are specified along with the structures in which it is embedded. Such a process of combination thus closely parallels the licensing of a phrasal constituent such as a VP jointly by a verb and its direct object.

The distinction between productivity and semiproductivity appears in derivational morphology as well. Although most derivational processes are only semiproductive, consider for example the interesting case of English expletive infixation (McCarthy 1982). The literature on this process has concerned the unusual positioning of the affix within a word (e.g. *manu-fuckin-facturer*). But it has not addressed where such derived words fit into the morphology in general. I think we can take it for granted that *auto-fuckin-matic* is not a listeme; and to say it is nevertheless part of the "virtual lexicon" is only to say it is the output of a productive process. Expletive infixation is certainly not an inflectional process—there is nothing at all in phrasal syntax that conditions it or depends on it. And in fact the availability of an expletive infix depends on phonological conditions not visible to syntax, so it cannot be available with the uniformity of an inflectional process. If anything, then, this is an instance of derivational morphology, but it is a productive process.

Suppose that we treat the infix as a triple of structures $\langle$PS, SS, CS$\rangle$ approximately like (7).

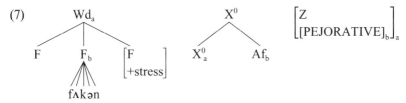

The phonology in (7) is an approximation to whatever is the proper environment for the infix: within a word, after an initial foot, immediately before a stressed foot. What makes it an infix is that the index *b* dominating the phonological content is dominated by the index *a* for its host word.[5] In the syntax, I have somewhat arbitrarily treated the form as a suffix. But in fact it could be anywhere—or even absent, since it has no syntactic consequences (so that it might be something like *hello*). In its semantics, the infix behaves like any other modifier, adding a property to its head. (I have not included any account of the fact that this affix is invariably associated with topic/focus stress and semantics.)

(5) and (7) will license matchings of freely generated phonological structure to freely generated syntax and semantics. In that respect they are like any other lexical item. They are however lexical items that are less than an X^0, that is, smaller than a syntactic word. This appears to be a plausible model for any regular morphological process, inflectional or derivational.[6]

One might want to say that such forms are stored in a special "affixal lexicon," separate from the "word lexicon." But in fact such a distinction is unnecessary, since affixes are inherently distinguished by their phonological and syntactic form. We can freely lump them into the lexicon along with *cat* and *forget*, because they can license only the kinds of correspondences they are built to license.[7]

Turning to semiproductive rules, the distinction between actual and virtual lexicon does make some sense here. The "virtual lexicon" here is the set of potential forms that are easier to understand or learn in context by virtue of the existence of lexical rules; these forms are nowhere listed. On the other hand, the actual lexicon contains the forms the language user lists, along with their actual specialized pronunciations and meanings.

I am advocating, therefore, that the fundamental distinction is not between lexical rules and phrasal rules, but between productive and semiproductive rules.[8] For instance, we can say that the regular English past tense is a productive rule of free combination. The various subregularities in irregular past tenses, on the other hand, are semiproductive rules, hence lexical rules. The existence of a listed semiproductive form such as *sang* blocks the use of a free combination such as *singed*, in a manner that we return to in chapter 6.

Putting all these pieces together: The theory of grammar must distinguish a notion of syntactic word, which can be identified with a maximal X^0—the X^0 that dominates morphologically derived words and compounds, and that defines a syntactic head around which phrasal arguments and modifiers cluster.[9] The theory must also distinguish a notion of phonological word, which may specify some minimal prosodic conditions such as the presence of at least one foot (McCarthy and Prince 1986). Both these notions are distinct from the notion of a lexical item or listeme, which stereotypically consists of a syntactic/phonological word (e.g. *dog*), but may also be larger (*kick the bucket*) or smaller (*-s* and *-fuckin-*).

The distinction between inflectional and derivational morphology is a morphosyntactic distinction. A morphological process is inflectional if it involves features that are independently active in productive phrasal syn-

tax; it is derivational otherwise. An inflectional process *must* provide a set of derived forms for all stems of the requisite sort, whereas a derivational process may or may not.

The distinction between productive and semiproductive processes cuts across the inflectional/derivational distinction. Although an inflectional process must provide derived forms for all stems, at least some of these forms may be provided by semiproductive processes or even suppletion, as is the case with the English past tense. Conversely, a derivational process may be entirely productive, as evidenced by expletive infixation.

The defining characteristic of semiproductive rules is that one needs to know whether each particular derived form exists, as well as (in many cases) particularities of its meaning and pronunciation. That is, the outputs of semiproductive rules must be either individually listed or understood by virtue of context. By contrast, productive processes predict the existence and form of all derived forms, which need not therefore be listed (but still may be). Productive affixes are treated here as lexical items that are smaller than X^0 and that undergo productive rules of sub-X^0 combination.[10]

5.5 Psycholinguistic Considerations

The basic psycholinguistic question about morphology is whether complex morphological forms are stored in long-term memory or composed "on-line" in working memory from stored constituents. The position taken in the last section translates readily into these terms. In the case of semiproductive regularities, one must know whether the derived form exists and exactly what it means. Hence such forms must be stored in long-term memory, and lexical rules are to be regarded as relations among entries in long-term memory. In the case of productive regularities, the affixes are stored as separate lexical entries, and at least some derived forms are composed on the fly in working memory.

This distinction appears to be borne out in a growing psycholinguistic literature. This research has been particularly stimulated by the connectionist proposal of Rumelhart and McClelland (1986), which claims that all past tenses, regular and irregular, are accounted for by a uniform associationist process, and by the critique of this account by Pinker and Prince (1988). Here is a brief summary of some experimental results, drawn from Pinker and Prince 1991.

The behavior of irregular past tense verbs is affected by their frequency, whereas that of regular past tenses is not. For instance, lower-frequency irregulars are more likely to be overregularized by children and to be uttered incorrectly by adults when under time pressure (Bybee and Slobin 1982). Ratings of naturalness for past tenses of regular verbs correlate significantly with rated naturalness of their stems, but naturalness ratings for irregular past tense forms correlate less strongly with their stem ratings but significantly with past tense form frequency (Ullman and Pinker 1991). Prasada, Pinker, and Snyder (1990) asked subjects to utter past tense forms in response to a stem flashed on a screen. Lower past-frequency irregulars took significantly longer to utter than higher past-frequency irregulars, but there was no such difference with regular-past-tense verbs. In a study reported by Marin, Saffran, and Schwartz (1976), agrammatic aphasics displayed errors with regular inflected forms to a much greater extent than with irregulars. Pinker and Prince argue that all these differences are consistent with irregulars' being stored and regulars' being generated on line, as advocated here.

In addition, Jaeger et al. (1996) had subjects undergoing PET scans produce past tenses in response to verb stems flashed on a screen. The group of subjects producing regular pasts showed a much different involvement of brain areas than those producing irregular pasts. The areas for the regular verbs were almost a subset of those for the irregulars, but not quite. (In addition, reaction time patterns were different, irregulars being generally slower than regulars.) Again this suggests that the brain processes involved in semiregular morphophonology are different from those involved in productive affixation. (See also papers in Feldman 1995, especially Schreuder and Baayen 1995 and Chialant and Caramazza 1995.)

As Pinker and Prince (1991) point out, however, the fact that a word is constructed by a productive process does not preclude its being listed as well. In fact, in *learning* a productive rule, a child presumably first has to learn a number of derived forms separately in order to extract the generalization. Once the productive process is learned, do the previously listed derived forms simply vanish? That doesn't seem like the brain's way.

Interestingly, some experimental work has verified this speculation. Baayen, Van Casteren, and Dijkstra (1992) found that, in comprehension, reaction times to plurals with a low-frequency stem were in proportion to the frequency of the stem and not to the frequency of the plural form alone. In contrast, reaction times to plurals with a high-frequency stem showed a significant effect of frequency of the plural form itself. Thus high-frequency nouns (but not low-frequency nouns) behave as if they have independent representations for their singular and plural forms. Baayen, Levelt, and Haveman (1993) have extended this finding to production: in a picture-naming task, nouns (such as *eye*) whose plural is more frequent than their singular were slower in production than nouns whose singular is more frequent than their plural (factoring out overall frequency effects). Their explanation is that for the "plural-dominant" nouns, the plural is actually listed as a separate lexical item, and so the singular and plural are in competition for word selection, slowing the process down. Stemberger and MacWhinney (1988) arrive at a similar conclusion with respect to English past tenses: low-frequency regular past forms are constructed on line, but high-frequency regular past forms are stored.[11]

Notice that this approach is consistent with the existence of nouns that appear in plural form without a corresponding singular, such as *scissors* and *troops* ('soldiers'). These are just listed, the same as *eyes*. What is not consistent with this approach would be the existence of singular count nouns that for semantic reasons should have a plural but in fact do not. I don't know of anything like this (though see note 3).

5.6 "Optimal Coding" of Semiproductive Forms

Let us return now to the issue of how forms derived by semiproductive processes, say *shelve*, are listed in the lexicon.[12] We are under the following two constraints. First, because the process is semiproductive, a speaker must list in long-term memory that the word in question exists. Second, by the time the sentence containing *shelve* is composed, the phonology, syntax, and meaning of *shelve* must be completely filled out.

There are two possible solutions. The first possibility is that *shelve* is listed in its entirety in the lexicon, just like, say, the underived form *mumble*. Let's call this the *full entry theory*. The second possibility is that *shelve* is not listed in its entirety—that its entry contains less complete information, but that, in the process of its being used in a phrasal structure, its full information is filled in from the lexical rule that relates it to *shelf*. Let's call this the *impoverished entry theory*. (Henderson (1989) and Marslen-Wilson et al. (1994) present surveys of parallel positions in psycholinguistics.)

A fairly standard assumption among linguists is that the impoverished entry theory is ultimately correct. This is expressed, for instance, by assumption 5 of chapter 1, namely that the language faculty is nonredundant and that the lexicon appears in terms of an "optimal coding" that expresses "exactly what is not predictable." However, to repeat the point made in chapter 1, although "conceptual necessity" requires that the lexicon encode what is not predictable, it does not require that the lexicon encode *only* what is not predictable. In fact, section 5.5 cited psycholinguistic evidence that even some regular plurals are lexically listed (in some form or another), casting doubt on the assumption of nonredundancy and optimal coding. (Remember, we are talking about the mental lexicon, not some mathematically optimal abstract object, so psycholinguistic evidence is absolutely relevant.)

Why is optimal coding appealing? The obvious reason is that it translates the notion of "lexical generalization" directly into some measure like number of bits of information encoded in the lexicon. If there is a generalization among a number of items, it takes fewer bits to store them than if they were unrelated (and therefore in the traditional view of memory as a filing system, less "space"). In principle, then, this is a nice way to conceptualize matters.

However, if we try to work out an impoverished entry theory rigorously, a number of discomfiting formal issues arise. First, notice that the impoverished entry theory cannot simply say that the full information found in the phonological and semantic representation of the lexical item in its sentential context is "filled in." Rather, we must posit a grammatical process that accomplishes this filling in on the basis of lexical rules and/or syntactic context. Let us call this process *Lexical Assembly*. Presumably Lexical Assembly applies in working memory as part of the on-line composition of sentences. (If it applied to long-term memory, lexical items would be filled in in long-term memory, violating the basic assumption of the impoverished entry theory.)

This said, let us construct an approximate version of the lexical rule for English denominal verbs like *saddle* and *shelve*. The rule will have a phonological part that says the phonology of the base form remains (in the default case) unchanged, a syntactic part that says the derived form is a verb dominating the base noun,[13] and a conceptual part that specifies a variety of possible meanings built on that of the base.

(8) Base form   Wd$_a$ N$_a$ [X]$_a$

       Derived form   Wd$_b$ [$_V$ N$_a$]$_b$ a. [Y PUT [X]$_a$ $\left\{ \begin{matrix} \text{i.} & \text{IN} \\ \text{ii.} & \text{ON} \end{matrix} \right\}$ Z]$_b$

                                  b. [Y GET [X]$_a$ $\left\{ \begin{matrix} \text{i.} & \text{OUT-OF} \\ \text{ii.} & \text{OFF} \end{matrix} \right\}$ Z]$_b$

                                  c. [Y PUT Z $\left\{ \begin{matrix} \text{i.} & \text{IN} \\ \text{ii.} & \text{ON} \end{matrix} \right\}$ [X]$_a$]$_b$

In the conceptual structures in (8), Y and Z are the arguments of the derived verb; they are realized syntactically as subject and object respectively. The options in (8a–c) are illustrated by the examples in (9).

(9) a. i. *smoke* a ham = put *smoke* in a ham
      ii. *roof* a house = put a *roof* on a house
        (also *saddle* a horse, *water* flowers)
   b. i. *milk* a cow = get *milk* out of a cow
        (also *smoke* a cigar)
      ii. *skin* a banana = get the *skin* off a banana
   c. i. *pocket* the money = put money in one's *pocket*
        (also *bottle* the wine, *house* the immigrants)
      ii. *shelve* the books = put the books on a *shelf*
        (also, in my daughters' dialect, *roof* a frisbee)
        (*halve* illustrates yet another semantic option)

How will these derived verbs be listed? Suppose they were semantically perfectly predictable. Then, one might suppose, the verb *saddle* could be listed as shown in (10).

(10) ["saddle" + rule 8aii]

But what does "saddle" mean in (10)? It stands for the lexical noun whose phonology is *saddle*—but this noun can't be identified without spelling out all the information in the noun itself. Hence the verb ends up taking as many bits as the noun from which it is derived, missing the point of optimal coding.

The obvious alternative is to have the verb contain a "pointer" to the noun. In computer science–like notation, we might draw something like this:

(11) [x + rule 8aii]

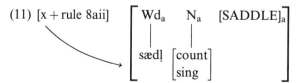

$$\begin{bmatrix} \text{Wd}_a & \text{N}_a & [\text{SADDLE}]_a \\ | & | & \\ \text{sædl} & \begin{bmatrix} \text{count} \\ \text{sing} \end{bmatrix} & \end{bmatrix}$$

This looks somewhat better. But what is a pointer formally? It is an index attached to x that uniquely identifies the target lexical entry. Which raises the question, What does it take to uniquely identify a lexical entry?

One possibility is that each lexical entry is individuated by an index, say a numerical index, the entry's "address." In this case, if the noun *saddle* has the index 349, then the pointer reduces to a citation of this index, as in (12).

(12) [349 + rule 8aii]

This is all well and good, but how do we go beyond the idealization of semantic regularity and build more realistic lexical entries for this class of verbs? (13) lists some of these verbs with paraphrases corresponding somewhat more closely to their meaning. The italicized material is the part not predictable from the base noun and the lexical rule; the material in brackets designates selectional restrictions on an argument.

(13) a. smoke = put smoke into [*food*] *by hanging in an enclosure over a fire*

   b. smoke = get smoke out of [*a cigar, pipe, etc.*] *by putting in the mouth and puffing*

   c. saddle = put a saddle on [*horse, donkey, etc.*] *in canonical position*

   d. roof = put *permanently attached* roof*ing material* on roof of [*a building*]

   e. roof = put object on a roof *by throwing, kicking, etc.*

   f. plate = put [*food*] on a plate *for serving*

Extending the form in (12) to encompass these gives something like (14).

(14) [349 + rule 8aii; [HORSE] [IN CANONICAL POSITION]]

But this is incoherent, because it does not specify how Lexical Assembly is to incorporate the extra semantic information with that provided by the lexical rule.[14]

Another such case concerns exocentric compounds line *yellowjacket* ('a bee with a yellow "jacket"'), *redcoat* ('British soldier of the 1770s with a red coat'), *big top* ('circus tent with a big top'), *redhead* ('person with red hair'), *blackhead* ('pimple with a black "head"'). Assuming a lexical rule something like (15),

(15) Base form(s) Wd_a $[A]_a$ $[X]_a$
                     Wd_b $[N]_b$ $[Y]_b$
     Derived form $[Wd_a\,Wd_b]_c$ $[_N\,A_a\,N_b]_c$
                     $[Z\ WITH\ [Y]_b\ THAT\ IS\ [X]_a]_c$

these would have lexical entries like those in (16).

(16) a. [2,491 + 63,120 + rule 15; [BEE]]

  b. [16,246 + 2,489 + rule 15; [BRITISH SOLDIER OF 1770S]]

Like (14), these leave it to Lexical Assembly to figure out that the residual conceptual information such as [BEE] is to be filled in for Z in the derived form of rule (15).

Now, again, let's remove the idealization of semantic regularity and see how *redhead* is specified as meaning 'a person with red *hair on the* head'.

(17) [16,246 + 59,821 + rule 15; [PERSON] [HAIR ON ...]]

This is even less coherent than (14). Still worse would be a case like *pothead* ('person who habitually smokes pot'). How can Lexical Assembly figure out how to put these pieces together?

One might respond to this difficulty by stipulating that these isolated pieces are indexed into their proper places in the structure for the derived form in the rule. (I won't try to find a way to state this.) But this too is problematic. Consider that different lexical items put their idiosyncratic material in different places. Consequently, each lexical entry must pick out the particular parts of the rule to which it adds extra information. In other words, each lexical entry must individuate the relevant parts of the derived form of the rule. In terms of bits of information, this amounts to reconstructing (much of) the derived form of the rule within the lexical entry itself—just what the impoverished entry theory was supposed to successfully avoid.

Matters are complicated still further by the existence of multiple forms related to each other through a nonexistent root (this is a primary argument against the impoverished entry theory in Jackendoff 1975).

(18) a. aggression, aggressive, aggressor (*aggress)

  b. retribution, retributive (*retribute, *retributor)

  c. aviator, aviation (*aviate, *aviative)

  d. fission, fissile (*fiss, *fissive, *fissor)

How is a lexical entry for such items to be formulated? One possibility, suggested by Halle (1973), is that the lexicon *does* list *aggress*, *retribute*, and so on, but marks them with a diacritic [−lexical insertion]. Presumably, the morpheme *cran-* in *cranberry* would be similarly marked. Under this assumption, all the words in (18) are related to such hypothetical roots in the normal way.

But consider what such a position entails: *aggress* has every property of a lexical entry except that of being used as a lexical item in sentences—the defining factor of lexical entries. The claim made by such a diacritic is that the lexicon would be simpler if *aggress* just lacked this annoying feature and could be inserted. Of course, we do sometimes find back-formations such as *aggress*, in response to the need for a verb to express the requisite concept and to avoid the clumsy periphrastic *commit aggression*. But to say this is due to overriding a feature [−lexical insertion] is a little odd. Consider what it would mean to learn that a lexical item had such a feature. On this analysis, we would say that for a child to over-generalize a word (say *I fell the horse* 'I made the horse fall') would be to create a lexical item; to learn that there is no such causative form would be to mark that form [−lexical insertion]. So the mental lexicon ought to be littered with such failed attempts at generalization, among which happen to be forms like *aggress* and *retribute*.

A more attractive solution conceptually is that failed lexical forms like causative *fall* simply wither away (I gather that the reasons this might happen are still obscure to researchers in acquisition; but in any event, they are the same as those that would prompt a child's adding a feature [−lexical insertion]). They therefore become part of the virtual lexicon; that is, they are not listed, though they are potential forms made available by lexical rules. This is, I believe, the correct option for the use of *aggress* as a neologistic back-formation.

However, this doesn't help us with the relations among *aggression*, *aggressive*, and *aggressor*. A way to relate such words without making use of the hypothetical root is to arbitrarily choose one member of each set as the fully listed form and to list the other members as impoverished entries, making use of multiple lexical rules. Suppose 2,136 is the address for the full entry *aggression*, rule 75 is the rule creating *-tion* nominals from verbs, and rule 86 is the rule creating *-ive* adjectives from verbs. Then (19) might be the entry for *aggressive*. (*Rule 75* is preceded by minus rather than plus to indicate that the rule is invoked in such a way that Lexical Assembly *removes* rather than adds the *-tion* affix.)

(19) [2136 − rule 75 + rule 86]

This works, but it leaves totally indeterminate which member of the set should be the fully specified one. (Aronoff (1976) does give arguments for the priority of one form, though.) We get equally valued solutions by treating *aggressive* or *aggressor* as the fully specified form. So here the impoverished entry theory forces upon us an embarrassment of nota-tionally indistinguishable solutions.

Let us turn now to the full entry theory of lexical listing. It is easy to see that none of these formal issues arises. There is no need for a process of Lexical Assembly. There is no problem of integrating idiosyncratic information in a composed lexical entry with predictable information borrowed from its root, because the predictable information is present in the entry of the composed item, where it forms a structural matrix in which the idiosyncratic information is already embedded. There is no need for entries marked [−lexical insertion], because a word like *aggression* is fully specified and does not need to borrow information from its hypothetical root. And all the members of rootless families like (18) are fully listed, so there is no need to arbitrarily choose which one is basic and therefore fully listed.

What seems to be lost in the full entry theory, though, is any notion that semiregularities "save" anything: *shelve* takes no fewer bits to list than an underived word of similar complexity. In order to make sense of the full entry theory, then, we need to develop an alternative notion of what constitutes "informational cost" in the lexicon. In Jackendoff 1975 I proposed that the notion of "cost" be measured in terms of nonredundancy or "independent information content." The idea is that lexical entries are fully listed, but that lexical rules render parts of these entries redundant, so the "cost" of learning them and listing them is less. On the other hand, idiosyncratic content not predicted by a lexical rule costs "full price." In the case of derived forms for which there is no lexical root, one "pays" for the information that would constitute the root without having to list the root separately; at the same time one gets the derivational morphology more "cheaply" because of the lexical rule. Finally, in cases like the rootless families in (18), one "pays" for the root information only once, as is desired.

Although such a notion of cost can be made formally coherent (I think), its implementation in a real system admittedly remains somewhat hazy. It seems to me, though, that such relatively recent computational notions as distributed memory (Rumelhart and McClelland 1986) and Pinker and Prince's (1988) theory of irregular verb morphology make the idea a bit more plausible than it was in the heyday of von Neumann–style computational theories of mind. (See also Pollard and Sag 1987 on inheritance hierarchies.) Let me speculate that the appropriate interpretation of "informational cost" will make more sense once we understand more about the neural implementation of long-term memory.

In any event, we have a trade-off between, on one hand, a theory of lexical redundancy that is easy to implement in simple cases but rapidly gets out of hand formally, and, on the other, a theory that is harder to understand in terms of implementation but raises none of the same formal problems. At least the fact that this trade-off exists should lead to some doubt about the assumption that the lexicon is listed in terms of "optimal coding," the most extreme version of the impoverished entry theory.

5.7 Final Remarks

In this discussion of the lexicon I have left many important issues un-addressed, for instance the categorial status of affixes in morphosyntax, the notion of morphosyntactic head in sub-X^0 syntax (Selkirk 1982; Williams 1981), whether semiregular affixes have separate lexical entries, how derivational morphology affects argument structure (Lieber 1992; Randall 1988), the precise form of lexical rules, the nature of polysemy—and indeed the extent to which there need be any morphosyntactic structure at all (Anderson 1992, chapter 10). I have also ignored the question of how morphophonology works, other than saying it must be to a certain extent independent of morphosyntax, an issue to which I turn in the next chapter.

What I think I *have* done here is to lay out a framework in terms of which issues of lexical structure can be integrated into a larger theory of the architecture of grammar. Within that, however the structure works out, it works out. Once the issues of syntactic word versus phonological word versus listed lexical item, morphosyntax versus morphophonology, inflection versus derivation, and productivity versus semiproductivity have been set straight, the relation of composed lexical items to the phrasal grammar becomes (for my taste) a great deal clearer.

Chapter 6
Remarks on Productive Morphology

6.1 Introduction

Chapter 5 suggested that, unlike standard Chomskian architectures, the tripartite architecture should support lexical insertion/licensing of items not only of the size of words (X^0), but also of sizes larger and smaller than words. We now look at smaller-sized lexical entries in more detail; chapter 7 turns to larger-sized items.

To review the problem: Why do we want listemes smaller than X^0? The argument concerns productive morphology, cases in which, upon learning a new word, a speaker knows automatically that a certain morphological form of it must exist and what that form must be; a typical example is the regular plural of English nouns. Viewing the lexicon as the long-term memory store of listemes (not just as a formal characterization of all possible X^0 forms of the language), it makes little sense in general to store both singular and plural forms of English nouns as listemes. In fact section 5.5 cited some psycholinguistic evidence suggesting that although high-frequency regular plurals are stored, the rest are not.

However, if plural nouns are not stored as such, then the plural affix must somehow be represented in long-term memory in such a way that it can freely combine with nouns. For a first approximation, this affix conforms easily to the tripartite architecture: it is a correspondence between a phonological form, a syntactic feature (or functional category) in S-Structure, and a conceptual function. In very skeletal form, it would look something like (1) (repeating (5) from chapter 5).[1]

(1)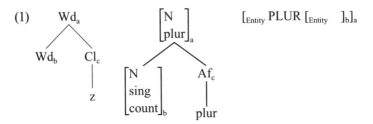

This chapter will be devoted to showing where some traditional issues in morphology can be situated in the present framework, so that solutions more sophisticated than (1) can be formulated. I do not intend by any means to break new ground in morphology, or even to come to terms with much of the existing literature. I wish only to provide a place for morphology that makes sense in the present scheme of things. The basic idea, however, is that dividing a morpheme this way into phonological, syntactic, and semantic parts plus the correspondence among them enables us to parcel out various standard problems of morphology in a sensible fashion.

In particular, it has often been noted that the notion of an inflectional or derivational morpheme as a constant matching of phonology, syntax, and semantics, although perhaps a useful first approximation, is not nearly flexible enough for what really occurs in language. This chapter will deal with ways in which such flexibility can be introduced by loosening different aspects of the correspondence between phonological, syntactic, and conceptual structure in (1).

As observed in chapter 5, it is only for productive morphology that the present architecture pushes one toward extracting separate lexical entries for the morphemes in question. Semiproductive morphology, which predicts the *possibility* but not the *existence* of forms (and need not completely predict their meaning), is better accounted for by lexical rules than by principles of free combination. Lexical rules, it will be recalled, mediate between fully listed but related forms. It should also be recalled that the productive/semiproductive distinction cuts across the inflectional/derivational distinction; for instance, English expletive infixation and the derivation of -*ly* adverbs from adjectives are productive but not inflectional. The present chapter therefore will be concerned exclusively with productive morphology, since it is here that the tripartite architecture has somewhat novel consequences for lexical listing.

Readers conversant with LFG and HPSG may find the present approach somewhat foreign, in that these frameworks deal with both productive and semiproductive morphology by means of lexical rules, distinct from rules of phrasal combination. However, I do not see anything essential in those frameworks that prohibits extending rules of free combination to units smaller than the word. Koenig and Jurafsky (1994), for instance, working in a Construction Grammar/HPSG framework, propose the same division of morphology as chapter 5, dealing with semiproductive morphology through lexical rules but with productive morphology through "on-line" composition. The theoretical shift proposed here is to replace the question "Is this process in the 'lexicon' or the 'grammar'?" with the question "Is this process a relation in long-term memory (i.e. among forms listed in the lexicon) or a construction in working memory (i.e. 'on the fly')?"

On the other hand, readers conversant with GB and the Minimalist Program may find this approach foreign for a different reason: inflectional affixes here do not constitute heads of larger functional categories, complete with specifiers and complements. In the present approach, lexical licensing in syntax is established at S-Structure; therefore the lexicon must establish correspondences at a point in syntax where inflections look like affixes adjoined to a major category. Syntax may well contain processes that move verbs to their inflections or vice versa, but if so, these processes have already occurred by the time lexical licensing takes place.

The issues I will take up, all too briefly, are the place of traditional morphophonology (section 6.2), phonological and class-based allomorphy (6.3), suppletion of composed forms by irregulars (6.4), and the status of zero affixation (6.5).

6.2   The Place of Traditional Morphophonology

The *SPE* model (Chomsky and Halle 1968) took the problem of morphophonology to be (2).

(2) a. What are the underlying forms of morphemes and morpheme sequences?
   b. What are the phonological processes that operate on them to produce surface phonological forms (or phonetic forms)?

Let us try to translate these questions into the present framework; along the way we will see their relation to the approach advocated by Optimality Theory (Prince and Smolensky 1993).

The crucial issue is what is meant by "underlying forms." First of all, for the purposes of deriving phonetic forms, we are interested specifically in *phonological* underlying forms; their relation to morphosyntax and conceptual structure is a separate issue, which we will take up presently. Where do phonological underlying forms come from?

Each lexical entry in long-term memory lists among other things a piece of phonological structure, the entry's lexical phonological structure or LPS (I ignore allomorphy for the moment, returning to it in section 6.3). In the course of processing a sentence in working memory, there must be a level of phrasal phonological structure in which LPSs can be identified, so that lexical access (and therefore lexical correspondence) can be established. Following the terminology of previous chapters, let us call this the Syntactic Interface Level of phonology (SIL$_{PS}$, or SIL for short).[2] A first hypothesis, paralleling our discussion of PIL/CIL in chapter 4, is that all lexical and phrasal phonological properties that are relevant to syntax can be localized at a single SIL in working memory. (If lexical correspondences and phrasal correspondences were to turn out to occur at different levels of phonology, it would be too bad, but we shouldn't rule this possibility out in advance.)

Under this construal, the issue of phonological underlying forms breaks into two parts:

(3) a. What phonological information is present in LPSs?
    b. What phonological information is present in SIL?

The standard *SPE*-type story is that questions (3a) and (3b) have essentially the same answer: SIL is nothing but a concatenation of LPSs. On this picture, phonological structure has no independent generative power of its own; all that is present in SIL is the sequence of LPSs coming out of the lexicon, linearly ordered and partially bracketed by virtue of the syntactic structure from which they are "interpreted." (This view is present also in the Minimalist Program, where the process of "interpretation" is called Spell-Out; recall the discussion in chapter 2.)

Consider also the relation of SIL to the "other end" of phonology, phonetic form (PF). As discussed in chapter 2, PF is to be regarded as the Auditory-Perceptual Interface Level of phonology (A/PIL$_{PS}$), connected to auditory and motor representations by further sets of correspondence rules. In the *SPE* story as standardly construed, all phonological properties of PF not present in the concatenation of LPSs are inserted in the course of phonological derivation, through a sequence of rule applications.

However, the present architecture allows another possibility. For instance, think about the status of rules of syllable structure. It is widely acknowledged that syllable structure is predictable and therefore need not be present in LPS. In an *SPE*-type model, this structure is not present in SIL, either; rather, syllabic bracketing is inserted in the course of derivation.[3] Within the present framework, an alternative is that syllable structure *is* present in SIL, but it is invisible to the PS-SS correspondence rules—including to lexical entries, which are part of these correspondence rules. The status of syllabic bracketing would thus mirror the status of much of the recursion in syntactic bracketing; the latter is present for purposes of relating syntax to semantics but is largely invisible to phonology. In other words, to recall the discussion of chapter 2, one should not view syntactic bracketing as "erased" by derivational rules, "after" which new bracketing is "introduced" by phonology. Rather, the two kinds of bracketing exist autonomously in different modules and are essentially invisible to each other.

Similarly, consider the possibilities for dealing with other kinds of underspecification in LPSs. To take the simplest sort of case, consider Turkish vowel harmony, in which the LPS of an affix specifies only the height of its vowel(s), and the rest of the vowel's features are determined by context on the left. Again there are two possibilities. First, SIL could correspond exactly to LPS and contain underspecified vowels, which are then filled in by the phonological derivation (the *SPE*-type solution). Alternatively, vowel harmony could be a well-formedness constraint on fully specified structures at SIL. In this case, an LPS with an underspecified vowel will unify with a fully specified vowel in SIL, contributing an index that links SIL to syntax. (4) contrasts the two solutions (*I* is the underspecified high vowel subject to vowel harmony).

(4) *Hypothesis 1*
 LPSs: ev, Im
 SIL: evIm → A/PIL (PF): evim
 Hypothesis 2
 LPSs: ev, Im
 SIL: evim → A/PIL (PF): evim

A further problem arises in cases where LPSs are intercalated in SIL, as in Semitic morphology. Here it makes little sense to have an SIL in which the LPSs are clearly distinct, as in hypothesis 1; but hypothesis 2 is fairly straightforward.

(5) *Hypothesis 1*
    LPSs: k-t-b (root), CaCaC (inflection)
    SIL: ??? → A/PIL: katab
    Hypothesis 2
    LPSs: k-t-b, CaCaC
    SIL: katab → A/PIL: katab

A by now standard approach to this phenomenon (McCarthy 1982) deconstructs SIL so that the two LPSs are independently identifiable in it.

(6)

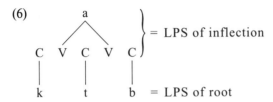

The association lines between the root and the CV skeleton could be supplied either by the phonological derivation (as per hypothesis 1) or by phonological conditions on SIL (as per hypothesis 2).

Let us be a little careful about how hypothesis 2 works here. In the course of lexical licensing, both the root and the inflection unify with the entire word. As a consequence, the entire phonological word receives *two* linking indices, one linked with the syntax of the root and one linked with the syntax of the inflection.[4]

Now notice that, however this is solved, we have begun to appeal to a somewhat more abstract notion of licensing, in which unification of LPS with SIL is not a simple mapping of contiguous segments onto contiguous segments. A further example arose already in chapter 5, in the formulation of English expletive infixation, where the LPS of the host word (say *Susquehanna*) had to unify with a discontinuous portion of SIL (*Susquefuckinhanna*).

A consequence of accumulating many such cases is that SIL begins to look less like a simple concatenation of LPSs and more like PF. One might ask, therefore, whether it is possible to go all the way and identify SIL entirely with PF, eliminating *SPE*-type derivations altogether. The price would have to be a considerably more abstract relation between LPS and SIL. This seems to me the correct way to characterize the approach of Optimality Theory within the present framework. We could think of many of the violable constraints of Optimality Theory as constraining a "soft unification" of LPSs with SIL, a unification in which not all pieces have to match. For instance, the constraints Parse and Fill of Optimality Theory can be taken as together stipulating a one-to-one match between segments in LPS and segments in SIL. But if these constraints are for some reason violated because of higher-ranking constraints, then "soft unification" can proceed anyway, thereby linking SIL with syntax despite the incomplete match of SIL with the lexicon.

Finally, it is necessary to mention "process" views of morphology such as Anderson's (1992) "a-morphous morphology." Anderson argues that because there exist morphological processes that delete or metathesize segments, one cannot in general treat the LPS of an affix as a sequence of segments; rather, it must be thought of as a rule that applies to a stem. Beard's (1988) Separation Hypothesis includes a similar position. In this treatment, the affixes are not independently identified in SIL; rather, one can view the application of affixes as part of the process matching the LPS of the stem to SIL.[5] In these views, it is still possible to perform purely phonological manipulations on SIL to derive PF. Thus at this scale of description they are a mixture of the two other architectures.

This is not the place to discuss the relative merits of these treatments of morphophonology. My only intention here is to situate morphophonology within the present architecture; with the proper construal, any of the treatments appears compatible with the framework.[6] At the same time, the framework forces us to recognize a clear separation between the long-term memory store of LPSs and the working memory assembly of LPSs in SIL. This seems to me to clear up a certain amount of vagueness that (for me at least) has been inherent in the notion of "phonological underlying form" for some time.

An interesting symmetry obtains between the treatments of morphophonology discussed in this section and the contrast of two approaches to semantic composition discussed in chapter 3. In *simple composition*, the LCSs of the words in a sentence are combined transparently into a "semantic level," with no further material added in the course of "interpretation" of syntactic structure. Pragmatic information is added "later" by separate processes to provide a level of contextualized interpretation. This parallels the *SPE* model of phonology, in which LPSs of the words are concatenated to create a level of underlying phonological form, then phonological rules are used to derive the separate level of phonetic form. Parts (a) and (b) of figure 6.1 sketch these architectures.

By contrast, in the theory of *enriched composition* advocated in chapter 3, LCSs combine in various intricate ways, so that individual LCSs are

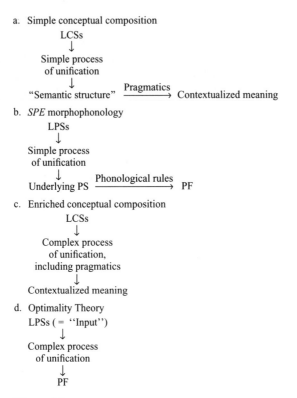

a. Simple conceptual composition

   LCSs
    ↓
   Simple process
   of unification
    ↓
   "Semantic structure" —Pragmatics→ Contextualized meaning

b. *SPE* morphophonology

   LPSs
    ↓
   Simple process
   of unification
    ↓
   Underlying PS —Phonological rules→ PF

c. Enriched conceptual composition

   LCSs
    ↓
   Complex process
   of unification,
   including pragmatics
    ↓
   Contextualized meaning

d. Optimality Theory

   LPSs (= "Input")
    ↓
   Complex process
   of unification
    ↓
   PF

Figure 6.1
A symmetry between treatments of morphophonology and of semantic composition

not entirely discrete from each other in phrasal conceptual structure, and features from different LCSs can coconstrain each other in order to promote overall well-formedness of conceptual structure. Moreover, pragmatic information is integrated intimately into the composed form in the process of combining LCSs. Thus there is no separation of levels into one that consists just of combined LCSs and one that incorporates context. This parallels my construal of the phonological architecture behind Optimality Theory. In Optimality Theory, LPSs can be considerably distorted in the process of unifying with SIL, in order to ensure overall well-formedness of phrasal phonological structure. Moreover, all sorts of phonological information is present in SIL that does not come from LPSs, for instance syllable structure. Finally, the hypothesis of Optimality Theory is that the level at which LPSs are combined (i.e. SIL) and the

level of phonetic form are identical. Parts (c) and (d) of figure 6.1 sketch
these architectures.

What is one to make of these parallelisms? At the very least, they
should make clearer the symmetry of issues that arise in dealing with the
PS-SS interface and the SS-CS interface. It is only by stepping back and
considering both interfaces at once—and trying to develop a compatible
view of them—that one can recognize these symmetries. Still, it is an
empirical question whether the issues should be resolved the same way in
both interfaces. Phonology and semantics are certainly different enough
on other grounds that it is hard to expect architectural uniformity. Yet we
now have interesting bases of comparison, which do push us toward a
possible uniformity that could not have been perceived before. The questions thus acquire a richer texture, which I take to be a sign of progress.

6.3 Phonological and Class-Based Allomorphy

The matching of LPS, LSS, and LCS in (1) assumes that there is only
a single phonological realization corresponding to a syntactic affix; any
variation in its phonological form is accounted for by regular rules of
morphophonology. Of course, this assumption is false: it is not uncom-
mon for an affix to have phonologically conditioned allomorphs. A simple
example from Spencer (1991, 121), citing Lewis (1967), is the Turkish passive suffix, which is realized phonologically as /In/ after /l/, /n/ after vowels,
and /Il/ elsewhere (where /I/ is the high vowel subject to vowel harmony).

(7)   *Root*   *Passive*
   a. al-   alın   /In/ after /l/
   b. oku-   okun   /n/ after vowels
   c. yap-   yapıl   ⎫
      sev-   sevil   ⎬ /Il/ elsewhere
      tut-   tutul   ⎭
      gör-   görül

If the three allomorphs were entirely independent, there would be no
problem: a single morphosyntactic structure could be linked to the three
morphophonological structures disjunctively. However, (7) presents a
more complex problem. So far we have viewed lexical licensing simply as
unifying a lexical item's LPS with SIL in phonology, its LSS with PIL/
CIL (S-Structure) in syntax, and its LCS with conceptual structure. By
virtue of this unification it adds its linking index between the three levels
in working memory. Under this construal, though, the "elsewhere" case

(7c) in principle should be able to unify with any word. The problem, then, is to properly formulate the blocking of the default allomorph by the more specialized ones.

In order to do so, I must elaborate the notation for LPS slightly. I will mark the constituent that the lexical item licenses (i.e. the actual affix) with a superscript F (for "figural"), to distinguish it from the allomorph's contextual conditions. Using this notation, (8) presents a possible lexical entry for this affix. (I omit the conceptual structure.)

(8)

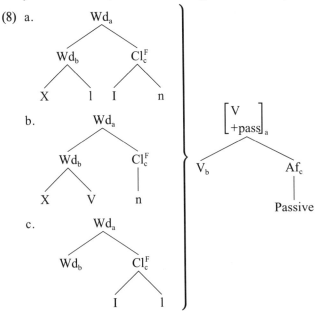

We now have to formulate lexical licensing slightly more carefully. In particular, we have to distinguish the figural constituent from the context. We want the lexical item to license only the figural constituent; it just *checks* the context. Checking can be accomplished formally by attempting to unify the contextual features of the lexical item with SIL and S-Structure (again omitting conceptual structure for the moment). If the contextual features can be unified, I will say the lexical item is *anchored* in SIL and S-Structure.

Given the notion of anchoring, we can now state lexical licensing involving multiple allomorphs as (9). The idea, parallel to standard formulations of blocking, is that only the allomorph with the most specific context is allowed to license the correspondence of its figural constituent to S-Structure.

(9) *Lexical licensing*
  a. *Allomorphic blocking*
     If the LPS of a lexical item L has alomorphs $A_1, \ldots, A_n$, and more
     than one of these can be anchored at the same position in SIL, call
     the one with the most specific context the *designated allomorph*,
     A^*. (If only one can be so anchored, it is A^* by default.)
  b. *Licensing*
     If possible, unify the figural constituent of A^* with SIL and the LSS
     of L with S-Structure, adding the linking index of L to both structures.

To see how (9) works, consider how it licenses *tutul* and *alın* in SIL but
fails to license **tutun* and **alıl*. Suppose SIL contains *tutul*. Of the allomorphs in (8), only (8c) has the proper contextual features to be anchored
by *tutul*; hence by default it counts as A^*. The figural constitutent of
(8c), /Il/, unifies with *ul* in SIL and therefore can be linked to Passive in
S-Structure.

Suppose instead that SIL contains *tutun*. Again this anchors only allomorph (8c). But this time the figural constituent of (8c) cannot unify with
un. Therefore the affix cannot be linked to Passive in S-Structure.

Now suppose SIL contains *alin*. This anchors two allomorphs in (8):
(8a) and (8c). Of these two, (8a) is more specific, so it is designated as A^*.
In turn, its figural consituent, *In*, unifies with *in* in SIL and therefore the
affix can be linked to Passive in S-Structure. On the other hand, suppose
SIL contains *alıl*. This again anchors (8a) and (8c); (8a), the more specific,
is chosen as A^*. But this time the figural constituent of (8a) cannot unify
with *ıl*, so the affix cannot be linked to Passive in S-Structure. Table 6.1
sums up these analyses.

In (8) the allomorphy is based on phonological conditions. Aronoff
(1994) describes a different sort of allomorphy: *class-based* allomorphy, in
which the choice of allomorph is a consequence of an arbitrary lexical

Table 6.1
Summary of lexical licensing and blocking in Turkish passive affix

SIL	tutul	tutun	alın	alıl
Anchored allomorphs	(8c)	(8c)	(8a,c)	(8a,c)
A^*	(8c)	(8c)	(8a)	(8a)
Figural constituent of A^*	Il	Il	In	In
Corresponding part of SIL	ul	un	in	ıl
Link to passive licensed by (8)	yes	no	yes	no

classification of the host. One of Aronoff's simpler examples (pp. 72–74) concerns Russian nominal cases. The phonological realization of case endings depends on the inflectional class of the noun, which in turn is determined not entirely reliably (i.e. semiproductively) by syntactic gender. Class 1 includes most masculine and neuter nouns; class 2 is mostly feminine but includes a few masculines; class 3 is mostly feminine but includes one masculine and a few neuters; class 4 consists of all plurals of all genders. Aronoff argues that such lexical marking of inflectional class is autonomous of both syntactic and phonological structure—"morphology by itself"—though it may be related through semiproductive rules to syntax or phonology (depending on the language). Since the possibility of a word's belonging to an inflectional class depends on its syntactic category, this feature makes most sense as part of lexical syntactic structure. Aronoff's analysis of the dative affix therefore comes out as (10) in the present notation.[7]

(10)

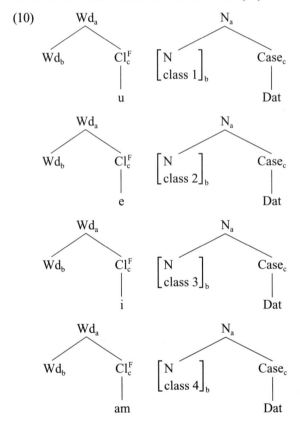

These lexical pairings of morphophonological and morphosyntactic structures are notational variants of Aronoff's "realization pairs." In this particular case there is no default form and therefore no blocking, but in principle such a situation is possible.

6.4 Suppletion of Composed Forms by Irregulars

We next turn to the problem of true irregularities, where the existence of an irregular form blocks the licensing of a regular composed form. Just to be extreme, let us deal with the suppletion of the regular past tense of *go*, **goed*, by *went*. I will assume that in less extreme cases such as *sing/sang*, the phonological similarity between the stem and the irregular form is a matter of semiproductive regularity, hence a lexical rule. Thus the problem such cases pose for lexical licensing is exactly the same as for total suppletion.

In working this out correctly, the key will be in loosening the connection between PS-SS linking and SS-CS linking to some degree. As a consequence it will become impossible consistently to list lexical entries that are complete ⟨PS, SS, CS⟩ triples. I therefore diverge from, for example, Lieber's (1992) "lexeme-based" morphology, which in effect treats every lexical entry as a complete triplet. Rather, I concur with Beard's (1987, 1988) Separation Hypothesis and Halle and Marantz's (1993) Distributed Morphology in granting PS-SS linking and SS-CS linking some independence from each other.

To see what is happening in the blocking of **goed* by *went*, we need to state lexical entries for *go*, past tense, and *went*. Here is a first approximation for *go*; I now revert to including LCS, as it is crucial to the story.

(11) Wd_a V_a $\left\{ \begin{array}{l} [_{Event} \text{ GO } ([_{Thing} \quad]_A, [_{Path} \quad]_A)]_a \\ [_{State} \text{ EXTEND } ([_{Thing} \quad]_A, [_{Path} \quad]_A)]_a \\ \dots \textit{(other readings)} \end{array} \right\}$

      go

The two readings in the LCS are those exemplified by *John went to LA* and *The road goes to LA* respectively;[8] there may well be other readings. The crucial point for what follows is that the past tense of *every* reading of *go* is *went*, and this must follow from the analysis.

Next consider the regular past tense. Since lexical licensing takes place at S-Structure, the morphosyntactic structure relevant for licensing has Tense adjoined to the verb; it is not a separate functional projection. (In the case where Tense is not syntactically adjoined to the verb, it is realized as a form of *do*.) Thus the relevant case of past tense has the following entry, for a first approximation; note its parallelism to the entry for plural in (1).[9]

(12)

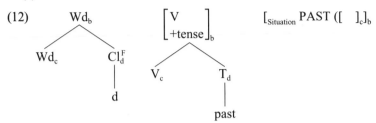

(13) gives the phonological and syntactic structure for *went*.

(13)

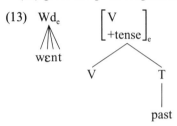

Notice that some of the morphosyntax is not linked to phonology. Rather, the phonological word *went* stands in for the whole syntactic complex. This corresponds to the notion of "fusion" in Halle and Marantz 1993.

How does *went* get its meaning, though? The brute force way would be to link it to a set of meanings parallel to those of *go*, but incorporating PAST. However, this would miss the generalization that the set of meanings is exactly the same; this is what makes *went* a form of *go*.

Just to push the point further, consider the phonologically irregular present *does* of the verb *do*. Like *go*, *do* has a series of alternative LCSs, including empty (*do*-support), light verb (*do a job*), part of various anaphoric forms (*do so*, etc.), and 'tour' (*do London*).[10] Moreover, the English present tense has a number of alternative LCSs, including present of stative verbs, generic of active verbs, scheduled future (*We leave tomorrow morning*), "hot news" (*Churchill dies!*), and stage directions (*Hamlet leaves the stage*). *Does* has exactly the product set of the readings of *do* and present tense. The theory should not have to treat this as a coincidence.

The solution lies in how the entries for *go* and *past* are formulated. Until now, linking indices have extended across phonology, syntax, and semantics. In order to account for *went*, we have to weaken the bonds tying the three components together, separating the PS-SS linking from the SS-CS linking. (14) gives revised versions of *go* and *past*; the presubscripts *a*, *b*, *c*, and *d* notate PS-SS linkings, and the postsubscripts *x*, *y* the SS-CS linkings.

(14)

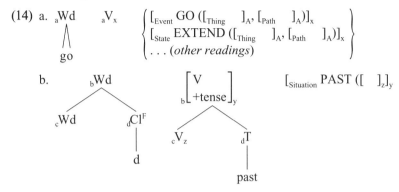

We can now give the entry for *went* as (15), in which the syntax corresponds idiosyncratically to the phonology but invokes the SS-CS indices of (14a,b) in perfectly regular fashion.[11]

(15)

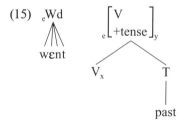

The upshot is that *went* becomes syntactically and semantically a past tense form for *go*; only in its phonology is it idiomatic. If one wants to think of (15) as a branch of the entry for *go*, that is fine. But one should also think of it as a branch of the entry for past tense. Its position with respect to the two is symmetrical.

Having dissociated the PS-SS linking from the SS-CS linking, we now have a place in the theory for a distinction made frequently in the literature. Levelt (1989), for instance, speaks of the distinction between *lemmas* and *lexical forms*. In our terms, a *lemma* is a linkup between an LSS and an LCS. Lemmas are individuated by their postsubscripts. Hence the pairing of the verb and any of the conceptual structures in (14a) is one lemma, and the pairing of the tensed verb and the conceptual structure in

(14b) is another. A *lexical form* is a linkup between an LSS and an LPS. Lexical forms are individuated by their presubscripts. Hence the pairing of the verb and the phonological string /go/ in (14a) is one lexical form, that between past tense and /-d/ in (14b) is another, and that between the tensed verb and /wɛnt/ in (15) is still another. Each reading of *went* thus expresses two lemmas at once with a single lexical form.[12]

Notice, by the way, that if a word is morphologically regular, there is never any branching among its linking indices. In such a case, the dissociation of PS-SS and SS-CS linking is effectively invisible, and we return to the stereotypical notion of the morpheme as a unitary mapping of PS, SS, and CS. It is the irregular cases in their great variety that undermine the traditional notion; the present notation makes it feasible to differentiate the possibilities.

It is not enough, of course, to formulate a lexical entry for *went*. We also have to block **goed*. Like allomorphic blocking, this has to be stated as part of lexical licensing. Essentially, lexical licensing must choose the most inclusive lexical form as the only candidate for licensing, so that the composite form never has a chance to unify in SIL. This condition can be added at the beginning of our previous lexical licensing rule (9), which with suitable editing emerges as (16). The idea behind the new clause, (16a), is that a listed lexical form takes precedence over a composite of multiple lexical forms.

(16) *Lexical licensing (revision)*
  a. *Blocking of composed forms by irregulars*
     If one or more sets of lexical forms can exhaustively unify their LSSs with a given syntactic constituent C_S, and one set consists of a single lexical form, call that one the *designated lexical form*, L*. (If only one set can so unify, its member(s) is/are L* by default.)
  b. *Allomorphic blocking*
     If the LPS of L* has allomorphs $A_1, \ldots, A_n$, and more than one of these can be anchored at the same position in SIL, call the one with the most specific context the *designated allomorph*, A*. (if only one can be so anchored, it is A* by default.)
  c. *Licensing*
     If possible, unify the figural constituent of A* with SIL and the LSS of L* with S-Structure, adding the linking index of L* to both structures.

How does this block *goed*? Suppose we have licensed the SS-CS correspondence shown in (17). Then there are two sets of lexical forms that can unify with the tensed verb; one is the set consisting of *go* and past tense, and the other is the set consisting only of *went*.

Condition (16a) says that *went* is the designated lexical form; condition (16b) says that /wɛnt/ is the designated allomorph. Hence, if SIL contains /go+d/, it never has a chance to link to the syntax and therefore cannot be licensed.

In most inflectional languages, there are inflectional affixes that realize more than one morphosyntactic feature at a time. A simple case is the English verbal suffix /−z/, which corresponds to present tense plus third person singular agreement. We can treat such composite affixes along the same lines as *went*, except that the compositionality appears within the structure of the affix itself instead of spreading into the verb. (18) gives a possible lexical entry for this affix.[13]

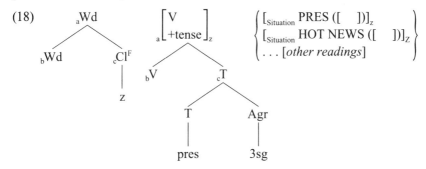

In paradigms that are partially compositional (e.g. separate tense and agreement affixes are distinguishable in some forms but not others), the transparently composed forms can be treated as such; the irregular cases, listed in the manner of (18), will block the licensing of regular composition.

6.5   The Status of Zero Inflections

What about the English present tense, which, except in the third person singular, is realized phonologically with no inflectional ending on the verb? We know that present tense must be realized in the morpho-syntax—present is not just the absence of past—since it surfaces as *do* in environments where tense cannot attach to the verb. So what is its lexical entry?

One possibility is that it is parallel to past tense, except that its LPS contains no segmental information.[14]

(19)

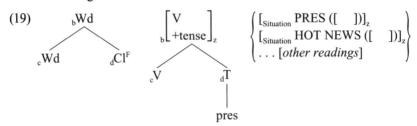

Such a solution, however, grates against one's sense of elegance. A solution that stipulated no LPS at all would be preferable.

(20)

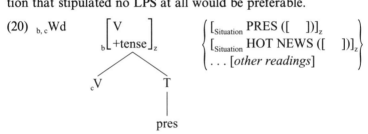

Notice here that the T node in morphosyntax is completely unlinked: it corresponds to nothing in either conceptual structure or phonology. The double indexation of Wd in (20) indicates that the form of the host verb and the form of the tensed verb are identical. (Alternatively, the LPS could have $_b$Wd dominating $_c$Wd, but this would be just a notational variant.)

As motivation that (20) is the proper sort of entry, we observe that it is only one of three sorts of situations in which a constituent of a lexical entry is unlinked. A second is the existence of "theme vowels": inflectional endings that depend on inflectional class but that express no morpho-syntactic information (i.e. information that is used for syntactic purposes such as agreement). An entry for a theme vowel in the simplest case might look something like (21), where the clitic constituent is not linked to anything.

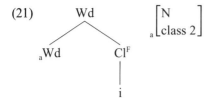

(21)

In addition, there may be pieces of conceptual structure that have no syntactic or phonological realization but must be present as part of one's understanding of a sentence. A clear example is the reference transfer functions discussed in section 3.3. The function allowing use of *Ringo* to name a picture of Ringo, for instance, could be stated as a correspondence rule like (22), a ⟨SS, CS⟩ pair with structure not unlike that of a lexical entry. Notice how the indexing between syntactic structure and conceptual structure here parallels that between phonological structure and syntactic structure in (20).

(22) $NP_{x,y}$ [VISUAL-REPRESENTATION-OF ([$]_x$)$]_y$

Here the syntactic structure is doubly indexed, so it links both to the thing being represented and to its representation. That is, the conceptual function VISUAL-REPRESENTATION-OF is another kind of zero morph.[15]

We conclude that it would be useful for the theory to permit unlinked pieces of LPS, LSS, and LCS. This poses a minor difficulty for lexical licensing as conceived so far. Until now, we have considered structures in SIL, S-Structure, and conceptual structure to be licensed just in case they can be linked with each other. Now we have encountered cases in which a lexical item apparently licenses a piece of SIL (a theme vowel), S-Structure (English present tense), or conceptual structure (reference transfer functions) that is not linked to other structures. This suggests that it is necessary to separate the *licensing* function of the lexicon from its *linking* function. With normal stereotypical morphemes the two functions go hand in hand; but here we find licensing without linking. In fact, chapter 4 mentioned lexical items that license phonology but do not link to either syntax or semantics, for instance *fiddle-de-dee*. So such a licensing function without linking is independently necessary.

To make this explicit, I will further revise (16). Its three parts now determine licensing of morphosyntactic structure in S-Structure, morphophonological structure in SIL, and the link between them.

(23) *Lexical licensing (further revision)*

    a. If more than one set of lexical forms can exhaustively unify their LSSs with a given syntactic constituent C_S, and one set consists of a single lexical form, call that one the *designated lexical form*, L*. (If only one set can so unify, its member(s) is/are L* by default.) L* licenses C_S.

    b. If the LPS of L* has allomorphs $A_1, \ldots, A_n$, and more than one of these can be anchored at the same position in SIL, call the one with the most specific context the *designated allomorph*, A*. (If only one can be so anchored, it is A* by default.)

    If the figural constituent of A* unifies with a constituent C_P of SIL, then A* licenses C_P.

    c. If the LSS of L* is linked to A*, add a linking index between C_P and C_S.

Consider how (20) works in this version of licensing. The LSS of L* is $[_{V,+tense}$ V $[_T$ pres]]. This licenses the present tense in S-Structure. L* has only one allomorph, but this allomorph lacks a figural constituent. Therefore A* licenses nothing in SIL, and no linking index is added. Similarly, in (21), the LSS of L* is a class 2 noun. Its single allomorph licenses but does not link the theme vowel.

I should add that the global conditions on licensing and linking of SIL, S-Structure, and conceptual structure have not yet been stated; it is these that determine whether a derivation converges or crashes. Certainly not all the distinct configurations for blocking have yet been enumerated, and the connection of lexical licensing to conceptual structure has not yet been stated. And there are doubtless many pitfalls still to be avoided. However, I leave the matter at this point.

6.6 Why the Lexicon Cannot Be Minimalist

In the traditional view of generative grammar, a lexical item is a matrix of syntactic, phonological, and semantic features that is inserted into a D-Structure representation and "later" interpreted. In the present view, a lexical item is instead a correspondence rule that licenses parts of the three independent phonological, syntactic, and conceptual derivations. We have seen in this chapter that the way this correspondence is stated is not simple and that many of the standard problems of morphology concern the connections among alternative LPSs and the separation of

PS-SS connections from SS-CS connections. In the process, we have considerably elaborated the theory of linking indices, which seemed so simple and innocent in previous chapters. It seems to me that whatever theory of the lexicon one adopts, similar complications must necessarily appear. Moreover, in this chapter we have set aside all matters of semiproductive regularities discussed in chapter 5, which add further complexity to the stew.

In this light, the idea of the lexicon as "simply" a list of exceptions is revealed as but a naive hope. To me, the considerations raised in this chapter and in chapter 5 show that no proposal regarding phonology, syntax, or semantics can be taken seriously unless it includes in some reasonable detail an account of the associated LPSs, LSSs, and LCSs and how they combine into phrasal structures.

Chapter 7

Idioms and Other Fixed Expressions

7.1 Review of the Issues

Every so often in the past chapters, I have asserted that it is necessary to admit idioms as phrasal lexical items, that is, as lexical items larger than X^0. This chapter will draw out the arguments in more detail and integrate idioms into the tripartite architecture and lexical licensing theory.[1]

Let us start by seeing how idioms bear on various assumptions about the lexical interface. First, as pointed out a number of times already, a standard assumption is that the lexicon consists (mostly) of words (assumption 4 of chapter 1). Idioms, which are multiword constructions, are taken to be a relatively marginal and unimportant part of the lexicon.

Second, under the standard architecture, lexical items enter syntax by means of a rule of lexical insertion that inserts them into D-Structure (assumption 3 of chapter 1). By assumptions 2 and 4, lexical insertion *substitutes* a lexical item for a terminal element (a lexical category or X^0 category) in a phrase structure tree. Thus standard lexical insertion creates a problem for idioms, which do not look like X^0 categories.

Third, under the standard architecture, the semantic interpretation of syntactic structures is performed compositionally after lexical insertion (at D-Structure in the Standard Theory, S-Structure in EST, LF in GB and the Minimalist Program). This too raises a problem for idioms: how are they marked at the time of lexical insertion so that they receive noncompositional interpretations at this later stage?

Fourth, a lexical entry is often assumed to include only information that cannot be predicted by rules (assumption 5). All redundancies among lexical items are extracted and encoded in lexical rules. But since most idioms are made up of known lexical items (though often with wrong meanings), it is not clear how to formalize the extraction of their redundancies.

As stressed throughout, not everyone holds all four of these views; each one has been questioned many times. But I think it is fair to say they constitute the default assumptions that are adopted when dealing with issues outside the lexicon, as in Chomsky 1993, 1995.

In the course of the chapter we will question all four of these assumptions. We will see that the lexicon contains large numbers of phrasal items; that lexical licensing by unification is the proper way to get idioms into sentences; that idioms provide further evidence that the level at which lexical licensing applies in syntax is also the level of phonological and semantic correspondence; and that the lexicon must contain redundancy.

7.2 The *Wheel of Fortune* Corpus: If It Isn't Lexical, What Is It?

Before turning to idioms, let us ask in what larger space of linguistic entities they might be embedded. To set the context, it is of interest to consider a new source of evidence. Many readers will be familiar with the U.S. television show *Wheel of Fortune* or one of its overseas counterparts. This is a game show in which contestants try to win prizes by guessing words and phrases, using a procedure rather like the children's game Hangman. My daughter Beth collected puzzle solutions for me over a few months as she watched the show; she collected about 600, with no repetition.[2]

This *Wheel of Fortune* corpus consists mostly of phrases, of all sorts. (A full listing appears in the appendix.) There are compounds, for example (1),

(1) black and white film
   Jerry Lewis telethon
   frequent flyer program

idioms of all sorts,

(2) they've had their ups and their downs
   yummy yummy yummy
   I cried my eyes out
   a breath of fresh air
   trick or treat

names of people (3a), names of places (3b), brand names (3c), and organization names (3d),

(3) a. Clint Eastwood
     Count Dracula

    b. Boston, Massachusetts
       Beverly Hills
    c. Jack Daniels whiskey
       John Deere tractor
    d. American Heart Association
       Boston Pops Orchestra
       New York Yankees

clichés (which I distinguish from idioms because they apparently have nothing noncompositional in their syntax or meaning),

(4) any friend of yours is a friend of mine
    gimme a break
    love conquers all
    no money down
    name, rank, and serial number
    we're doing everything humanly possible

titles of songs, books, movies, and television shows,

(5) All You Need Is Love
    City Lights
    The Price Is Right
    The Pirates of Penzance

quotations,

(6) beam me up, Scotty
    may the Force be with you
    a day that will live in infamy

and foreign phrases.

(7) au contraire
    persona non grata
    c'est la vie

All these expressions are familiar to American speakers of English; that is, an American speaker must have them all stored in long-term memory. And there are parallels in any language. The existence of such "fixed expressions" is well known; but what struck me in watching *Wheel of Fortune* is how many there are. Consider that the show presents about five puzzles a day and is shown six days a week, and that it has been on the air for over ten years. This comes to something on the order of ten to fifteen thousand puzzles with little if any repetition, and no sense of strain—no worry that the show is going to run out of puzzles, or even that the puzzles are becoming especially obscure.

To get a rough idea of the distribution of the puzzle types listed in (1)–(7), the *Wheel of Fortune* corpus includes about 10% single words, about 30% compounds, 10% idioms, 10% names, 10% meaningful names, 15% clichés, 5% titles, and 3% quotations. Assuming (for the sake of argument) similar proportions in the total distribution of *Wheel of Fortune* puzzles, a speaker of English must be carrying around thousands of compounds, idioms, names, meaningful names, and clichés, and at least hundreds of titles and quotations that could be potential *Wheel of Fortune* puzzles.

As for names, think of all the names of people you know that could *not* be *Wheel of Fortune* puzzles because they're not famous enough—Noam Chomsky, Otto Jespersen, all your family, colleagues, neighbors, and old classmates—thousands more. As for titles and quotations, think of all the poetry you know, including lyrics of popular songs, folk songs, and nursery rhymes, plus advertising slogans. There are vast numbers of such memorized fixed expressions; these extremely crude estimates suggest that their number is of about the same order of magnitude as the single words of the vocabulary. Thus they are hardly a marginal part of our use of language.

It is worth adding to this list the *collocations* in the language—uses of particular adjective-noun combinations, for instance, where other choices would be semantically as appropriate but not idiomatic (in a broader sense): *heavy/*weighty smoker, strong/*powerful coffee, sharp/?strong/ *heavy contrast, weighty/*heavy argument,* and so forth. The vast number of such expressions is stressed by Mel'čuk (1995) and Schenk (1995).

How is all this material stored? Received wisdom gives us an immediate reaction: "I don't know how it is stored, but it certainly isn't part of the lexicon. It's some other more general-purpose part of memory, along with pragmatics, facts of history, maybe how to cook." But if it isn't part of language, what is it? Unlike pragmatics, facts of history, and how to cook, fixed expressions are made up of *words*. They have phonological, syntactic, and semantic structure. When they are integrated into the speech stream as sentences and parts of sentences, we have no sense that suddenly a different activity is taking place, in the sense that we do when we say or hear a sentence like *And then he went, [belching noise].*

I therefore want to explore the position that fixed expressions are listed in the lexicon. That is, I want to work out a more inclusive view of linguistic knowledge that includes this material, given that it is made out of linguistic parts. (I am hardly the first to suggest this. Langacker (1987) and Di Sciullo and Williams (1987) have done so relatively recently. Weinreich (1969) makes a similar point, citing estimates of over 25,000 fixed expressions; Gross (1982) makes similar estimates for French.)

First, it is worth asking why the "received view" would want to exclude clichés, quotations, and so forth from the lexicon. The likely reason is for the purpose of constraining knowledge of language—to make language modular and autonomous with respect to general-purpose knowledge. But in fact, the boundaries of modules must be empirically determined. One can't just "choose the strongest hypothesis because it's the most falsifiable" and then end up excluding phenomena because they're not "core grammar" (i.e. whatever one's theory can't handle). In order to draw a boundary properly, it is necessary to characterize phenomena on *both* sides of it, treating phenomena "outside of language" as more than a heterogeneous garbage can.

In the present case, in order to draw a boundary between the theory of words and that of fixed expressions, it is necessary to show what the theory of fixed expressions is like and how it is distinctively different from the theory of words. In fact, the theory of fixed expressions must draw heavily on the theories of phonology, syntax, and semantics in just the way lexical theory does, and it must account for a body of material of roughly the same size as the word lexicon. Hence significant generality is missed if there is such duplication among theories—and little motivated constraint is lost by combining them into a unified theory. In the course of this chapter, we will see that most of the properties of fixed expressions (and idioms in particular) are not that different from properties found in semiproductive derivational morphology.

Turning the question around, why would one want to *in*clude fixed expressions in the lexicon? In the context of the present study, the answer has to do with Representational Modularity. According to Representational Modularity, anything with phonological structure is the responsibility of the phonological module; anything with syntactic structure is the responsibility of the syntactic module; anything that correlates phonology, syntax, and meaning is the responsibility of the correspondence rule modules. On this construal, fixed expressions such as clichés, names, and

idioms necessarily are part of language: they are built up out of linguistic
levels of representation. There is no other faculty of the mind in which
they can be located.

7.3 Lexical Insertion of Idioms as X^0s

What motivation is there for assuming that the lexicon contains only
single words? In part, the reasons go all the way back to *Syntactic Structures* (Chomsky 1957), where, as mentioned in chapter 4, lexical items are
introduced by phrase structure rules like (8).

(8) N → dog, cat, banana, . . .

If this is how lexical items are introduced, then an idiom like *let the cat
out of the bag* will have to be introduced by a rule like (9).

(9) VP → let the cat out of the bag, spill the beans, . . .

The problem with this is that it gives the idiom no internal structure. As a
result, inflectional processes can't apply to *let*, because it isn't structurally
marked as a verb; passive can't move *the cat*, because it isn't marked as
an NP; and so forth. Only if we restrict lexical expansion to the level of
lexical categories can we properly create such internal structure.

This convention was carried over into the *Aspects* lexicon (Chomsky
1965) without alteration. Potentially the *Aspects* lexicon could have permitted phrasal lexical items: there is nothing to stop an idiom from being
substituted for a VP in a phrase marker and then itself having internal
syntactic structure that is visible to syntactic rules. But I don't recall such
a possibility ever being exploited. Rather, the word-only conventions of
Syntactic Structures were retained, and idioms were always taken to
require some special machinery.

One version of this special machinery (Chomsky 1981, 146 note 94)
treats *kick the bucket* as a lexical verb with internal structure.

(10) $[_V[_{VP}[_V$ kick$]$ $[_{NP}[_{Det}$ the$]$ $[_N$ bucket$]]]]$

Because (10) is dominated by a V node, it can be inserted into a V position in syntax. In cases where single-word lexical entries are minimally
plausible, such analyses have been accepted with little question. A good
example is the English verb-particle construction, for which the standard
question is whether (11a) or (11b) is the underlying form.

(11) a. Bill looked up the answer.
         (+ rightward particle movement)
     b. Bill looked the answer up.
         (+ leftward particle movement)

The criterion that lexical entries must be X^0 categories forces us to choose (11a) as the underlying form, with a syntactic structure something like (12); this analysis is widely assumed in the lore.

(12) $[_V[_V$ look] $[_{Prt}$ up]]

However, on purely syntactic grounds this is the wrong analysis, as pointed out as early as Emonds 1970; for in addition to idiomatic verb-particle constructions like *look up*, there are compositionally interpreted ones like (13a,b) that have the same alternation.

(13) a. put in/down/away the books
     b. put the books in/down/away

The particle-final version (13b) clearly is related to constructions with a full PP: *put the books in the box/down the chute/on the table*. Since a full PP must appear after the object, generality demands that (13b) be the underlying position for the particle as well. However, aside from idiomatic interpretation, (11) and (13) behave syntactically alike; hence generality also demands (11b) as the underlying form.

This leaves us in the position of requiring a discontinuous lexical item *look NP up*. But Emonds points out that similar idioms exist that contain full PPs, such as *take NP to task*, *take NP to the cleaners*, *bring NP to light*, *haul NP over the coals*, *eat NP out of house and home*, and *sell NP down the river*. Despite Chomsky's explicit assumption (1981, 146 note 94) that idioms are not "scattered" at D-Structure, it strains credulity to treat these as V^0s containing an adjoined PP, along the lines of (14).

(14) $[_V[_{VP}[_V$ sell] $[_{PP}[_P$ down] $[_{NP}[_{Det}$ the] $[_N$ river]]]]]

To allow for such a lexical entry, sub-X^0 syntax now has to include phrasal categories (as already assumed in (10), of course). But in addition, some of these internal phrasal categories are obligatorily postposed by some new sort of movement rule, to a syntactic position that just happens to make these idiomatic constructions look like ordinary VPs.[4] For those who find such a solution unappealing, the only alternative is to find a way to base-generate discontinuous idioms as such from the start, an option to which we will turn in section 7.4.

More generally, a well-known old fact about idioms is that virtually all of them have a syntactic structure that looks like an ordinary syntactic structure. If an idiom is simply a compound under a V node, one part of which undergoes movement, such a situation would be unexpected.

Even more generally, many idioms are complete sentences, for instance *the jig is up, keep your shirt on, that's the way the cookie crumbles*, and *the cat's got X's tongue*. It is bizarre to think of these as inserted under a V^0 node, or in fact under anything less than a full S: how could we explain why they have garden-variety sentential syntax?

Nevertheless, many theorists, even those sympathetic to the inclusion of idioms in the lexicon, have tried to maintain the received view of lexical insertion, in which every lexical item has to be a word. Consequently, lexical items larger than words have always created a problem. *Aspects*, for example, ends with an extremely inconclusive discussion of how to encode verb-particle constructions, among the syntactically simplest of idioms; Weinreich (1969) and Fraser (1970) go to great lengths trying to insert idioms in the face of the standard formulation of lexical insertion.

A possibility somewhat different from (10) is to more or less simulate the listing of *kick the bucket* with monomorphemic lexical entries, by stipulating that *bucket* has a special interpretation in the context of *kick* and vice versa (see Everaert 1991 for such an approach). But the information one has to list in such an approach is a notational variant of listing a lexical VP: the entries for *bucket* and *kick* have to mention each other, and both have to mention that the two items together form a VP. Under this approach, then, the theory of "contextual specification" for idiomatically interpreted morphemes in effect includes the very same information that would appear if *kick the bucket* were simply listed lexically as a VP—and in much less direct form. Given a body of fixed expressions as numerous as the single words, such clumsy encoding should be suspect.

Indeed, because of the complications of such "contextual specification," no one (to my knowledge) has really stated the details. In particular, it is (to me at least) totally unclear how to "contextually specify" idioms of more than two morphemes. For instance, in order to specify *let the cat out of the bag* one word at a time, contextual specifications must be provided for *let, cat, out of*, and *bag*, each of which mentions the others (and what about *the*?). Moreover, the correct configuration must also be specified so that the special interpretation does not apply in, say, *let the bag out of the cat*. I conclude that this alternative rapidly collapses of its own weight.

7.4   Lexical Licensing of Units Larger than X^0

Consider instead the view urged in chapter 4: that a lexical entry enters a grammatical derivation by being unified simultaneously with independently generated phonological, syntactic, and semantic structures. Under this assumption, it is possible to say that *kick the bucket, look up,* and *sell down the river* are listed syntactically in the lexicon as ordinary VPs.[5] (15a–c) are identical to (10), (12), and (14) except that the outer V^0 category is expunged. (For the moment I revert to traditional notation, recalling however that the phonological material is really coindexed with the syntax, not dominated by it.)

(15) a. $[_{VP}[_V \text{ kick}] [_{NP}[_{Det} \text{ the}] [_N \text{ bucket}]]]$
      b. $[_{VP}[_V \text{ look}] [_{PP}[_P \text{ up}]]]$
      c. $[_{VP}[_V \text{ sell}] [_{PP}[_P \text{ down}] [_{NP}[_{Det} \text{ the}] [_N \text{ river}]]]]$

Lexical licensing tries to unify these structures with VPs that are independently generated by the syntactic component. If it cannot, the derivation crashes. Thus the fact that idioms have ordinary syntactic structures follows readily.[6]

What about the direct object in *sell down the river*? Suppose we assume that unification preserves sisterhood and linear order but not adjacency.[7] Then this leaves open the possibility that the VP with which (15c) unifies contains an NP direct object in the usual position ordained by phrasal syntax. This NP will not be phonologically and semantically licensed by (15c), so it will have to be licensed by other lexical material. On semantic grounds, such an NP proves necessary in order to satisfy the argument structure of the idiom, just like the direct object of an ordinary transitive verb. Furthermore, just as an ordinary transitive verb doesn't have to syntactically stipulate the position of its direct object argument, the idiom doesn't either.

The present theory, of course, also claims that lexical licensing takes place at S-Structure. If this is the case, how does the verb within the idiom receive its agreement features? The same way any verb does: the syntax installs these features in S-Structure, and since they are not contradicted by the lexical item, unification proceeds normally.

To be slightly more explicit, we can give an idiom like *take NP to the cleaners* ('get all of NP's money/possessions') a lexical entry something like (16).

(16) ₐtake ₆to ꜀the ₄cleaners

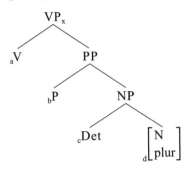

[_Event_ GET ([   ]_A_, [ALL OF [MONEY OF [   ]_A_]])]ₓ

Here the whole VP is indexed to the LCS (subscript x). The postsubscripts *A* in the LCS are the positions that are linked to subject and object position by the linking theory developed in Jackendoff 1990, chapter 11. Note that, as in (15c), the syntax of the direct object does not have to be stipulated in the LSS of the idiom. What makes (16) idiomatic, though, is that not all the syntactic constituents correspond to conceptual constituents: the PP and its NP complement are not linked to the LCS. Thus these constituents have no independent interpretation.

(16) as stated does not capture the intuition that the constituent words of the idiom are really the words *take, to, the,* and *cleaners*. Using some of the ideas from section 6.4, we can actually do a little better. Recall how we organized the lexical entry for *went*: it is a lexical form in which a syntactic complex [V-past] is linked idiosyncratically with a simple morphophonological unit /wɛnt/. However, the parts of this syntactic complex are linked into the *regular* lemmas that individually would be expressed as *go* and past tense.

The mirror image of this situation occurs with idioms. Here a VP such as that in (16) is linked idiosyncratically in a single lemma to an LCS. However, the X^0 categories that this VP dominates can carry the PS-SS indices associated with the independent words *take, to, the, cleaner,* and -*s*; thus the idiom actually needs no independent LPS and independent PS-SS linking. This way of arranging things guarantees that the irregular verb *take* will inflect properly with no further adjustment; *took to the cleaners* appears instead of **taked to the cleaners* under the very same allomorphic specification that *took* appears instead of **taked*. In other words, irregular inflectional morphology involves a single lexical form expressing multiple lemmas; an idiom involves a single lemma expressed by multiple lexical forms.

On the other hand, the licensing conditions of idioms are not quite symmetrical with those of irregular inflections. In the case of inflections, the lexically listed form completely blocks licensing of the composed form: *taked* never appears, for instance. However, in the case of idioms, the idiomatic (i.e. lexically listed) reading does not block the composed (i.e. literal) form if there is one. *Go for broke* has no literal reading, but *kick the bucket* does, and *John kicked the bucket* may indeed mean that John struck the pail with his foot. Hence the conditions on blocking for SS-CS connections must be more liberal than those for PS-SS connections. I leave the proper formulation open.

A number of questions arise for a licensing theory that includes items like (16). First, how large a unit is it possible to lexically license? This corresponds to the question within traditional theory of how large idioms can be: whether they can for instance include the subject of a sentence but leave the object (or something smaller than the object) as an argument. (See the debate between Bresnan (1982) and Marantz (1984), for example.) Idioms like *the cat's got NP's tongue* suggest that IP-sized units are possible—including inflection, as this idiom does not exist in alternative tenses and aspects. I don't think that any constraints on size or argument structure follow from lexical licensing theory per se. On the other hand, admitting phrasal units into the lexicon at least permits one to state the constraints formally, which is not the case in a theory where the formal status of phrasal idioms is relegated to a vaguely stated "idiom rule."

A second question for licensing theory is exactly how a phrasal lexical item is exempt from the need to link subphrases to conceptual structure. An answer to this would take us into more detail about licensing and linking than is possible here. But the basic idea is that full linking is necessary only for productive syntactic composition, that is, syntactic composition in the usual generative sense. In productive syntactic composition, the meaning of a phrase is a rule-governed function of the meanings of its parts. However, when a syntactic phrase is lexically listed, there is no need to build it up semantically from its parts—the meaning is already listed as well, so full linking of the parts is unnecessary.

Once we allow lexical licensing by listemes larger than X^0, it is possible to include in the lexicon all sorts of fixed expressions—not only verb-particle constructions and larger idioms, but also clichés and quotations

of the sort listed in the *Wheel of Fortune* corpus. So this part of the goal—
to incorporate fixed expressions into "knowledge of language"—has been
accomplished. The next step is to show how some of the peculiar properties of idioms are possible within lexical licensing theory.

7.5 Parallels between Idioms and Compounds

Another part of the goal is to show that the theory of fixed expressions is
more or less coextensive with the theory of words. Toward that end, it is
useful to compare fixed expressions with derivational morphology, especially compounds, which everyone acknowledges to be lexical items. I
want to show that the lexical machinery necessary for compounds is sufficient for most of the noncompositional treatment of idioms. Thus, once
we admit phrases into the lexicon, existing lexical theory takes care of
most of the rest of the problems raised by idioms.

Consider three classes of compounds. First, compounds of the simplest
type just instantiate a productive pattern with a predictable meaning,
redundantly. The *Wheel of Fortune* corpus includes such cases as *opera
singer* and *sewage drain*. There is nothing special about these items except
that they are known as a unit. Similar phrasal units are clichés/quotations
such as *whistle while you work*. Often such memorized units have some
special situational or contextual specification; for instance, *whistle while
you work* means literally what it says, but at the same time it evokes Dis-
neyesque mindless cheerfulness through its connection with the movie
Snow White.[8]

In a second class of compounds, an instance of a productive pattern is
lexically listed, but with further semantic specification. For instance, a
blueberry is not just a berry that is blue, but a *particular sort* of blue berry.
The difference between *snowman* and *garbage man* is not predictable: a
snowman is a *replica of* a man *made of* snow, and a garbage man is a man
who *removes* garbage.[9] Similarly but more so with exocentric compounds:
a redhead is a *person with* red *hair on his/her* head, but a blackhead is a
pimple with a black (*figurative*) head. As pointed out in section 5.6, the
italicized parts here must be listed in the lexical entry, above and beyond
the meanings of the constituent nouns.

A third type of compound instantiates a productive pattern, except that
some of the structure of the constituent parts is overridden phonologically, syntactically, or semantically. This case has three subcases:

1. Some part may not be a lexical item at all, as in the case of *cranberry*, '*particular sort of* berry', in which the morpheme *cran* exists only in the context of this compound (or did, until cranapple juice was invented).

2. Some part may be a word, but of the wrong syntactic category to fit into the pattern. An example is *aloha shirt* (from the *Wheel of Fortune* corpus), in which the greeting *aloha* is substituted for the first N or A in the compound pattern. The meaning, however, is semicompositional: 'shirt *of style associated with place where one says* aloha'.

3. Some part may be a phonological word of the right syntactic category but the wrong meaning. An example is *strawberry*, '*particular kind of* berry', which has nothing to do with straw.

Specifying the lexical entry of a compound thus involves two parts: listing a fixed phrase, and distinguishing which elements of the phrase are nonredundant and which are partially overridden. Under the full entry theory of section 5.6, the redundant parts—the elements that are independently existing words, and the morphological/syntactic structures that bind the elements together—have to be listed as part of the entry; but because they are predictable, they do not contribute to the independent information content or "cost" of the item.

Let us apply this approach to idioms. As observed a moment ago, clichés are cases in which combinations of independently listed items are listed redundantly—but they *are* listed, so that *whistle while you work* is a known phrase, a possible *Wheel of Fortune* puzzle, but *hum as you eat* is not. Idioms differ from clichés, of course, in that their meaning is not entirely a function of the meanings of their constituents. In other words, idioms always have overrides and therefore fall in with the third class of compounds described above.

Within this class, we find the same three subclasses. First, we find idioms containing nonwords, for instance *running amok*. There are also idioms containing words in which the normal meaning of one of the words is completely irrelevant, so it might as well be a nonword, for instance *sleeping in the buff* (*Wheel of Fortune* corpus)—*buff* normally denotes either a color or a polishing operation, so its use in this idiom is completely unmotivated.

Second, there are idioms containing words with an approximately correct meaning but of the wrong syntactic category. Four examples from the *Wheel of Fortune* corpus are *in the know* (verb in noun position), *they've had their ups and downs* (prepositions in noun position), *wait and see attitude* (verbs in adjective position), and <u>*down*</u> *and dirty* (preposition in adjective position, and the whole can appear prenominally).

Third, the most interesting cases are words in an idiom that are of the right syntactic category but have the wrong meaning. An important wrinkle not present in compounds appears in idioms because of their syntactic structure: the deviation in meaning can appear at either the word level, the phrasal level, or some odd combination thereof. Here are two examples from the *Wheel of Fortune* corpus:

(17) a. eat humble pie
     b. not playing with a full deck

Eat humble pie, which means roughly 'humbly acknowledge a mistake', is not totally noncompositional: *humble* clearly plays a role in its meaning. Less obviously, *eat* can be read metaphorically as 'taking something back' or 'accepting'. The only part that seems completely unmotivated to me is *pie*. (David Perlmutter (personal communication) has pointed out that this sense of *eat* also occurs in the idioms *eat crow* and *eat one's words*.) Similarly, *not playing with a full deck* can be paraphrased roughly as 'not acting with a full set of brains', where *playing* means 'acting', *full* means 'full', and *deck* (of cards) means 'set of brains'. That is, this fixed expression is a minimetaphor in which each of the parts makes metaphorical sense.[10]

Thus the lexical listing of idioms like these must override in whole or in part the meanings of the constituent words and the way they are combined in the literal meaning. This is admittedly a more complex process than the rather simple overrides cited for compounds, possibly the only place where the theory of morphology may have to be seriously supplemented in order to account for idioms.

7.6 Syntactic Mobility of (Only) Some Idioms

Another well-known old fact about idioms is that they have strangely restricted properties with regard to movement. (Schenk (1995, 263) extends this observation to fixed expressions in general.) The classic case is the resistance of many idioms to passive: examples such as (18a–d) are impossible in an idiomatic reading (signaled by #).

(18) a. #The bucket was kicked by John.
     b. #The towel was thrown in by Bill.

    c. #The breeze was shot by the coal miners.
    d. #The fat was chewed by the boys.[11]

Chomsky (1980) uses this fact to argue for deep structure lexical insertion. I confess to finding the argument obscure, but the idea seems to be that something specially marked as an idiom in syntax cannot undergo movement.[12] Wasow, Nunberg, and Sag (1984), Ruwet (1991), Nunberg, Sag, and Wasow (1994), and Van Gestel (1995) point out that this is a counterproductive move, given that there are significant numbers of idioms that occur *only* in "transformed" versions (Ruwet and Van Gestel present examples from French and Dutch respectively).

(19) a. *Passive*
        X_i is hoist by pro_i's own petard
        X has it made
        X is fit to be tied
    b. Tough-*movement*
        play hard to get
        hard to take
        a tough nut to crack
        easy to come by
    c. Wh-*movement and/or question formation*
        What's up?
        How do you do?
        NP_i is not what pro_i's cracked up to be
    d. *All kinds of things*
        far be it from NP to VP

Also recall the idiomatic interpretations of *n't* and *shall* in inverted yes-no questions.

(20) a. Isn't John here?
        (Compare to *I wonder whether John isn't here*)
    b. Shall we go in?
        (Compare to *I wonder whether we shall go in*)

If lexical insertion takes place at D-Structure, somehow these idioms must be specified to undergo certain movement rules—but only those!

    On the other hand, if lexical insertion/licensing takes place at S-Structure, then it is natural to expect that some idioms (if not many) will stipulate "transformed" surface forms with which they must unify. At the same time, the inability of *kick the bucket*, *throw in the towel*, and the like to undergo passive is perfectly natural if these too stipulate surface forms.

The problem posed by S-Structure lexical licensing is then why some idioms, such as those in (21), happen to have mobile chunks.

(21) a. The hatchet seems not to have been buried yet by those skaters.
    b. The ice was finally broken by Harry's telling a dirty joke.
    c. The line has to be drawn somewhere, and I think that it should be when people start claiming nouns are underlying verbs.
    d. The cat was believed to have been let out of the bag by Harry.

A key to the answer is suggested by Wasow, Nunberg, and Sag (1984), Ruwet (1991), and Nunberg, Sag, and Wasow (1994); a similar proposal is made by Bresnan (1978). In an idiom such as *kick the bucket*, *bucket* has no independent meaning and therefore no θ-role. On the other hand, the idioms in (21) can be taken as having a sort of metaphorical semantic composition.

(22) a. bury the hatchet = reconcile a disagreement
    b. break the ice = break down a (fragile rigid) barrier to social interaction
    c. draw the line = make/enforce a distinction
    d. let the cat out of the bag = reveal a secret

As a result, the LCSs of these idioms can be partitioned into chunks that correspond to "subidiomatic" readings of the syntactic idiom chunks: *bury* means 'reconcile' and *the hatchet* means 'disagreement', for example.

This permits us to construct a lexical entry for *bury the hatchet* something like (23). (In the interests of clarity, I retain the phonological structure shared with the words *bury*, *the*, and *hatchet*.)

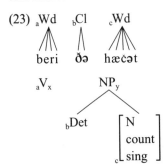

[RECONCILE ([ ]ₐ, [DISAGREEMENT]_y)]ₓ

Let's unpack this. The LCS is of course a raw approximation, containing only the critical parts of argument structure. The subscript x on the whole LCS says that this maps into the verb. The empty argument subscripted A will be filled by the conceptual structure of the external argument of the sentence. In an ordinary transitive verb, the second argument would also be subscripted A, so that it would link to the direct object. But in this case it is mapped into a stipulated constituent in the syntax by the subscript y, namely an NP consisting of Det + N. In turn, these syntactic pieces map into the phonology.

What is crucial here is that the syntactic structure does not stipulate a VP constituent: the V and the NP are not syntactically connected in any way. Therefore the NP is free to be anywhere in S-Structure, as long as it heads a chain whose lowest trace can be θ-marked as the second argument of the verb. That is, *the hatchet* behaves exactly like any other "under-lying object" in syntax, receiving its θ-role via the principle RUGR of section 4.4.

Notice that the phonology does not stipulate adjacency of the three morphemes either. As a result, not only can *the hatchet* be displaced, but *the* and *hatchet* can be separated by modifiers such as *proverbial* and *metaphorical*, which do not interfere with unification in syntax and which can be semantically integrated with the LCS of the idiom.

This account with "disconnected" syntax depends on the possibility that each piece can be connected with a piece of the LCS. By contrast, in *kick the bucket*, there is no possibility of distinguishing *the bucket* as an argument in the LCS, so the lexical entry has to look like (24), with a fixed VP.

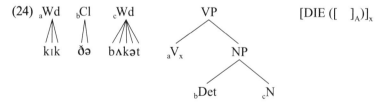

(24) $_a$Wd $_b$Cl $_c$Wd   VP   [DIE ([$]_A$)]$_x$

      kɪk   ðə   bʌkət $_a$V$_x$ NP

                                   $_b$Det $_c$N

In other words, *the hatchet* is linked to *bury* via its θ-role; but *the bucket* has to be linked to *kick* syntactically because it has no θ-role. Hence *the hatchet* is movable and *the bucket* is not.

On the other hand, since *the hatchet* does not contrast semantically with any other freely substitutable expression, it cannot be used in syn-tactic positions that entail contrast, for instance as topic: *The hatchet, we wouldn't dare bury* is only grammatical in the literal reading. Thus the fact that an idiom chunk can be moved by passive and raising does not entail that it can always be moved.

This approach is confirmed by an observation made by Abeillé (1995) and Schenk (1995). Suppose a passivizable idiom chunk contains a free position, for example *pull X's leg*. Although *leg* does not contrast with anything and thus cannot be focused or topicalized, X may, in which case it can carry *leg* along by pied-piping, yielding examples like *MARY's leg, you'd better not pull—she has a lousy sense of humor.* (This includes clefting: *It was MARY's leg, not JOHN's, that we were trying to pull.* So this analysis is not confined to movement.)

The story is not so simple, though. Paul Postal (personal communication) has pointed out that there are some idioms that have a plausible semantic decomposition but like *kick the bucket* do not readily undergo passive.

(25) raise hell = 'cause a serious disturbance'
     *Hell was raised by Herodotus. (though ?*A lot of hell will be raised by this proposal*)

(26) give the lie to X = 'show X to be a falsehood'
     *The lie was given to that claim by John. (though ?*The lie was given to that claim by John's subsequent behavior*)

For such idioms, it would be possible to say that despite their semantic decomposition, they are lexical VPs rather than a collection of syntactic fragments. That is, having a decomposition is a necessary but not a sufficient condition for mobility of idiom chunks. This concurs with Ruwet's (1991) conclusion. (However, see Abeillé 1995 for further complications that I do not pretend to understand.)

To sum up, the treatment of idioms benefits from the theory of lexical licensing developed in chapter 4. Multiword structures are easily inserted into complex syntactic structures if the process in question is unification rather than substitution. The fact that many idioms are rigid in syntactic structure, and that some of them have rigid "transformed" structures, follows from the fact that lexical licensing takes place at S-Structure rather than D-Structure. The fact that some idiom chunks are still movable follows from the possibility of assigning them independent bits of meaning in the idiom's LCS, so that they can be integrated with the verb of the idiom by normal θ-marking.[13]

Returning to our main issue: by adopting a theory in which lexical items larger than X^0 can license syntactic structures, we can incorporate clichés and idioms into the lexicon. Furthermore, many of the curious properties of idioms are altogether parallel to those already found within lexical word grammar, so they add no further complexity to grammatical theory. As for the remaining properties of idioms, they may have to be added to grammatical theory—but they had to be added *somewhere* in the theory of mind in any event. The point is that those generalizations that do exist can be captured; by contrast, a theory that relegates idioms to some unknown general-purpose component of mind incurs needless duplication.

7.7 Idioms That Are Specializations of Other Idiomatic Constructions

One interesting class of idioms in the *Wheel of Fortune* corpus are *resultative* idioms, listed in (27).

(27) a. cut my visit short
     b. I cried my eyes out
     c. knock yourself out ('work too hard')
     d. you scared the daylights out of me

These are idiomatic specializations of the resultative construction, which has the syntactic structure (28a) and the interpretation (28b).

(28) a. [$_{VP}$ V NP PP/AP]
     b. 'cause NP to go PP/to become AP, by V-ing (NP)'

To show what I mean by *idiomatic specializations*, I first must briefly discuss the nature of the resultative construction. (29a–d) are standard examples of this construction.

(29) a. The gardener watered the tulips flat. ('the gardener caused the tulips to become flat by watering them')
     b. We cooked the meat black. ('we caused the meat to become black by cooking it')
     c. The professor talked us into a stupor. ('the professor caused us to go into a stupor by talking')
     d. He talked himself hoarse. ('he caused himself to become hoarse by talking') ("fake reflexive" case)

It has been argued (Jackendoff 1990, chapter 10; Goldberg 1992, 1995) that the resultative is a "constructional idiom," a match of syntactic and conceptual structure that is not determined by the head verb. Although the verb is the syntactic head of the VP, it is not the semantic head; rather,

its meaning is embedded in a manner constituent, as indicated roughly in
(28b). As a result, the argument structure of the VP is determined by the
meaning of the constructional idiom, essentially a causative inchoative of
the sort expressed overtly by verbs such as *put* and *make*.[14]

Under this approach to the resultative, the construction is listed in the
lexicon just like an ordinary idiom, except that it happens to have no
phonological structure: it is a structure of the form ⟨∅, SS, CS⟩, where SS
happens to be a whole VP. (28) presents the matching, with (28b) as a
very informal account of the conceptual structure. At the same time, since
the syntactic structure and conceptual structure provide open places for
the V, NP, and PP/AP; the construction is productive; hence it differs
from ordinary idioms, whose terminal elements are fixed.

To see this more clearly, consider a related constructional idiom that is
more transparent: the "*way*-construction" exemplified in (30).

(30) a. Bill belched his way out of the restaurant.
    b. We ate our way across the country.

Note that in these sentences the intransitive verb cannot license anything
in the rest of the VP; and the NP in direct object position, *X's way*, is not
exactly a normal direct object. Goldberg (1993, 1995) and I (Jackendoff
1990) argue that this construction too is an idiom, listed in the lexicon
with the following structure:[15]

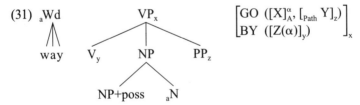

(The conceptual structure in (31) is coded in the notation of Jackendoff
1990; it says essentially 'Subject goes along Path designated by PP, by V-
ing'. The fact that the subject functions as semantic subject of GO and of
the main verb is encoded by the binding of the arguments designated by α,
as mentioned in section 3.7. See also Goldberg's treatment for further
complications in meaning and for discussion of Marantz's (1992) coun-
terproposal.)

(31) licenses correspondences of syntactic structure and conceptual
structure that do not follow canonical principles of argument structure
mapping. As a result, the verb is not what licenses the argument structure

of the rest of the VP; rather, the construction does. Furthermore, the odd noun *way* is the only phonological reflex of the construction. Again, because there are open places in syntactic structure and conceptual structure, the construction is productive, unlike ordinary idioms. Thus a construction like this offers yet another source of enriched semantic composition, in addition to the types discussed in chapter 3.

As with the resultative, there exist fixed expressions built out of the *way*-construction. For instance, the form *wend* occurs only in the expression *wend one's way PP*; the form *worm* appears as a verb only in the expression *worm one's way PP*. In addition, there is the expression *sleep one's way to the top*, 'reach the top of a social hierarchy by granting sexual favors', in which *sleep* and *top* must be taken in a special sense. If the lexicon allows listing of instances of a productive pattern with further specification and/or overrides (as argued for compounds in section 7.5), then it is natural to expect such specialized forms of the productive construction, containing cranberry morphs and/or special metaphorical meanings.

Returning to the idioms in (27), these bear the same relation to the resultative construction as *wend one's way PP* does to the *way*-construction. It is interesting that different specializations pertain to different arguments of the construction. In (27a), for instance, the idiom is *cut NP short*, where the free argument is the direct object; but in (27d) it is *scare the daylights out of NP*, where the free argument is the prepositional object. In (27b) the idiom is the whole VP *cry NP's eyes out*, where NP has to be a bound pronoun. It shares this bound pronoun with the *way*-construction and many other idioms such as *gnash NP's teeth* and *stub NP's toe* (in which, incidentally, the verbs are cranberry morphs).

How does the lexicon express the relation of a specialized fixed expression to a more general construction of which it is an instance? It seems to me that this relationship is actually not so different from that between subordinate and superordinate concepts such as *robin* and *bird*. In either case, both members of the relationship have to be listed in memory. Indeed, as is well known, it is not unusual for a subordinate concept to override features of its superordinate, for instance in stipulating that an ostrich, though a bird, is flightless. In other words, the general cognitive machinery necessary for working out hierarchical relationships of concepts seems not inappropriate for working out hierarchical relationships among lexical constructions and idioms built on them.[16]

7.8 Relation to Construction Grammar

Such an account of constructional idioms and their lexical specializations
makes sense, of course, only in a theory of the lexicon that permits phrasal
lexical items, that is, in a theory of lexical licensing rather than lexical
insertion. This approach makes clear contact with work in Construction
Grammar (Fillmore, Kay, and O'Connor 1988; Fillmore and Kay 1993;
Goldberg 1995), whose premise is that a language typically contains a
substantial number of syntactic constructions that (1) are not entirely
derivable by principles of "core grammar" and (2) receive specialized
interpretations. Typical examples for English are shown in (32).

(32) a. *The more* he likes her, *the more* she dislikes him.
   b. Bill hates chemistry class, *doesn't he?*
   c. *One more beer and* I'm leaving. (Culicover 1972)
   d. Fred doesn't even like Schubert, *let alone* Mahler. (Fillmore,
      Kay, and O'Connor 1988)
   e. *Day by day* things are getting worse. (Williams 1994)

Since these constructions, like the *way*-construction, are listed as triples
of partly specified phonological, syntactic, and conceptual structures, the
boundary between "lexicon" and "rule of grammar" begins to blur. For
instance, Williams (1994) notes that *day by day* belongs to a semiproductive family of idioms of the form N_1-P-N_1: *week after week, inch by inch,
piece by piece, bit by bit, cheek to cheek,* and *hand over hand* (plus the
outlier *hand over fist,* with two different nouns). Or are they compounds?
It's hard to tell, because they resist modification, other than perhaps *inch
by agonizing inch.*

Another such family includes compound prepositions like *in consideration of, with respect to, in touch with, under penalty of, in search of, in
need of, in spite of, in synch with, in line with,* and *by dint of* (with a cranberry morph). I call these expressions compounds because, as in other
products of sub-X^0 composition, the internal noun resists any determiner
or other modification (**in the consideration of*, etc.).[17] However, a quite
similar group *does* allow some syntactic flexibility: *in case of war/in that
case, for the sake of my sanity/for Bill's sake, on behalf of the organization/
on Mike's behalf.* Hence the latter group looks more like a syntactic construction. We thus have two very closely related constructions, one of
which looks morphological, the other syntactic. This helps point up the
necessity of treating idiosyncratic syntactic constructions in a way as close
as possible to semiproductive morphology.

How far might one want to push this line of thought? Along with Fillmore and Kay (1993), Goldberg (1995), and in some sense Langacker (1987), one might even want to view the "core rules" of phrase structure for a language as maximally underspecified constructional idioms. If there is an issue with the Construction Grammar position here, it is the degree to which the "core rules" are inherently associated with semantics, in the way specialized constructions like (32) are.

To elaborate this issue a little, consider Goldberg's (1995) argument (related to that in Jackendoff 1990) that the double object construction in English always marks the indirect object as a beneficiary of some sort; she infers from this that the *V-NP-NP* construction carries an inherent meaning. However, a larger context perhaps leads to a different conclusion. Languages differ with respect to whether they allow ditransitive VPs: English does, French does not. The *possibility* of having such a configuration is a syntactic fact; the *uses* to which this configuration is put (i.e. the SS-CS correspondence rules that interpret ditransitive VPs) are semantic. And in fact, although English ditransitive VPs are used most prominently for Beneficiary + Theme constructions (so-called *to*-datives and *for*-datives), the same syntax is also recruited for Theme + Predicate NP, hence the ambiguity of *Make me a milkshake* (*Poof! You're a milkshake!*). And ditransitive syntax also appears with a number of verbs whose semantics is at the moment obscure, for instance *I envy you your security*, *They denied Bill his pay*, *The book cost Harry $5*, and *The lollipop lasted me two hours*. At the same time, there are verbs that fit the semantics of the dative but cannot use it, for example *Tell/*Explain Bill the answer*.

In addition, other languages permit other ranges of semantic roles in the ditransitive pattern. Here are some examples from Icelandic (33) and Korean (34) (thanks to Joan Maling and Soowon Kim respectively):

(33) a. Þeir leyndu   Ólaf   sannleikanum.
        they concealed [from] Olaf(ACC) the-truth(DAT)
     b. Sjórinn svipti   hanni   manni   sínum.
        the-sea deprived her(ACC) husband(DAT) her
        'The sea deprived her of her husband.'
        (Zaenen, Maling, and Thráinsson 1985)

(34) a. John-un   kkoch-ul   hwahwan-ul yekk-ess-ta.
        John-TOP   flowers-ACC wreath-ACC tie-PAST-IND
        'John tied the flowers into a wreath.'

b. John-un   cangcak-ul motakpul-ul   ciphi-ess-ta.
   John-TOP logs-ACC   campfire-ACC burn-PAST-IND
   'John burned the logs down into a campfire.'

This distribution suggests that there is a purely syntactic fact about whether a particular language has ditransitive VPs. In addition, *if* it has them, the SS-CS correspondence rules of the language must specify for what semantic purposes (what three-argument verbs and what adjunct constructions) they are recruited. It is not that French can't say any of these things; it just has to use different syntactic devices. And although the grammar of English no doubt contains the form-meaning correspondence for datives described by Goldberg, the availability of *that form* as a target for correspondences seems an independent, purely syntactic fact, also part of the grammar of English.

A similar case, concerning the contrast between English and Yiddish topicalization, is discussed by Prince (1995). On her analysis, the broader uses of Yiddish topicalization are not a consequence of a movement rule that permits a wider range of constituents to be moved; instead, they are available because this syntax is linked with a larger range of discourse functions. Yiddish speakers learning English tend to get the syntax right—they do not apply verb-second, for instance. But they tend to use the English construction with Yiddish discourse functions, yielding "Yinglish" sentences such as *A Chomsky, he's not.* The point of her argument is that there is a certain amount of independence between the existence of a syntactic construction and what meaning(s) it can express.

If one wishes to adopt the stance of Construction Grammar, then, it seems one should maintain that among the most general constructions, the bread and butter of the syntax, are constructions that are purely syntactic, the counterpart of phrase structure rules. These then would be phrasal lexical items that are of the form $\langle \emptyset, SS, \emptyset \rangle$. These could then be specialized into particular meaningful constructions, in the same way as meaningful constructions such as the resultative can be specialized into idioms.

But in principle there should be no problem with a theory that blurs these boundaries: a strict separation of lexicon and phrasal grammar, like a strict separation of word lexicon and idiom lists, may prove to be yet another methodological prejudice. I find this an intriguing question for future research.

7.9 Summary

To summarize the main points of this chapter:

1. There are too many idioms and other fixed expressions for us to simply disregard them as phenomena "on the margin of language."

2. From the point of view of Representational Modularity, what counts as "part of language" is anything stored in memory in phonological and/ or syntactic format.

3. The standard assumptions about lexical insertion make it difficult to formulate a general theory of idioms; but these assumptions are in any event unsatisfactory on other grounds.

4. The alternative theory of lexical *licensing* conforms to Representational Modularity. It permits fixed expressions in the lexicon as a matter of course: like words, they are fixed matchings of ⟨PS, SS, CS⟩.

5. The theoretical machinery necessary for the noncompositional aspects of morphology (especially compounds) goes a long way toward providing an account of the noncompositionality of idioms as well, in particular allowing for the listing of partly redundant instances of a productive pattern, the further specialization of such instances, and the possibility of overrides.

6. At least some of the syntactic mobility of idioms can be accounted for in terms of how they map their meanings onto syntax.

7. This approach to idioms extends readily to syntactic constructions with specialized meanings, and perhaps to more general phrase structure configurations as well.

In short, within a theory of lexical licensing, it does not necessarily cost very much in the generality and constraint of grammatical theory to add a theory of idioms, other fixed expressions, and constructions, properly enlarging the scope of linguistic knowledge.

Chapter 8

Epilogue: How Language Helps Us Think

8.1 Introduction

It may seem out of place to conclude a book about technical linguistics with a chapter on how language helps us think. However, some interesting answers to this question emerge from the architecture for language developed here and from Representational Modularity. Part of my goal in this book is to emphasize the continuity of technical linguistic theory with the other cognitive sciences. Hence I find it interesting to turn from the nitty-gritty of lexical licensing to one of the most general issues a theory of linguistics may confront. Many outside of linguistics have speculated on it, but without an informed view of language. By contrast, few inside of linguistics have tried. Emonds (1991) makes some relevant remarks (in reaction to which this chapter developed); Chomsky's (1995) minimal speculations were mentioned in chapter 1. Bickerton (1995) thinks through the question much more comprehensively, and I will draw on some of his ideas in the course of the discussion.[1]

Part of the difficulty in attacking this question is that it seems altogether natural that language should help us think—so natural as almost to require no explanation. We differ from other animals in being smarter, in being able to think (or reason) better; and we differ from other animals in having language. So the connection between the two seems obvious. In this chapter, therefore, I must first show that the fact that language helps us think *does* require an explanation, before being able to give an idea of what the explanation might be like.

From the way I have phrased the question, it should be clear that I am emphatically not expecting an absolute connection between language and thought; otherwise I would have entitled the chapter "Does Language

Enable Us to Think?" Rather, I will be promoting a somewhat more complex position.

1. Thought is a mental function completely separate from language, and it can go on in the absence of language.

2. On the other hand, language provides a scaffolding that makes possible certain varieties of reasoning more complex than are available to nonlinguistic organisms.

Thus the question of how language helps us think may be focused further.

3. How much of our increased reasoning power is due simply to our big brains, and how much of it is specifically due to the presence of a language faculty and why?

For reasons discussed in sections 1.1.6 and 2.6, we continue to think of mental functions in computational terms. In particular, we have found it useful to think of brain processing in terms of the construction of representations within representation modules and the coordination of these representations by interface modules. Thus particular mental functions are to be localized in particular representation or interface modules. In addition, we have taken care to ask how the information that appears in working memory (in speech perception and/or production) is related to long-term memory knowledge of language (lexicon and grammar).

Seen from a larger perspective, then, this chapter is an exercise in showing how to tease apart which linguistic phenomena belong to which modules. For cognitive scientists interested in other faculties of mind, this may be taken to provide a model for how mental faculties can be deconstructed, a formal and functional approach that can complement investigation into brain localization.

8.2   Brain Phenomena Opaque to Awareness

In working out a computational theory of brain function, it immediately becomes necessary to claim that certain steps behind common sense are hidden from conscious experience. Such a claim supposes that we can distinguish two sorts of phenomena in the brain: those that are present to awareness—that show their face as something we experience—and those that are not (with perhaps some in-between cases as well). The immediate question that arises, then, is which information within the brain contributes directly to the character of conscious experience and which only indirectly.

We can immediately observe that experience is connected to *working* memory and not *long-term* memory. We can be aware of a (long-term) memory only if the memory is recovered into working memory. Hence, for example, the lexicon and the rules of grammar are not accessible to awareness. Only their consequences, namely linguistic expressions, are consciously available.

In earlier work (Jackendoff 1987a; henceforth *C&CM*) I proposed the further hypothesis that the distinction between conscious and unconscious information can also be made partly in terms of the levels of representation available to the brain—that some levels much more than others can be seen mirrored directly in the way we experience the world. If this is the correct approach, it makes sense to ask which of the levels of representation are the ones most directly connected to awareness.

Let us start with a simple case, far from language. Notice how the images in your two eyes are subtly different. If you alternately close one eye and then the other, you see the image change. But in normal binocular vision, the two images are fused into a single image, which contains an element of depth not present in either eye separately. How does your brain do that? No matter how hard you think about it, you can't catch yourself in the act of fusing the two images into one. Phenomenologically, it just happens, as if by magic. Explaining exactly how the brain does this is a major preoccupation of vision research (e.g. Julesz 1971; Marr 1982; Crick 1994). But even when we figure out how the brain does it, we still won't be able to catch ourselves in the act! And this is true of peripheral information in general. We can't be aware of the frequency analysis our auditory system performs on an incoming sound wave; we just hear a sound (Bregman 1990). We can't be aware of the input from stretch receptors in the proprioceptive system; we just feel a weight (Lackner 1985).

In fact, it seems plausible that all peripheral sensory representations in the brain are totally inaccessible to awareness. A crude diagram like figure 8.1 (next page) schematizes the situation: what we might call the "outer ring" of representations is completely unconscious.

Once we have established that *some* representations are unconscious, the obvious question that arises is exactly *which* are unconscious. Is it only the peripheral ones, or are there more? Section 8.4 will try to show that there are indeed more, and subsequent sections will work out interesting consequences for the relation of language and thought.

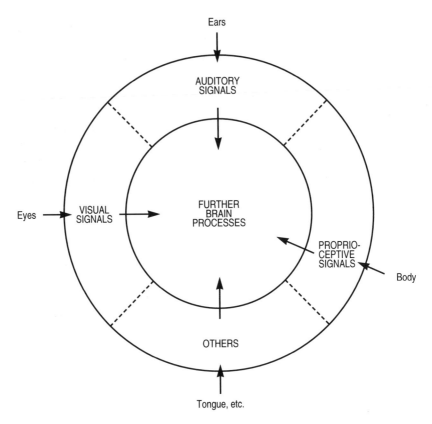

Figure 8.1
An outer shell of sensory representations is unconscious

Note that I am not asking the questions everyone seems to ask, namely "What Is Consciousness?" or "What Is Consciousness For?" (This includes, for instance, Hofstadter 1979, Searle 1992, Baars 1988, and Block 1995.) I suspect that many people who insist on this question (though perhaps not the authors just cited) really want to know something like "What makes human life meaningful?" And in many cases—my students have often been quite explicit about this—they are just hoping that somehow we'll be able to bring back some magic, some hope for a soul or the possibility of immortality. By contrast, I am asking a less cosmic and more structural question, simply, "Which representations are most directly reflected in consciousness and which ones are not, and what are the consequences for the nature of experience?" If you don't care for this question, I am the first to acknowledge that it's a matter of taste; but I hope to convince you that my question can still lead to a certain kind of progress.

8.3   Language Is Not Thought, and Vice Versa

Let us focus more closely on the relation of language and thought. We very often experience our thought as "talking to ourselves"—we actually hear words, phrases, or sentences in our head—and it's very tempting therefore to characterize thought as some sort of inner speech. I want to argue, though, that thought cannot be simply bits of language in the head, that it is a different kind of brain phenomenon. These arguments are by no means new (see Dascal 1995 for some history of the dispute), but it's worth rehearsing them again in this context.

First, thinking is largely independent of what language one happens to think in. A French speaker or a Turkish speaker can have essentially the same thoughts as an English speaker can—they're just in French or Turkish.[2] The point of translation between languages is to preserve the thought behind the expression. If different languages can express the same thought, then thoughts cannot be embalmed in the form of any single language: they must be neutral with respect to what language they are expressed in. For instance, the same thought can be expressed in English, where the verb precedes the direct object, and in Japanese, where the verb follows the direct object. Hence the form of the thought must not depend on word order. *Language*, by contrast, *does* depend on word order: you (or your brain) have to choose a word order in order to say a sentence— or even just to hear it in your head. Consider also bilinguals who can "think in two languages." We would like to be able to say their thoughts are essentially the same, no matter which language they are "thinking in." This is possible only if the form of thought is *neither* of these languages. In chapter 2, following earlier work (Jackendoff 1983, 1987a, 1990), I took the position that the nonlinguistic level of conceptual structure is one of the forms in which thought is encoded, and in terms of which inference takes place.[3]

In fact, we find dissociations of ability in linguistic expression (syntax and phonology) from reasoning, for example children with Williams syndrome (Bellugi, Wang, and Jernigan 1994). These individuals at first glance seem rather precocious, because they chatter away in animated fashion, using all kinds of advanced vocabulary. But their language skills turn out to be an isolated high point in an otherwise bleak intellectual landscape; they evidently cannot use their advanced language to reason very well.

Another such case is the linguistic idiot savant studied by Smith and Tsimpli (1995). This is an individual retarded in nearly every respect except for the learning of languages, in which he displays remarkable ability, having acquired substantial fluency in Danish, Dutch, Finnish, French, German, Greek, Hindi, Italian, Norwegian, Polish, Portuguese, Russian, Spanish, Swedish, Turkish, and Welsh. Interestingly, although his word-for-word translation and use of grammatical inflection is excellent, he is poor at making use of contextual relevance to refine his translations, suggesting a dissociation between using language and understanding it in any depth.

In these cases, then, linguistic expression is highly structured but is not connected to commensurately complex meaning. Conversely, complex thought can exist without linguistic expression. Think about people like Beethoven and Picasso, who obviously displayed a lot of intelligence and deep thought. But their thoughts were not expressible as bits of language—their intelligence was in the musical and visual domains respectively. (Music and visual art are indeed modes of communication, but not *languages*; see Lerdahl and Jackendoff 1983 for discussion.)

For a much more mundane example, think of the motor intelligence displayed in the simple act of washing dishes. It is well beyond current understanding in computer science to program a pair of robot eyes and hands to wash dishes in the manner that we do, with the skill and flexibility that any of us can muster. I suspect it would be impossible to train an animal to carry out such a task, much less induce it to have the persistence to want to finish the job (this parallels in part Dennett's (1995) example of tending a fire). Yet very little of this skill is verbalizable.

It would seem to me, then, that humans display considerable intelligent behavior that is governed by representations outside of syntax and phonology. This may reveal the existence of further cognitive specializations in humans besides language, or it may be simply a consequence of the big brain affording more computational capacity in preexisting modules. Which is closer to correct, it seems to me, is a matter for future research.

Turning to animals, there are ample arguments for reasoning in nonhuman primates, going back to Köhler (1927) and continuing in a rich tradition to the present.[4] If apes and monkeys can think without language, at least to some degree, then we are forced to acknowledge the independence of thought from language. To make this point more vividly, it is of interest to consider a phenomenon called *redirected aggression*, described by Cheney and Seyfarth (1990). From extended observation of and experimentation with vervet monkeys in the wild, Cheney and Seyfarth show that if monkey X attacks monkey Y, there is a strong likelihood that monkey Y will shortly thereafter attack some other member of X's kin-group. Consider what reasoning must be attributed to Y to explain this behavior: Y must know (1) that X attacked Y, (2) that retaliation is a desirable response, (3) that this other monkey, call her Z, is a member of X's kin-group, (4) that kin-groups count as some sort of equivalence class for attack and retribution, and (5) that facts (1)–(4) give Y reason to attack Z. This seems to me like fairly complexly structured thought, and, other than the actual attack, the facts involved are related to perception only very abstractly. The level of conceptual structure has the appropriate degree of abstraction for expressing them. (Cheney and Seyfarth mount extended arguments against regarding this behavior as any sort of simple stimulus generalization; their explicit goal is to convince animal behaviorists that reasoning is indeed taking place.)

The picture that emerges from these examples is that although language *expresses* thought, thought itself is a separate brain phenomenon.

Bickerton (1995) claims, by contrast, that language itself is the form in which thought is encoded; Emonds (1991) makes a similar claim that it is language that permits "connected thought." However, neither of them addresses the question of what levels of linguistic representation support reasoning and how rules of inference can be defined over them. They seem to think that syntactic structure is an appropriate structure for thought. Yet syntactic structure does not carry such elementary semantic distinctions as the difference between dogs and cats (see chapter 4), so it clearly cannot support inference of any complexity.

Bickerton's and Emonds's claims rest in part on their assumption that θ-roles (the relations of who did what to whom) are syntactic notions: they argue that since reasoning involves computation of θ-roles, it must necessarily turn on syntactic structure. I have argued extensively (Jackendoff 1972, 1976, 1990, and many other places) that θ-roles are aspects of conceptual structure, not of syntax, so Bickerton's and Emonds's arguments are unfounded.

Bickerton also confuses the broad notion of syntax (i.e. the organization of any formal system) with the narrow notion of syntax (the organization of NPs and VPs). He says that since thought is (broadly) syntactic, it requires (narrow) syntax, which is simply false.

Finally, Bickerton calls the aspect of language used for reasoning, abstracted away from the particulars of the syntax and phonology of individual languages, "Language-with-a-capital-L." This seems to me to fall in with Chomsky's statement, quoted in chapter 1, to the effect that if only we had telepathy, language could be "perfect" and we could communicate pure thought. Along with Pinker (1992), I submit that the level of representation satisfying these desiderata is precisely conceptual structure, a level with which language communicates, but not itself a strictly linguistic level.[5]

8.4   Phonetic Form is Conscious, Thought Is Not

Next I want to point up a difference between language and thought with respect to consciousness. Compare *rhyming* with *entailment*. When we observe that two words rhyme, say *mouse* and *house*, we can easily see why: the ends of the two words sound the same, *-ouse*. That is, the relevant parts of words in a rhyming relationship are immediately transparent to awareness. By contrast, consider an entailment relationship, for instance if *Bill killed Harry*, then *Harry died*. This entailment is intuitively trivial. But exactly what parts of the first sentence are responsible for entailing exactly what parts of the second sentence? One is tempted to say "That's just what killing is: making someone die." But this merely restates the problem: there's nothing about the conscious *form* of the word *kill* that makes it obvious that it has anything to do with the *form* of the word *die*.[6] The relationship of entailment *feels* to us as obvious and mechanical as the relationship of rhyming, but at the same time we can't put our finger on what parts of the words make the entailment mechanical. Entailment involves an intuitive step, a step that is opaque to awareness.

In this light, we can regard the development of formal logic, from the Greeks to the present, as a series of attempts to make explicit the steps involved in reasoning, to lay bare the mechanical principles of thought. Such an enterprise has always been deemed necessary precisely because these principles are *not* evident in natural language. By contrast, until the advent of modern phonology, no one found it necessary to uncover the mechanical principles behind rhyming: they are self-evident.

Of course, a major difference between rhyming and entailment is that rhyming is a relation between the linguistic *form* of words—in particular their phonetic form—whereas entailment is a relation between the *meanings* of sentences, between the thoughts the sentences express. In *C&CM* I

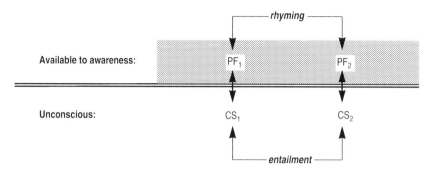

Figure 8.2
The forms governing rhymes are available to awareness; the forms governing entailment are not

proposed that this difference is a key to understanding why the former is transparent to awareness and the latter is not. Figure 8.2 schematizes my analysis. The idea is that phonetic forms are available to awareness—we can consciously analyze them into their parts, at least to a degree. We can hear directly the analysis into syllables, and with training that everyone has undergone in learning to read, the analysis into individual phonetic segments. (On the other hand, we cannot hear directly the analysis into distinctive features; this is why beginning linguistics students have such difficulty memorizing the features.) Thus the structures involved in judging rhymes are consciously available.

By contrast, conceptual structures, although *expressed* by conscious linguistic forms, are not themselves available to consciousness. Thus in figure 8.2, phonetic form$_1$ entails phonetic form$_2$ only indirectly, via a principled relationship between the conceptual structures they express. Since the conceptual structures are not consciously available, entailment has an intuitive, quasi-magical gap in the way it is experienced.

More generally, I am inclined to believe that thought per se is *never* conscious. This may sound radical, but consider: When we engage in what we call conscious thinking, we are usually experiencing a talking voice in the head, the so-called stream of consciousness, complete with segmental phonology, stress, and intonation. In other words, we are experiencing something that has all the hallmarks of phonetic form. For most of us, this voice never shuts up—we have to do Zen or something to make it quiet in there. But we know that phonetic form is not the form of thought; it is rather a consciously available expression of the thought. If we can catch ourselves in the act of thinking, then, it is because the linguistic images in our heads spell out some of the steps.

Remember too that there are those times when an inspiration jumps into awareness; it comes as if by magic. Of course, as good cognitive scientists, we're not allowed to say it's magic. Rather, we have to assume that the brain is going about its business of solving problems, but not making a lot of conscious noise about it; reasoning is taking place without being expressed as language. So when the final result pops out as a linguistic expression ("Hey! I've got it! If we just do such and such, everything will work fine!"), it comes as a surprise.

So far, then, I'm advocating that we become aware of thought taking place—we catch ourselves in the act of thinking—only when it manifests itself in linguistic form, in fact phonetic form.

This is an oversimplification, however, because there exist other conscious manifestations of thought, such as visual images. For instance, if I say *Bill killed Harry*, you may have a visual image of someone sticking a knife into someone else and of that second person bleeding and falling down and ceasing to breathe, and you say "Oh yes, Harry died!" So you might suspect that the connection between the two thoughts is made in the visual image, a mental phenomenon that does appear in consciousness.

The problem with this solution was pointed out by Bishop Berkeley back in the 18th century; the modern version of the argument appears in Fodor 1975. An image is too specific. When I said *Bill killed Harry*, your image had to depict Bill stabbing or strangling or shooting or poisoning or hanging or electrocuting Harry. Any of these count as killing. And Harry had to fall down, or expire sitting down, or die hanging from a rope. Any of these count as dying. So how can any of them be *the* concept of killing or dying? That is, the thoughts expressed by the words *kill* and *die*, not to mention the connections between them, are too general, too abstract to be conveyed by a visual image.

A second problem, emphasized by Wittgenstein (1953), concerns identification. How do you know that those people in your visual image are Bill and Harry respectively? There's nothing in their appearance that gives them their names. (Even if they're wearing sweatshirts with *Bill* and *Harry* emblazoned on them, that still doesn't do the trick!)

A third problem: What is the visual image that corresponds to a question like *Who killed Roger Rabbit?* This sentence clearly expresses a comprehensible thought. But there is nothing that can be put in a visual image to show that it corresponds to a question rather than a statement, say

Someone unknown killed Roger Rabbit. In fact, what could the image be even for *someone unknown*? The situation is still worse when we try to conjure up a useful image for *virtue* or *social justice* or *seven hundred thirty-two*.

My view is that visual images, like linguistic images, are possible conscious manifestations of thought, but they are not thoughts either. Again, this is nothing new.

But now let me put this together with figure 8.1. Figure 8.1 distinguishes a sort of shell of sensory representations that are completely unconscious. In the case of vision such representations encode such things as fusion of the two retinal images, edge detection, and stabilization of the visual field in spite of eye movements. In the case of language they include at least the frequency analysis of the auditory signal and any further stages prior to the conversion into phonetic form.

I am now suggesting that there is also a central core of representations that is inaccessible to consciousness. In the linguistic faculty these include at least syntactic structure and conceptual structure; outside of language these include for example the multimodal spatial representations (section 2.6) that coordinate vision, touch, and action. Thus the representations that *are* conscious form a sort of intermediate ring between the sensorimotor periphery and the cognitive interior. Figure 8.3 is a crude picture of this. (Figure 8.2 can be regarded as a segment of figure 8.3.) Since we act on the world as well as perceive it, figure 8.3 includes not only sensory information coming into the brain but also motor instructions going out. Only the representations in the shaded ring are conscious. The outer peripheral ring is unconscious, as in figure 8.1, and the inner cognitive core is also unconscious.

Figure 8.3 schematizes a position I have called the *Intermediate Level Theory of Consciousness*, worked out in a good deal more detail in *C&CM*. With respect to language and thought, the idea is that the *form* of our experience is driven by the form of language, especially by phonetic form. We experience language as organized sequences of sounds. On the other hand, the *content* of our experience, our understanding of the sounds, is encoded in different representations, in particular conceptual structure and spatial representation. The organization of this content is completely unconscious.

Thought often drives language: the presence of a conceptual structure in working memory often causes the brain to develop a corresponding linguistic structure, which we may either pronounce or just experience as

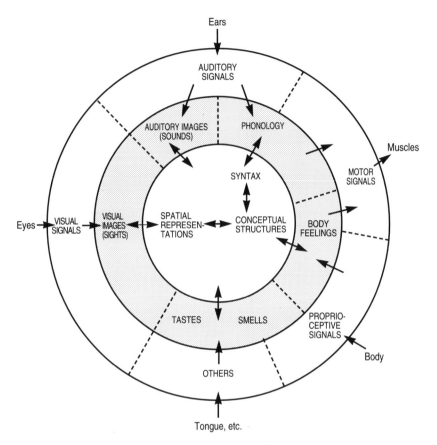

Figure 8.3
The Intermediate-Level Theory: peripheral and central representations are inaccessible to consciousness

linguistic imagery. Conversely, linguistic structures in working memory (most often created in response to an incoming speech signal) invariably drive the brain to try to create a corresponding conceptual structure (the meaning of the heard utterance). Consequently many of our thoughts have a conscious accompaniment: the linguistic structures that express them.

Thought can be driven by other modalities as well. For instance, consider figure 8.4. In response to viewing a tree in the world, the visual system constructs a representation of the form of the tree—and, through the appropriate interface modules, it also drives the conceptual system to

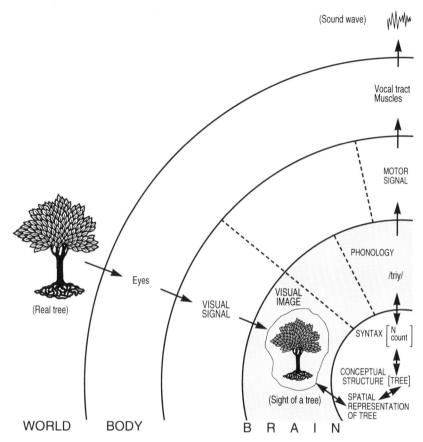

Figure 8.4
What is conscious in seeing a tree and talking about it

retrieve the *concept* of a tree, a combination of its conceptual and spatial representations (*C&CM*, chapter 10; Jackendoff 1996a). That is, our understanding of what we see is a consequence not only of visual images but also of the conceptual organization connected to those images. As in the case of language, we have no direct awareness of our understanding of trees; we have only a perceptual awareness of the visual form of what we are seeing. The visual form is in the intermediate shell of brain processes in figure 8.3, but the understanding is in the unconscious central core.

In turn, the unconscious central core links the visual perception with language. If the visual/spatial system drives the conceptual system to develop a conceptual structure for the tree, then conceptual structure, through its lexical and phrasal interface with syntax and phonology, can drive the language faculty to create an utterance such as "Hey, a tree!" Thus, in figure 8.4, the two conscious parts, the visual image and the word, are linked together by the unconscious concept of a tree.

Part of the idea behind figure 8.3 is that the same general architecture is preserved in other organisms, at least those with higher mammalian brain structure (though not necessarily reptiles or Martians). For instance, a monkey will have essentially the same linkages among representations as we do, lacking only the link provided by language. In fact, an organism might have other modalities of experience that humans don't have. Bats presumably have some kind of experience through their echolocation modality whose quality we can't imagine—*hearing* shape and distance and motion! This follows from the Intermediate-Level Theory, which says that somewhere between sensation and cognition lies a level of representations that is conscious. We can thus envision taking the basic model of figure 8.3 and adding and subtracting different modalities of experience to imagine the forms of experience for different organisms.

The overall spirit of this analysis, of course, derives from Representational Modularity, since it presumes that the representations underlying different mental functions can be formally segregated from each other and linked via interface modules. In figure 8.3 the different sectors of each ring stand very roughly for different representation modules.

A crucial part of the analysis comes from the nature of interface modules. We saw in chapter 2 that, almost as a point of logical necessity, we need modules that interface between faculties: a module that dumbly, obsessively converts conceptual structure into syntax and vice versa; another that dumbly, obsessively converts visual images into spatial representations and vice versa; and so forth. As we saw in chapters 2 and 3, part of the nature of interface modules is that they effect only a partial correspondence between representations; much information in each of the linked representations is invisible to the interface module. Moreover, the mapping performed by an interface module is often many-to-many, so that information content is by no means well preserved across the interface.

In particular, not all aspects of conceptual structure lend themselves to visual imagery or linguistic form, so the interface modules just do the best they can. The places where they fail are just those places where we have found gaps between the conscious forms of linguistic and visual experience on one hand and the needs of thought and reasoning on the other.

8.5 The Significance of Consciousness Again

Let us continue to look at figure 8.3, and ask what it says about consciousness. Section 8.2 mentioned that many people want to ascribe to consciousness some cosmic significance—they want to say our consciousness is what makes us human, it's connected to our highest capacities, it's what separates us from the animals. If anything like figure 8.3 is correct, the significance of consciousness can't be anything like that. If there is anything that makes us human, that has enabled us to build great civilizations, it is our capacity for reasoning—*which isn't conscious!* Consciousness is not directing our behavior. Rather, it is just a consequence of some intermediate phenomena along the chain of connection between perception (the periphery) and thought (the core).

This goes strongly against intuition, of course. But it stands to reason that it should. The conscious phenomena are all we can know directly about our minds. As far as consciousness is concerned, the rest of the mind simply doesn't exist, except as a source of miracles that we get so accustomed to that we call them "common sense." Hence we naturally ascribe any intellectual powers we have to consciousness. I submit that, if we really look at the department of so-called miracles, we find that most of the interesting work of intelligence is being done in that department—not in the conscious department. (My impression is that this has certainly been one of the lessons learned from research in artificial intelligence.)

Notice that this conclusion does not demean our humanity in any way. We can still do whatever we can do. Maybe it does reduce the chance that it would be interesting to have a consciousness that continues beyond our death—an immortal soul: with neither sensory input nor conceptual representations, there certainly wouldn't be much to experience. But, after all, wishing for something doesn't make it true. We'll have to look for reasons other than the hope of immortality to find our lives meaningful.

This completes the first part of this chapter, in which I've tried to dissociate language from thought and to show that they are distinct brain phenomena. According to this picture, the mere fact of having language does not make thought possible, nor does language have a direct effect on thought processes. In the rest of the chapter I want to suggest three ways in which language has important *indirect* effects on thought processes.

8.6   First Way Language Helps Us Think: Linguistic Communication

The first way language helps us think is fairly obvious. By virtue of having language, it is possible to communicate thought in a way impossible for nonlinguistic organisms. Language permits us to have history and law and science and gossip. The range of things we can think about is not limited to what we can dream up ourselves—we have all of past and present culture to draw upon. That is, language permits a major enhancement in the *range* of things the thought processes can pertain to—the conceptual structures that can be accumulated in long-term memory—even if the construction of conceptual structure and the inferential processing operating on it may be exactly the same.

Without language, one may have abstract thoughts, but one has no way to communicate them (beyond a few stereotyped gestures such as head shaking for affirmation and the like). Without language, there is no way to communicate the time reference of events: for instance, does a pantomimed action describe a past action or a desired future action? Without language, one may have thoughts of being uncertain whether such and such is the case, but one cannot frame questions, which communicate one's desire to be relieved of that uncertainty. And so on.

As a result of our having language, vastly more of our knowledge is collective and cumulative than that of nonlinguistic organisms. To be sure, other higher mammals have societies and even perhaps protocultures (Wrangham et al. 1994). But the collectivity and cumulativity of human thought, via linguistic expression, almost certainly has to be a major factor in the vast expansion of knowledge and culture in human societies. Good ideas can be passed on much more efficiently.

8.7   Second Way Language Helps Us Think: Making Conceptual Structure Available for Attention

The enhancement of thought by virtue of linguistic communication might strike many readers as a sufficient connection between language and thought. But I want to dig a little deeper, and explore the relation between language, thought, and consciousness that emerged in the Intermediate Level Theory sketched in figure 8.3.

8.7.1   Introduction
Imagine what it would be like to be an organism just like a human except lacking language. According to figure 8.3, you could see and hear and feel

exactly the same sensations, perform the same actions, and in particular think exactly the same thoughts (have the same conceptual structures). There would be two differences. First, the one just discussed: you couldn't benefit from linguistic communication, nor could you make your knowledge available to others through the linguistic medium. So the range of things you could think about would be relatively impoverished.

But I want to concentrate on another difference, the phenomenological difference: you couldn't *experience* your thought as linguistic images. That is, a whole modality of experience would be simply absent—a modality that, as pointed out earlier, is very important to human experience.

What would the effect be? Let's return to the monkeys who practice redirected aggression. Recall what happens: monkey X attacks monkey Y, and then monkey Y attacks not monkey X, but monkey Z, who happens to be a member of X's kin-group. (It's not always that bad: sometimes Y will act nicely toward Z instead, as if to indirectly make up with X or appease X.) Recall that something like the following pieces of reasoning are logically necessary to account for this behavior:

(1) a. X attacked me.
     b. An attack on me makes me want to take retaliatory action
         (alternatively, to make up).
     c. The members of an attacker's kin-group are legitimate targets for
         retaliation (or making up).
     d. Z is a member of X's kin-group.
     e. Therefore, I will attack (or make up with) Z.

As we noticed earlier, factors (1b), (1c), and (1d) are abstract, that is, not connected directly to perception in any way—(1c) especially so. Now what seems so intuitively strange about this chain of reasoning is that we can't imagine a monkey saying things like (1a–e) to herself. And indeed she doesn't, because she doesn't have language. Yet thoughts very much like those expressed by (1a–e) *must* be chained together in the monkey's head in order to account for the behavior.

How do we escape this conundrum? Given the discussion up to this point, the answer is fairly clear: the monkey has the thoughts, but she doesn't hear the corresponding sentences in her head, because she has no linguistic medium in which to express them. Consequently, the monkey doesn't *experience* herself as reasoning through the chain in (1). All she experiences is the outcome of the reasoning, namely an urge to attack monkey Z, and perhaps an image of herself attacking monkey Z. The monkey's experience might be like our sudden urges, for no apparent reason, to go get a beer from the fridge. By contrast, humans do have the linguistic medium, and so, when they have thoughts like those expressed in (1), they may well experience the thoughts as a conscious plotting of revenge.[7]

The point is this: Only by having a linguistic modality is it possible to experience the steps of any sort of abstract thought. For example, one can't directly *see* that monkey Z is a member of X's kin-group—this is an abstract predicate-argument relationship, encoded in conceptual structure. But this relationship can be made explicit in consciousness by using the linguistic structure *Z is kin to X*. Similarly, the notion of retaliation—performing some action *for a particular reason*—is unavailable to non-linguistic consciousness. A reason *as a reason* cannot be represented in a visual image. But by using the word *because* to relate two propositions, the linguistic modality can make reasons as such available in consciousness. More generally, of all the representations available to consciousness, only phonetic form has constituent structure even remotely resembling the predicate-argument organization of conceptual structure. The correspondence between conceptual constituency and phonetic constituency is not perfect by any means (chapters 2 and 3), but it is a great deal more transparent than, say, that between conceptual constituency and visual images.[8]

Still, after reading the argument up to here, you may well say, "So what?" The fact that these thoughts appear in experience doesn't change them, and it doesn't change the steps of reasoning that can be performed on them. Language is just a vehicle for externalizing thoughts; it isn't the thoughts themselves. So having language doesn't enhance *thought*; it only enhances the *experience* of the thought. Maybe thinking is more fun if we can experience it, but this doesn't make the thought more powerful. And that is about where I left matters in *C&CM*.

8.7.2   The Relation between Consciousness and Attention

However, I now think this is not the end of the story. I want to suggest that, by virtue of being available to consciousness, language (in particular phonetic form) allows us to *pay attention* to thought, yielding significant benefits. To see this, let us set language aside for a moment and think about the relation between consciousness and attention.

It is often pointed out that consciousness and attention are intimately linked. An often-cited example involves driving along, conversing with a passenger. On the standard account, you are said to be unconscious of the road and the vehicles around you—you navigate "without awareness"—until your attention is drawn by some complicated situation, perhaps a lot of traffic weaving through the intersection up ahead, and you have to suspend conversation momentarily while attending to the traffic. From anecdotal experiences like this, it is often concluded that consciousness is a sort of executive (or traffic cop) that resolves complicated situations in the processing of information, and that we are only conscious of things that are hard to process. (I understand Minsky (1986) as taking essentially this position, for instance.)

Notice that such a view goes well with the idea that consciousness is a top-level mental faculty, deeply entwined with our higher intelligence, free will, and so forth. In working out the Intermediate-Level Theory of Consciousness (figure 8.3), I have challenged that overall prejudice, and so I am automatically suspicious of drawing such a connection between consciousness and attention.

Let us therefore look a little more closely at the situation of driving and conversing at the same time. Are you really *unconscious* of your driving? You may not remember what you did afterward, and you are certainly not paying serious attention to it, but at the same time you are not completely unaware of what you are doing, in the way, say, that you are unaware of your saccadic eye movements or of the flow of serotonin in your brain, or for that matter of what is going on in your environment when you are asleep. Rather, I think it is fair to say that when you are driving and conversing, you are at least vaguely aware of the flow of traffic. It's not as if you're blind. (Searle (1992), among others, suggests a similar reanalysis.)

Consider also another situation. Suppose you are just lying on a beach, idly listening to the waves, wiggling your toes in the sand, watching people go by. There is no sense of anything being hard to process, it's just utter relaxation. But surely you are conscious of all of it. Analyses that view consciousness as a high-level decision-making part of the mind tend not to take such cases into account.

We certainly need to make a distinction between fully attentive awareness and vague awareness. But *both* are states of consciousness—something is in the field of consciousness. The goings-on that you are only vaguely aware of may be less vivid or immediate, but they are still "there" for you. To account properly for such phenomenology, we must make our terminology a bit more precise than common language, because we often *do* say "I wasn't conscious of such and such" when we mean something like "Such and such didn't attract my attention."

My sense is that consciousness has nothing at all to do with processing difficulty or executive control of processing: that is the function of *attention*. Attention, not consciousness, is attracted to those parts of the perceptual field that potentially present processing difficulty: sudden movements, changes in sound, sudden body sensations, and so forth.

We are therefore led to ask another of those superficially obvious questions: What happens in the brain when one pays attention to something? Most research on attention seems to have focused on what it takes to *attract* attention, or on the maximal capacity of attention (see Allport 1989 for a survey). I am asking a different question: What good does attention do once it is focused on something?

A traditional approach to attention (e.g. Broadbent 1958) takes the position that the function of attention is to filter out incoming information that would "overwhelm" the processing capacity of the brain. On this view, the function of attention is to keep out everything not attended to. I would prefer a more positive characterization of the same intuition: the processing capacity of the brain for dealing with incoming signals is indeed limited, but resources can be distributed in different ways. If resources are distributed more or less evenly, the result is a more or less uniform degree of detail throughout the perceptual field. Alternatively, resources can be distributed unevenly, so as to enhance certain regions, but at the price of degrading others. I take attention to be this function of selective enhancement.

There seem to be at least three things that we can do with a percept when we pay attention to it, things that we cannot do with nonattended material. First, as just posited, focusing attention on something brings more processing resources to bear on it, so that it can be resolved faster and/or in greater detail. In turn, this extra detail is what makes the consciousness more vivid and immediate. Because the remaining phenomena are allotted fewer processing resources, they are not resolved in as much detail, and so they are vaguer in consciousness. On the other hand, if attention is not particularly focused, say when lying on the beach, the quality of consciousness is perhaps more uniform across the perceptual field.

A second thing that happens when we pay attention to an object is that we can "anchor" it: stabilize it in working memory while comparing it with other objects in the environment, shifting rapidly back and forth, or while retrieving material from memory to compare with it. We can also anchor the percept while "zooming in" on details and attending to *them*. Another aspect of anchoring is the ability to track moving objects against a background, if we pay attention to them—or, more difficult, to track one moving object amidst a swarm of similar objects (Culham and Cavanagh 1994).

A third thing that happens when we pay attention to something is that we can individuate it and remember it as an entity in its own right. If we take in a particular visual figure just as part of the texture of the wallpaper, for example, we will never remember it. But once we pay attention to it, we can go back and pick out *that very one*—or notice that it isn't there if it has been erased. Formally, the process of noticing an entity amounts to constructing a constituent in conceptual structure that encodes this entity. This constituent may or may not have further features; but it is enough to permit us to construct a corresponding linguistic referring expression, at the very least an indexical: *That!* (perhaps accompanied by a pointing gesture).

I have been saying sometimes that attention is drawn by an object in the world, sometimes that it is drawn by a percept in the head. Which is right? If we want to be precise, we have to say "a percept." Attention is a process going on in the brain—so it cannot be directed by things moving out there in the external world. Attention is not a little person in the brain watching the world and pointing a spotlight at interesting things out there so they can be seen better. Rather, attention has to be directed by the character of brain phenomena that have occurred in response to things in the external world that may be of potential interest to the organism—a crucial difference. It all has to happen inside the brain.

This now raises an interesting question, which I think has not been asked in exactly this way before: Of all the brain phenomena that may take place in response to, say, a sudden motion or noise in the world, which ones are capable of being focused on by attentional processes? If we consider the phenomenology of attention, an answer suggests itself: *We can pay attention only to something of which we are conscious.* We may not *understand* what we are paying attention to (in fact that may be the reason we are paying attention to it)—but we must certainly be *aware* of it. In other words, the representations that fall into the intermediate ring of figure 8.3 play some necessary role in the functioning of attention; perhaps we can think of these representations as being potential "handles" by which attention "grasps" and "holds onto" percepts.

This puts a new twist on the more or less standard story that consciousness drives attention. Instead of thinking of consciousness as the smart (or even miraculous) part of the mind that determines which percepts need attention, I am claiming that consciousness happens to provide the basis for *attention* to pick out what might be interesting and thereby put high-power processing to work on it. In turn, the high-power processing resulting from attention is what does the intelligent work; and at the same time, as a by-product, it enhances the resolution and vividness of the attended part of the conscious field.[9]

8.7.3 Language Provides a Way to Pay Attention to Thought

Returning to language, we will now be able to see the reason for this detour on consciousness and attention.

Remember two points: first, language provides a modality of consciousness that other animals lack; second, language is the only modality that can present to consciousness abstract parts of thought like predicate-argument structure, kinship relations, reasons, hypothetical situations, and the notion of inference. Thus only through language can such concepts form part of *experience* rather than just being the source of intuitive urges.

At the point where we left off in section 8.7.1, we could see that although it might be more fun to experience one's reasoning through language, such experience would not yet help reasoning in any way. Attention, though, adds a new factor: having linguistic expressions in consciousness allows us to pay attention to them. And now the extra processing power of attention can be brought into play.

Consider yet again the monkey who is calculating some redirected aggression. Let's make it instead a person, say Bill, who has a language faculty and with it linguistic awareness. Instead of Bill just experiencing an urge to attack whoever it is, say Joe, Bill's concepts may drive his language faculty to produce some utterance (he may actually say it, or he may just hear it in his head).

(2) I'm gonna KILL that guy!

First of all, notice that the language faculty forces Bill to package his thought in some particular way, in accordance with lexical items and meaningful constructions that happen to exist in English. The existence of prepackaged lexical items that are selected to express the thought can themselves refine thought: Bill's generalized sense of aggression gets molded into a threat to murder Joe, as opposed to, say, just insult him.

Now, if Bill doesn't pay attention to his utterance, it's just mumbling and has no further effect—it's just a simple statement of generalized aggression, a bit of texture in the auditory wallpaper. But suppose Bill does listen to himself—suppose he pays attention to his utterance. Then the sentence gets anchored, more computing power is devoted to it, and details can develop.

(3) KILL? Or just mangle, or just insult?
    That guy? Or someone else, or his whole family?
    Gonna? When? Tomorrow? Next week?
    Why? What do I hope to accomplish? Is there a better way?
    How? Should I shoot him? Stab him? Poison him? Club him?
    What then? What will happen if I kill him?

Attention to some of these details may lead to elaboration of further details.

(4) Club him? With what? A baseball bat? A fence post? . . .

And any promising options may be remembered. Notice again that this detail is all a concequence of attention being paid to the *phonetic form.* Without the phonetic form as a conscious manifestation of the thought, attention could not be applied, since attention requires some conscious manifestation as a "handle."

We should also notice hidden in these ruminations of Bill's the expression of some concepts that would not be available without language, for example the notion "next week." What does it take to think about weeks? A nonlinguistic organism can obviously detect patterns of light and darkness and respond to diurnal patterns. But it takes the lexical item *day* to abstract this pattern out as a sort of object, so that attention can be drawn to it as a constancy. The phonetic form of the lexical item is a perceptual object that anchors attention on the pattern and allows it to be stored as a repeatable and retrievable unit in memory.

What about a *week*—a unit of seven days? This is a completely nonperceptual unit. I don't think it could be conceived of at all without linguistic anchoring. Even if such a unit were potentially available as a concept, it couldn't be accessed without having language to hold it in attention, which enables us to stow such a unit away for future use. I think it fair to say that although nonlinguistic organisms may be able to develop a concept of a day, they will never attain the concept of a week.

Finally, the phonetic form *next week* provides a conscious handle on an actual point in time. This handle provides a constituent in conceptual structure for a token point in time that can later be reidentified. This suggests that it is the existence of time expressions in language that enables us to identify points in the past and future and keep track of them.

To sum up this section: Language is the only modality of consciousness in which the abstract and relational constituents of thought correspond even remotely to separable units. By being conscious, these phonetic constituents become available for attention. Attention in turn refines the associated conceptual structures, both by anchoring and drawing out details and by concretizing or reifying conceptual units that have no stable perceptual base.

8.8 Third Way Language Helps Us Think: Valuation of Conscious Percepts

The third way language helps us think is related to the second. To understand it, we have to step back yet again and examine another property of consciously available percepts.

What is the difference between the appearance of something that looks familiar and that of something that doesn't look familiar? In general, nothing: as you get used to the appearance of some novel picture, let's say, the appearance doesn't change—it just somehow feels different than when it was novel. The same is true for the sound of a new tune as you gradually get to know it. Or, for the classic case, suppose you're a subject in a psychological experiment and you're asked which nonsense syllables are the same as ones you were given yesterday. What is the difference between the familiar ones and the novel ones? They all sound more or less like nonsense, except that some come with this feeling of familiarity and some don't.

I will call this feeling of familiarity or novelty attached to a percept a *valuation* of the percept. We can even have this sense of familiarity without clearly knowing what we are seeing—"I'm sure I know you from somewhere, but I'm damned if I can remember who you are or when we met." When we have a déjà vu experience, we somehow get a feeling of familiarity attached to an object or situation that we rationally know we have never experienced before; that is, déjà vu is an error or illusion of valuation.

The familiar/novel distinction is not the only valuation that the brain applies to percepts. Another one is the distinction between percepts that are taken to be imaginary and those that are taken to be real. ("Is this a dagger which I see before me?") This valuation is a bit trickier to isolate, because things we judge to be real tend to be vivid and substantial in consciousness, whereas things we judge to be imaginary tend to be fuzzy and fleeting. But in certain limiting cases, it is possible to see that the valuation can make an independent difference. Suppose you are trying to make your way through a thick fog, and you are just not sure what you're seeing. You detect a blurry motion: is it something really out there, or do you just think it is? Was that noise you heard real, or just your imagination? When for some reason perception is impeded, the very same percept may come to be judged either real or imaginary, and there is nothing clear about its appearance that helps us make the decision.

Another sort of limiting case is dreams, where things may seem quite real that upon awakening are judged imaginary. "Don't be frightened: it was only a dream!" we say. Like déjà vu, this is an error or illusion of valuation.

A related valuation concerns whether a percept is externally or internally initiated. Consider a visual image you may get as a result of my telling you "Imagine a pink elephant," and compare it with a similar image you might get as a result of drinking too much, where it "just pops into your head." The former image, you feel, is under your control; the latter is not. Yet both are in fact generated by your own brain activity, and you can't catch yourself in the act of making either image happen. There's just a mysterious, miraculous "act of will"—or its absence.

Or think of the sense of blinking your eyes voluntarily as opposed to doing it automatically. The movements themselves are essentially the same, and both ultimately require similar nerve activation of the muscles. But they feel different, namely in or out of your control.

Of course, the hallucinations of schizophrenics are errors in both of these latter valuations: they hear voices that they take to be real and externally generated ("God is really speaking to me," they say), whereas the voices are in fact imaginary and internally generated.

The general idea, then, is that our cognitive repertoire contains a family of valuations, each of which is a binary opposition that can determine part of the "feel" of conscious percepts. These three and a number of others are discussed in *C&CM* chapter 15 (where they were called "affects," a term I was never quite comfortable with). Valuations of percepts have not to my knowledge been singled out for attention elsewhere in the literature.[10] What is curious about them is that they are not part of the *form* of consciousness; as stressed above, they are more like a feeling associated with the form.

But if we have language, we *can* give these feelings some form: we have words like *familiar, novel, real, imaginary, self-controlled, hallucination* that express valuations and therefore give us a conscious link to them. This conscious link permits us to attend to valuations and subject *them* to scrutiny: Is this percept really familiar, or is it a case of déjà vu? Is it real, or is it a dream? And so forth. A dog awakening from a dream may be disturbed about what happened to the rabbit it was chasing; but it cannot formulate the explanation "It was a dream." Rather, something else attracts its attention, and life goes on. But with language, we can fix on this valuation as an independent object in its own right and thereby explain the experience—as well as recognize a category of experiences called "dreams."

The plot thickens. Because phonetic forms are percepts too, they can themselves be subject to valuation. For instance, what is going on when we judge that some sentence is *true*? There is nothing about the literal sound of a true sentence that is different from the literal sound of a false sentence, yet we say "It sounds true to me." That is, the sense that a sentence is true or false is also—from a psychological point of view—a kind of valuation. It is altogether parallel to a judgment that a visual percept is something really out there. Similarly, the concept that we express by *suppose that* or *if* is a valuation that suspends judgment, parallel to evaluating some visual image as imaginary and internally produced.

Now let us combine this with the previous point. Like other valuations, the valuations of language can be expressed in language, with words like *true, not, if,* and so forth. Therefore, by virtue of their phonetic form, these valuations can be attended to as independent objects in their own right and focused on, and so we get full-blown recursion: a thought about the valuation of another thought, the larger thought having its own valuation. We can express thoughts like "Suppose I am incorrect about such and such ... then such and such other belief of mine is also false." That is, it is precisely because thoughts map into phonetic forms that it is possible to reason about reasoning. There is no other modality in which valuations can be given palpable form so they can be attended to and thought about.

And certainly a crucial source of the power of our reasoning is its ability to examine itself.

I do not see any evidence that nonlinguistic organisms can engage in such metareasoning. Apes and dolphins can be very clever in solving certain kinds of problems, and they can be uncertain about how to solve a problem, but I do not think they can *wonder why they are uncertain*. They may be able to believe something,[11] but they cannot wonder why they believe it and thereby be motivated to search for evidence. It takes language to do that.[12]

8.9 Summing Up

The first half of this chapter established that language is not itself the form of thought and that thought is totally unconscious. However, thought is given a conscious manifestation through the phonetic forms that it corresponds to. The second half of the chapter suggested three ways in which having language enhances the power of thought:

1. Because language allows thought to be communicated, it permits the accumulation of collective knowledge. Good ideas don't get lost. This conclusion is certainly nothing new.
2. Language is the only modality of consciousness that makes perceptible the relational (or predicational) form of thought and the abstract elements of thought. Because these elements are present as isolable entities in consciousness, they can serve as the focus of attention, which permits higher-power processing, anchoring, and, perhaps most important, retrievable storage of these otherwise nonperceptible elements.
3. Language is the only modality of consciousness that brings valuations of percepts to awareness as independent elements, permitting them to be focused on and questioned. Moreover, since phonetic forms and their valuations are also percepts, having language makes it possible to construct thoughts about thought, otherwise unframable.

Although these conclusions may seem in the end intuitively obvious, I've tried to find my way more carefully to them, in the course of which I've challenged some fairly standard preconceptions about the nature of consciousness. The interest of the argument lies, I think, in the intricacies of the connections among language, thought, consciousness, and attention. In turn, untangling these intricacies depends heavily on the mental architecture posited by Representational Modularity.

8.10   The Illusion That Language *Is* Thought

One nice thing that emerges from the present analysis is an explanation
for the commonsense identification of thought with language. As pointed
out in section 8.5, all we can know directly of our own minds are those
brain phenomena that are conscious; in the terms of section 8.7, these are
the only ones we can pay attention to. Hence these are the phenomena to
which we ascribe responsibility for our behavior. Since the phonetic forms
accompanying thought are conscious and the thoughts themselves are
not, it is altogether natural to think that the phonetic form *is* the thought.
Consequently language is quite naturally taken to be the substrate for the
act of reasoning. This illusion that language is thought has been the
source of endless philosophical dispute (Dascal 1995). We now can see
why the illusion is so intuitively persuasive.

Recognizing this illusion allows us to examine the dark side of our initial question: why language can be a *less* effective tool for reasoning than
we are often prone to assume. There are at least five sorts of gaps where
language does not adequately express the structure of thought. In each
case, illusions develop in reasoning because language is all we have to pay
attention to.

1. The smallest unit of thought that can be expressed as an independent
percept is a word. Because a word is a constant percept in our experience,
we treat the thought it expresses as a constant thought—even though in
fact we bend and stretch the concepts expressed by words every which
way, especially in the process of combining them into sentences by coercion and cocomposition (chapter 3). Just within the ambit of this chapter,
consider how the word *unconscious* in common usage means anything
from being out cold to being vaguely aware (but not noticing)—not to
mention the technical use of the term I've applied here to particular brain
processes. It takes careful analysis to notice the disparity among these
usages, and when we're done we don't know whether the word expresses
one bendable concept or a family of more rigid, related ones. Intuition is
not much of a guide.

This issue arises not only with fancy words like *unconscious*, but even
with simple, obvious words. For instance, considerable current research is
devoted to studying the semantics of prepositions. It proves to be a difficult problem to decide whether the preposition *in* expresses the same
concept in *the coffee in the cup* and *the crack in the cup* (I think so), and
whether the preposition *into* expresses the same concept in *jump into the*

pool and *crash into the wall* (I think not). Whatever the correct answer turns out to be, the nature of the problem is clear: in both cases, the use of the identical word invites us to presume we are dealing with the identical concept. Yet closer examination brings to light the unreliablity of such presumptions. (See Herskovits 1986, Vandeloise 1991, and Jackendoff 1996b for examples.)

2. The opposite side of this problem is the delegitimation of concepts for which no sufficiently precise word exists. A prime example arises with the concepts of reasoning and belief (see notes 7 and 11). If one insists that a belief is propositional, that reasoning involves relations among propositions, and that propositions are linguistic (thereby at least partly succumbing to the illusion that language is thought), then there is no term available in the language for how animals' minds organize their perception and memory and create novel behavior on the basis of this organization. One is not *allowed* to say they have beliefs and reasoning. The forced move is to attribute to them abilities for which there *are* words, for example "instinct" or "associative learning," often prefixed by "mere." The effect is to inhibit examination of what mental ability animals actually have, because there happens to be a gap in our vocabulary just where the interesting possibilities lie.

3. Not only do we fail to recognize gaps, we tend to treat all existing words as though they have references in the real world, along the lines of concrete words like *dog* and *chair*. This tendency means we're always reifying abstract terms like Truth and Language, and constructing theories of their Platonic existence—or having to spend a lot of effort arguing, through careful linguistic analysis, against their reification.

4. As pointed out by Lewis Carroll (1895) as well as by Wittgenstein (1953), we don't really know how we ultimately get from one step in reasoning to the next. How do we know that if A implies B and B implies C, then A implies C? And how do we know that any particular chain of reasoning is an example of this rule? At bottom, we always have to fall back on a certain feeling of conviction, which can't be justified through any more general laws. That is, sooner or later we hit a stage of pure valuation with no language to make it conscious. Yet we think we are reasoning completely "rationally" (i.e. explicitly). Worse, we often get this feeling of conviction when it's utterly unwarranted; we are prone to delude ourselves and yet feel perfectly justified. Just as in any other application of attention, the default situation is that we don't pay attention to our valuations unless we have to, unless we find ourselves in trouble.

5. As a refinement of the previous point, our sense of conviction is too often driven by our desires, by what we *want* to be true. We are less likely to question our convictions if they lead to desired conclusions. At the same time, such gaps in reasoning all seem perfectly rational, because they are supported—to a great enough extent—by language.

None of these gaps would be possible if language really were the form of thought. If it were, all reasoning would be completely up front, and there would be no room for weaseling around. Behind much of the development of formal logic lies the desire to provide a more satisfactory form of language, in which all terms are precise and context-free, and in which the steps of reasoning are entirely explicit—that is, in which the idealizations in points 1–5 are not illusory but true.

By contrast, in the present perspective, in which language is only an imperfect expression of thought and furthermore is the only form in which many important elements of thought are available for conscious attention, these illusions are just what we would expect. And they are in large part irremediable precisely because of the architecture of the system—because of the way the interaction of language, thought, consciousness, and attention happened to evolve in our species. At the same time, as flawed as the system is from such an ideal point of view, it's all we've got, and we might as well enjoy it. There is no question that it has given our species a tremendous boost in its ability to dominate the rest of the environment, for better or for worse.

Appendix

The *Wheel of Fortune* Corpus
Collected by Beth Jackendoff

Note: The classifications given here are only heuristic and are not intended to be of any particular theoretical significance.

Compounds

A-N Compounds
acoustic guitar
Arabian horse
Australian accent
black and white film
black eye
black hole
blue cheese
British accent
catalytic converters
cellular phones
circular staircase
Cornish game hen
early American furniture
electrical outlet
elementary school
favorite son
grizzly bear
Mexican peso
miniature golf
mobile army surgical hospital
modern art
natural childbirth
overdue library book
permanent wave
polar ice cap
private eye

public education
Scholastic Aptitude Test
substitute teacher
subterranean parking
white flag

N-N Compounds
Academy Award winners
airline pilot
apple dumpling
April shower
ballpoint pen
beef stew
bench press
birdhouse
boot camp
Broadway play
campfire ghost stories
cellophane wrapper
chain gang
charm bracelet
chicken noodle soup
coffee break
cold wave
college entrance examination
computer screen
costume designer
cover girl
death penalty

Dixieland jazz
Dolby noise reduction
dream sequence
exclamation point
executive secretary
field goal
goal post
high school sweetheart
high school graduation
hot water heater
jazz band
Jerry Lewis telethon
joke book
junk food
light bulb
magazine section
maximum security prison
meter maid
milk chocolate
mountain spring water
music video
New York ticker tape parade
ocean liner
ocean view
oil painting
opera singer
oxygen tent
pancakes
peanut butter
pearl necklace
piano bench
piggyback ride
pillbox hat
pocket calculator
puppet show
push-button telephone
rearview mirror
retirement home
rhubarb pie
roast beef sandwich
robber baron
roulette wheel
ruby slippers
salt substitute
sewage drain

shower cap
skin cancer
soccer ball
soda pop
strawberry margarita
teddy bear
travel agent
tulip bulb
TV dinner
Volkswagen bug
wedding anniversary
wedding vows
weenie roast
wheelbarrow race
wind chimes
wine cellar
youth hostel

Participial Compounds (V-ing-N, N-ed-N, N-V-er)
baked beans
best-selling novel
blackjack dealer
chafing dish
chicken-fried steak
coloring book
galvanized steel
Gatorade thirst quencher
haunted house
heat-seeking missile
heavy-handed
help wanted ad
high school marching band
homogenized milk
money-saving coupon
one-armed bandit
piano player
pie-eating contest
poached egg
popcorn popper
reclining chair
road runner
scheduled departure time
stock car racing
sweepstakes winner

swimming pool
telephone answering machine
tongue twister

N's-N Compounds
cashier's check
catcher's mitt
lover's leap
pig's knuckles

Verbal Compounds
backorder
jump-start
lip-sync

Num-N-N Compounds
five-story building
twelve-round heavyweight bout
two-dollar bill

[A-N]-N Compounds
frequent-flyer program
front-row seats
high-rise building
long-haired cat
modern-day hero
Olympic-size swimming pool
open-heart surgery
round-trip airfare
third-string quarterback
white-water rapids

Odds-and-Ends Compounds
aloha shirt
bed-and-breakfast
blackmail scheme
copycat
country and western band
crew cut
deep-sea diving
honor bound
lost-and-found column
morning wake-up call
nine-to-five work day
pop quiz
starter kit

Idioms

Nonsyntactic Idioms
believe it or not
down and dirty
for example
in the know
johnny-on-the-spot
once upon a time
running rampant
sitting pretty
that'll be the day
they've had their ups and their downs
wait-and-see attitude
yummy yummy yummy

Resultative Idioms
butter him up
cut my visit short
I cried my eyes out
knock yourself out
you scared the daylights out of me

Other VP Idioms
bridge the gap
corner the market
don't lose your balance
eat humble pie
flying high
give it your best shot
go for it
going from bad to worse
hit the road
I blew it
I'm at the end of my rope
I'm at your mercy
it's as clear as day
it took my breath away
I've had it up to here
keep your shirt on
knocking on heaven's door
never throw in the towel
not playing with a full deck
sleeping in the buff
stand pat
you're whistling in the dark

NP Idioms
a breath of fresh air
bridge over troubled water
food for thought
forty winks
pie in the sky
point of view
red-blooded Americans
rite of passage
son of a gun
stick-in-the-mud
table of contents
the last straw
the life of the party

PP Idioms
all in a day's work
down in the dumps
in touch with one's feelings
off the top of my head
right on the money

S Idioms
hold everything
that's a laugh
that takes the cake
trick or treat

Other
clean as a whistle
fit as a fiddle
flip-flopping
no end in sight
would you like to take it for a spin

Names

Addis Ababa, Ethiopia
Alabama
Al Capone
Alec Guinness
Ali Baba
Athens, Greece
Barney Rubble
Beverly Hills
Bill Murray

Boise, Idaho
Boston, Massachusetts
Chicago, Illinois
Clint Eastwood
Count Dracula
Crocodile Dundee
David Lee Roth
Debby Thomas
Dick Van Patten
Dinah Shore
Donald Trump
George Lucas
George Orwell
Jesse Jackson
John F. Kennedy
Kenny G
Kurt Thomas
Leonard Nimoy
Maid Marian
Michael Dukakis
Mohammed Ali
Monte Carlo, Monaco
Narcissus
New Hampshire
Oklahoma
Palm Springs, California
Pat Sajak
Paul Bunyan
Peggy Lee
Rip Van Winkle
Robin Hood
Robin Williams
Santa Claus
Santiago, Chile
Sarajevo
Spike Lee
Sylvester Stallone
The Queen Mary
Vanna White
Walla Walla, Washington
Wally and Beaver Cleaver
Walt Disney
William Tell
Woodrow Wilson
Yugoslavia

Meaningful Names

American Heart Association
Battle of Britain
Boston Pops Orchestra
Brooklyn Bridge
Central Park
Cherokee Indians
Coney Island
Democratic Convention
Federal Express
Flying Walendas
Georgetown University
Golden Gate Bridge
Granny Goose potato chips
Great Depression
Honest Abe
Hostess Twinkies
Industrial Revolution
International Red Cross
Ivory Coast
Ivy League
Jack Daniels whiskey
John Deere tractor
Marlboro man
Marx Brothers
Miami Dolphins
Mickey Mouse Club
Milky Way galaxy
National Organization for Women
New York Yankees
Palm Springs, California
Philippine Islands
Pittsburgh Pirates
Playboy bunny
Pop Warner Football League
Pythagorean theorem
Queen of Spades
Rocky Mountain National Park
San Francisco Bay area
Sergeant Joe Friday
Sierra Nevada mountains
Singer sewing machine
Southern Hemisphere
Star of David
Stetson cowboy hat

Strategic Defense Initiative
The Big Apple
The Blues Brothers
The Grateful Dead
The Iron Man Triathlon
The Roaring Twenties
The Spirit of Saint Louis
The Third Reich
theory of relativity
United States Capitol
United States Olympic Team
United States Senate
Waldorf salad
walkie talkie
Winchester rifle
World Hockey Association
Wrigley Field

Clichés

a day that will live in infamy
a toast to your health
all hands on deck
any friend of yours is a friend of mine
baby-blue eyes
bring home the gold
business suit and power tie
by a strange twist of fate
changing of the guards
conquer the world
cowboys and Indians
don't be so persnickety
don't cry over spilt milk
drama on the high seas
everything he touches turns to gold
fair weather
faster than a speeding bullet
follow these easy guidelines
gimme a break
good things come in small packages
haven't I seen you someplace before
he couldn't punch his way out of a
    paper bag
herbs and spices
high as a kite
home sweet home

hot and humid weather
if the shoe fits wear it
I'll show you the door
in the middle of the night
I wouldn't be surprised
just another face in the crowd
just around the corner
just between you and me
just when you thought it was safe
leave a message at the tone
let's get out of here
life begins at forty
like taking candy from a baby
living breathing organism
look on the bright side
looks like something the cat dragged in
love conquers all
mad scientist's laboratory
Monday through Friday
muscularly built
name, rank, and serial number
no money down
open twenty-four hours
our military heroes
pay to the order of
people are flocking to see it
pick on someone your own size
poke in the ribs
poke your head out the window
prime rib and baked potato
quiet as a mouse
reckless driving
rosy cheeks
satisfaction guaranteed
see you later
shape up or ship out
so near yet so far
standing room only
standing the test of time
steak and eggs
taped in front of a live audience
that's the way the cookie crumbles
the best that money can buy
the catch of the day
the face of an angel
there's a lot more where that came from

the right to bear arms
they're popping up everywhere
time marches on
time to go on a diet
time will tell
too close for comfort
too much time on my hands
use only as directed
wait and see
we're doing everything humanly
    possible
we've got to stick together
what's the big deal
will you please excuse me
yes or no
you can't judge a book by its cover

Titles

All You Need Is Love
April in Paris
City Lights
Consumer Reports
Friday the Thirteenth
Good Morning America
Hill Street Blues
Lady and the Tramp
Little House on the Prairie
Little Orphan Annie
Mary Tyler Moore Show
Material Girl
National Enquirer
Pirates of Penzance
Pumping Iron
Rock-a-Bye Baby
Rocky Mountain High
Spin the Bottle
Swing Low Sweet Chariot
The Adventures of Robin Hood
The Bionic Woman
The Goose That Laid the Golden Egg
The Little Drummer Boy
The Little Rascals
The Long and Winding Road
The People's Court
The Price Is Right

The Tortoise and the Hare
Vanity Fair
Watership Down
When Irish Eyes Are Smiling
White Christmas
You're a Good Man, Charlie Brown

Quotations

and the rockets' red glare
beam me up, Scotty
do you believe in miracles
it's Miller time
long long ago in a galaxy far far away
may the Force be with you
now I lay me down to sleep
smile, you're on Candid Camera
someone's in the kitchen with Dinah
there's no place like home
to fetch a pail of water
whistle while you work
you ain't seen nothin' yet

Pairs

flint and steel
Mork and Mindy
Popeye and Olive Oyl
Simon and Garfunkel
Sonny and Cher
Starsky and Hutch

Foreign Phrases

amour
au contraire
c'est la vie
creme de menthe
mademoiselle
persona non grata
tam-o'-shanter
terra firma

Notes

Chapter 1

1. An important boundary condition on the simplicity of the learning theory, one that is often neglected in the syntactic acquisition literature, is that we learn tens of thousands of words, very few of which submit to any sort of simple definition (Fodor et al. 1980). Word learning presents formidable theoretical problems in its own right (Macnamara 1982; Landau and Gleitman 1985; Pinker 1989; Bloom 1994; and many others); it appears that it requires a substantial built-in specialized learning procedure, including a rich conceptual system and considerable ability to infer the intentions of other speakers, as well as some prespecification of the constraints of grammar. So one might ask whether there is any point in simplifying the procedure for grammar acquisition any further than is independently necessary for word acquisition. I leave the issue wide open.

2. I thus regard the formal/computational approach as a perspective for understanding, rather than as some ultimate truth. Regarding it this way undercuts the criticisms of Searle and Edelman. Were one to take their arguments one step further, one might legitimately claim that indeed there aren't neurons in the head any more than there are computations: actually, there are only quarks and leptons, and consequently brain function must be explained only in terms of elementary particles. Dennett (1995) has called this absurd sort of argument "greedy reductionism": it demands too much of theoretical reduction and thereby prevents anyone from understanding larger scales of organization. I submit that neuroscience, like the computational theory of mind, is just another perspective, and that it is at least premature, if not altogether illegitimate, to expect the latter to be replaced entirely by the former.

3. A perhaps wild speculation: Chomsky's commitment to syntactocentrism may go still deeper, to his identification of the goals of generative grammar with those of "Cartesian linguistics" (Chomsky 1966). According to the Cartesians (on Chomsky's reading), humans are distinguished from animals by virtue of possessing a "creative principle" that enables them to produce behavior of infinite diversity; and this "creative principle" is most directly evinced by the discrete infinity of linguistic behavior. At the same time, the choice among this discrete infinity of behaviors is given over to the capacity of "free will," the character of which

Chomsky relegates to the category of humanly insoluble mysteries (while occasionally alluding to it as the basis of much of his political stance). For Descartes, I think, free will was taken to be a unitary capacity; hence it is eminently logical that the discrete infinity over which it chooses is localized at one point in the mind. Hence, by association, the creative aspect of language should be localized in a single source. I do not think Chomsky or anyone else has ever made this argument explicitly, but I think one may detect some version of it lurking in the background, tacitly linking a number of the important themes of Chomsky's thought.

In any event, if there was ever any credence to the argument from free will, it is dispelled by current views in cognitive science. There is no single source of control to be found in the brain, no "central executive"; rather, control is distributed widely, and action arises from the interaction of many semiautonomous centers. The notion that there is a unified source of free will is a cognitive illusion, what Dennett (1991) calls the "narrative center of gravity." This does not *solve* the mystery of free will, but it certainly encourages us to take quite a different starting point in the search space of possible explanations. And it undercuts any heuristic connection between free will and a single source of discrete infinity in language.

4. Unlike children, apes also require intensive training in order to learn signs, and they never acquire a vocabulary of more than a few hundred. Is what apes learn different from what children learn, or is it just that their method of learning is not as powerful? An interesting question, but not crucial for my present point.

5. See Wilkins and Wakefield 1995 for some discussion of the possible precursors of *this* stage.

6. If you find Pinker and Bloom's (1990) arguments for the selective advantage of syntax unpersuasive, compare language with music. Try to find an argument for the selective advantage of the grammatical organization of music (Lerdahl and Jackendoff 1983) that doesn't make Pinker and Bloom's arguments look brilliant by comparison. Personally, I find the reasons for evolution of a musical capacity a good deal more mysterious than those for language; if anything is a "spandrel" (to use the famous term of Gould and Lewontin 1979), it is music.

Chapter 2

1. Although I use the term *representation* out of respect for custom, I recognize that it may be misleading. Bluntly, I do not take it that mental representations "represent" anything, especially anything out in the world. That is, I reject the notion that intentionality in Searle's (1983) or Fodor's (1975, 1987) sense plays any role in mental representation. For me, what is crucial about a mental representation is only how it differs from other mental representations. That is, the notion makes sense only in the context of a structured space of distinctions, or "format of representation," available to the brain. Phonetic representation is one such space, encoding the possibilities for phonetic expression; motor representation is another. A phonetic representation has "meaning" only insofar as (1) it contrasts with other possible phonetic representations, (2) it can serve as input to phonetic-internal processes such as the computation of rhyme, (3) it can serve as

input to interface processes such as the production of speech instructions to the vocal tract. A similar conception applies to all other representations discussed in the present study—crucially, including conceptual representations. See Jackendoff 1992b, chapters 1, 2, and 8 for more extensive discussion.

2. The constraints of Optimality Theory, for instance, are ranked instances of "preferably does"-type rules.

Calling these principles "correspondence *rules*" may be misleading to those who think of a rule in terms of computing an output from an input. The permissive and default modalities of some of these rules may be especially jarring. Readers who prefer the term *correspondence constraints* should feel free to make the substitution.

3. Given that the distinctive feature set for signed languages is different from that for spoken languages, it is actually unclear whether a unified interface level for both spoken and signed languages is empirically possible—though if there are distinct interface levels, they are undoubtedly closely related. As long as we stay within a single modality of language, though, a single interface level for both articulation and perception seems plausible.

4. Even here, some qualification might be in order. It might be, for example, that the dropping of certain phonetic distinctions in rapid speech is best regarded as a matter not of PF but only of its motor realization—in which case *full interpretation* is a misnomer.

5. This is not quite accurate: intonational phrasing plays some role in such syntactic phenomena as Heavy NP Shift and Right Node Raising. Steedman (1990, 1991) develops an integrated theory of syntactic and intonational constituency, which works out some of these relationships. Concerned most heavily with the interpretation of topic and focus, Steedman concludes (if I may grossly oversimplify a complex exposition) that the surface structure of a sentence is essentially the set of its possible intonational phrasings. For reasons unclear to me, he finds this view simpler than one in which there is a single syntactic structure that is partially independent of intonational phrasing. One might wonder, though, whether Steedman's conclusion is a symptom of trying to conflate two partially related structures into one.

On the other hand, I agree with Steedman that topic and focus marking depend more directly on prosodic than syntactic constituency, and that this realization permits a simplification of some of the ugly conditions of focus assignment in Jackendoff 1972. And, along with most everyone else, I owe him a counterexplanation of intonation-dependent syntactic phenomena.

6. Kayne (1994) can be seen in the present perspective as proposing an alternative to (12b).

(12b′) If syntactic constituent X_1 corresponds to phonological constituent Y_1, and syntactic constituent Y_2 corresponds to phonological constituent Y_2, then

If and only if X_1 asymmetrically c-commands X_2, Y_1 precedes Y_2.

In Kayne's theory, all syntactic properties follow from asymmetrical c-command, and linear order plays no syntactic role; we can therefore eliminate linear order from syntactic theory and regard it as a purely phonological relation. I will not comment here on the virtues or vices of Kayne's proposal; rather, I will simply continue to assume the traditional view that dominance and linear order are independent variables in syntactic structure.

7. Of course, a theory of conceptual structures has to *notate* units in a particular linear order, but this is just an artifact of putting structures on paper. By contrast, the linear order of phonological and syntactic units *does* model a psychologically real distinction (with caveats concerning syntax if one adopts a suggestion like that in note 6).

8. There may be a further type of representation on the way from syntax to conceptual structure, such as the language-specific "semantic structures" proposed independently by Pinker (1989) and Bierwisch and Lang (1989). For reasons discussed in Jackendoff 1983, chapter 6, I personally doubt such an extra level of representation is necessary; but if it is, then we need two sets of correspondence rules to get from syntax to conceptual structure. An extra layer of correspondence rules doesn't change anything essential in the picture I am painting here. If anything, it only makes things worse for a strictly derivational theory.

   The basic observation used by Pinker and by Bierwisch and Lang to motivate this extra level is that not all aspects of meaning are germane to syntactic distinctions. For instance, no grammatical distinction depends on color; although many languages make a syntactic singular-plural distinction, no language makes a grammatical distinction between six and seven objects. They propose therefore that the "semantic level" include only those aspects of meaning that are relevant to syntax. My position is that this constraint is a consequence of the SS-CS correspondence rules: only certain aspects of conceptual structure are "visible" to the correspondence rules. Bouchard (1995) advocates a similar position, using the term *G(rammar)-Semantics* for the subset of conceptual structure accessible to the SS-CS correspondence rules.

9. The same is true for Lakoff's (1987) cases of Japanese and Dyirbal noun classes (the latter including his famous class of "women, fire, and dangerous things"). There are fortuitous semantic links among the members of these classes, but there is nothing semantically inevitable that makes them go together. One can change the semantic criteria for the classification of nouns without changing the syntactic classifier system.

10. Tenny (1987, 1992), however, makes a valiant and widely cited attempt to connect telicity with direct object position. Sections 3.2.1 and 3.8.2 discuss aspects of telicity further; in particular, note 15 to chapter 3 mentions some of the problems with Tenny's proposal. Her claim has been somewhat weakened in Tenny 1994.

11. The level of "argument structure" in Grimshaw 1990 and other works then emerges as an "interlevel" that helps compute the relation between syntactic structure and conceptual structure. If such a level is necessary, it appears to me

that it deals exclusively with the central grammatical relations subject, object, and indirect or second object. It does not seem to play a role in the linking of adjuncts and oblique arguments.

It is interesting in this light that whole theories of syntax have been developed whose main contribution is in the treatment of subjects, objects, and indirect objects, for example Relational Grammar and LFG. In particular, although the f-structure level of LFG includes all the constituents in a sentence, the main argumentation for f-structure and the main work it does in describing grammatical structure concerns the central grammatical relations exclusively. One might wonder, therefore, whether the function of f-structure might not be limited to regulating the relation between semantic arguments and the central grammatical relations. See Nikanne 1996 for discussion.

12. One can also see such a conception inside of the phonological component, where autosegmental theory views phonological structure as composed of multiple quasi-independent "tiers," each with its own autonomous structure, but each linked to the others by "association lines" established by correspondence rules. In other words, phonology is itself a microcosm of the larger organization seen here.

13. I say "relatively novel" because Multidimensional Categorial Grammar (e.g. Bach 1983; Oehrle 1988) recognizes the tripartite nature of derivations (though see note 20). HPSG likewise segments its structures into phonological, syntactic, and semantic attribute structures. Connoisseurs may notice as well a resemblance to the basic architecture underlying Stratificational Grammar (Lamb 1966).

One way the present conception differs from Categorial Grammar and HPSG, I think, is in the status of constituency across the three components. Because these other theories build up constituents "simultaneously" in the three components, there is a strong presumption that phonological and syntactic constituency coincide—which, as we have seen, is not correct. I am not familiar with proposals in these theories that account for the basic independence of phonological and syntactic constituency. On the other hand, one could imagine variants of the HPSG formalism that would build up constituency independently.

14. Various colleagues have offered interpretations of Fodor 1983 in which some further vaguely specified process accomplishes the conversion. I do not find any support for these interpretations in the text.

15. Because the mapping is not, strictly speaking, information preserving, I would prefer to abandon the term *translation module* used in Jackendoff 1987a.

More generally, let us return to the remarks in note 1. The caveats applied there to the term *representation* also apply here to *information*. "Mental information" does not "inform" anyone other than the modules of the brain with which it communicates via an interface. Moreover, it does not make sense to speak of, say, visual information simply being "sent" to the language system. One must not think of information passing through the interface as a fluid being pumped through "mental tubes" or as bits being sent down a wire. Rather, as I have stressed throughout this chapter, the correspondence rules perform complex negotiations between two partially incompatible spaces of distinctions, in which only certain parts of each are "visible" to the other.

16. It is of course possible for Fodorian modularity to incorporate the idea of interface mappings, solving the problem of communication among modules. However, since interface modules as conceived here are too small to be Fodorian modules (they are not input-output faculties), there are two possibilities: either the scale of modularity has to be reduced from faculties to representations, along lines proposed here; or else interfaces are simply an integrated part of larger modules, so they need not themselves be modular. I take this choice to be in part merely a rhetorical difference, but also in part an empirical one.

17. A less well known visual input to phonetics is the McGurk effect (McGurk and Macdonald 1976), in which lipreading contributes to phonetic perception. One can experience this effect by watching a videotape in which a person utters *da, da, da,* ... on the sound track but utters *ba, ba, ba,* ... on the synchronized video. It turns out that the video overrides the acoustics of the speech signal in creating judgments about what the utterance *sounds* like; the viewer has no conscious awareness of the disparity between lip position and the acoustic signal, and cannot help *hearing* the syllable *ba*. (Although Fodor (1983) does mention this phenomenon (footnote 13), the remark does not occur in the section on informational encapsulation, where it would offer a significant counterexample to his formulation.)

18. In turn, Landau and I draw on neuropsychological evidence that spatial representation has two subcomponents, the "what" and "where" systems, served by ventral (temporal) and dorsal (parietal) processing (Ungerleider and Mishkin 1982; Farah et al. 1988). This elaborates spatial representation in figure 2.3 into two submodules, further complicating the diagram but not changing its general character.

Incidentally, the organization sketched in figure 2.3 begins to break down Fodor's notion of a nonmodular central core. At least spatial representation and conceptual structure belong to the central core; they are both domains of "thought" rather than "perception." See chapter 8 and Jackendoff 1987a, chapter 12, for discussion.

19. The notion of "optimal fit," expressed in terms of sets of violable "preference rules," anticipates by about a decade the similar application of violable constraints in Optimality Theory (Prince and Smolensky 1993)—though the manner of interaction among constraints is slightly different. In turn, Lerdahl and I found antecedents for this approach in the work of the Gestalt psychologists (e.g. Koffka 1935).

20. Multidimensional Categorial Grammar (e.g. Bach 1983; Oehrle 1988) treats rules of grammar formally as functions that simultaneously compose phonological, syntactic, and semantic structures. In this theory, essentially every aspect of phonological, syntactic, and conceptual structure is potentially accessible to every other. Oehrle takes the empirical task of linguistic theory to be that of reining in this richness, of finding the subclass of such grammars that actually appear in natural language; he includes the standard GB architecture as a special case. The proposal sketched in figure 2.1 can be considered a different special case of Oehrle's architecture; under that construal, the argument here is that it is a more adequate way than the GB architecture to constrain multidimensional categorial

grammars. (However, see note 13 for a way in which Categorial Grammar might not be rich enough to account for language.)

On the other hand, suppose one tries to extend the multidimensional categorial approach across all the modules of the mind sketched in figures 2.2 and 2.3. The result is an n-tuple of structures, any one of which can in principle interact freely with any of the others. Such a conception would seem to abandon modularity altogether. By contrast, the present approach localizes the interaction between two kinds of representations in an interface module that knows nothing about any other representations or interfaces; so the overall conception is one of more limited communication among representations.

Chapter 3

1. Within Chomskian generative grammar, this is a presumption behind Baker's (1988) UTAH, for instance. Outside generative grammar, something very like this is presumed in Montague Grammar and Categorial Grammar; Dowty's (1979) minimal lexical decomposition of verbs is an unusual exception within these traditions.

2. Déjà vu: In Jackendoff 1972 I discussed two interpretations of Katz and Postal's (1964) hypothesis that "deep structure determines meaning," a virtual dogma of the mid-1960s incorporated into the Standard Theory (Chomsky 1965). On the weak reading, deep structure was to be construed as encoding whatever distinctions in syntax contribute to semantics. On the strong reading, it was to be construed as encoding *all* semantic distinctions, an interpretation that led inexorably to Generative Semantics. In Jackendoff 1972 I argued that only the weak reading was warranted by Katz and Postal's evidence (then went on to point out that it was still only a hypothesis, and to argue against even the weak form). A similar ambiguity lies in the conception of LF: Does it provide whatever grammatical information is relevant to meaning, or does it provide *all* information relevant to meaning? Simple composition is compatible with either reading; enriched composition is compatible with only the weaker.

3. Marjolein Groefsema (personal communication) has pointed out, however, that the principle can emerge in other restricted contexts where standard portions exist, for example among employees of a garden supply shop: *Would you bring up three potting soils from the cellar?*

4. Paul Bloom (personal communication) has pointed out the relevance to this case of the conceptual and proprioceptive sense of having a vehicle or tool act as an extension of one's body. For instance, hitting a ball with a tennis racket is phenomenologically not so different from hitting it with one's hand. He suggests that the reference transfers in (14a,b) and (15) are semantically supported by this deeper phenomenon of body sense and that the constraints on this reference transfer may thereby be explained. I leave the exploration of this intriguing possibility for future research.

5. As Paul Bloom (personal communication) has pointed out, the principle is actually slightly more general than this, given that speakers who are blind can use this reference transfer equally well.

6. The proper statement of the rule, I imagine, will provide an appropriate semantic characterization of which NPs the rule can apply to. I have no such characterization at the moment, so an informal list will have to do.

7. Alternatively, given appropriate context, predicates other than those from the object's qualia structure can be read into the (b) frames. For example:

(i) My pet goat was going around eating all kinds of crazy things. After a while he began (on) the newspaper, and enjoyed it a lot.

Here the goat is obviously not reading the newspaper but eating it. Hence, in general, qualia structure is used in these situations not to provide determinate readings, but to provide default readings in the absence of strong countervailing context.

8. This subsection and the next (though not the proposed solutions) were inspired by Franks 1995.

9. As Peter Culicover (personal communication) points out, there are certain in-between cases such as *gold tooth*, where one is not so clear whether the object is to count as a tooth or not, presumably because it not only looks like a tooth but also serves the function of one.

10. This problem is already cited in Jackendoff 1972, 217, as a "long-standing puzzle." I have no memory of where it originally came from.

11. Chomsky (1971) is arguing against a proposal in which focused expressions are *lowered* from Deep Structure topic positions into their Surface Structure location. But the argument works just as well against a raising-to-LF account.

12. One might avoid this problem by maintaining, rather plausibly, that the reconstruction is just *ruin his books*. However, I find the fuller reconstruction a more natural interpretation, especially if *wants to ruin his books by smearing* in the first clause is sufficiently destressed. Moreover, the putative reconstruction of the second clause under this interpretation is *ruin his books with glue*. In this case any other tool of destruction ought to be acceptable as well. However, I find ... *but Bill wants to do it with a KNIFE* quite odd as the final clause of (61). This suggests that *by smearing* is indeed retained in the reconstruction.

13. It is noteworthy that Fiengo and May (1994) use reconstruction of sloppy identity as a prime argument for the level of LF. However, all the cases of sloppy identity they examine use VP-ellipsis, which does not permit the Akmajian-type constructions (e.g. **John petted the dog, then Bill did to the cat*), so they do not consider the sort of evidence presented here.

Among Fiengo and May's main cases are so-called antecedent-contained deletions such as (i), where on their analysis the reconstruction of the elliptical VP escapes infinite regress only because the quantified object moves out of the VP at LF.

(i) Dulles suspected everyone who Angleton did.

An ideal refutation of their position would show that an Akmajian-type sentence can appear in an antecedent-contained deletion. It is difficult to construct pragmatically plausible examples that combine antecedent-contained deletion with an

Akmajian-type construction; however, (ii) seems fairly close when read with proper intonation.

(ii) Bill painted red cheeks with a BRUSH on every doll for which he had not yet done so with a SPRAY gun.

If (ii) is acceptable, *done so* cannot be reconstructed syntactically, and therefore LF cannot solve antecedent-contained deletion in full generality.

14. The dependency is often stated the other way, from positions on the trajectory to time. But, as Verkuyl (1993) stresses, the cart may stop or even back up in the course of the event, thus occupying the same position at different times. Hence the dependency is better stated with time as the independent variable.

15. Tenny (1987) claims to identify measuring-out relationships with syntactic direct argument position (direct object + subject of unaccusatives). However, her analysis neglects a vast range of data (Dowty 1991; Jackendoff 1996e). She does not adequately account for verbs of motion, where the path rather than the direct argument does the measuring out, and she does not consider the verbs of extension and orientation, which clearly counterexemplify her hypothesis. Moreover, in the present context, simply placing a "measured-out" argument in a particular syntactic position has nothing to do with quantifier scope effects, so the larger semantic generalization is missed entirely.

16. The fact that a clause encodes a question is sometimes taken to involve a syntactic feature [+wh] on the clause, an option that goes back to Katz and Postal 1964. However, there is really no syntactic justification for this feature other than a theory-internal need to make the selection of indirect question complements emerge as a syntactic fact. See Grimshaw 1979 for discussion.

17. Van Valin (1994) and Legendre, Smolensky, and Wilson (1996) independently suggest that the distinction between "moved" and "in situ" *wh* can be characterized a different way. In order for a clause to be interpreted as a *wh*-question, its conceptual structure requires some operator that marks the clause as a question (the "scope" of the question), plus a variable in the sentence that carries the θ-role of the questioned entity. In a language that "moves" *wh*-phrases, the SS-CS correspondence rules stipulate that the *wh*-phrase appears in a position specified by the scope of the question operator and that a trace appears in the variable position. By contrast, in a language with "in situ" *wh*-phrases, the SS-CS rules stipulate that the *wh*-phrase appears in the syntactic position of the variable, and nothing (or a question marker, as in Korean) appears in the syntactic position of the operator. To the extent that the so-called constraints on movement are actually constraints on the relation between the operator and the variable, both kinds of language will exhibit the same constraints on the occurrence of *wh*-phrases. (Though see Kim 1991 for some differences.) Brody (1995) makes a similar proposal for eliminating LF movement of in situ *wh*-phrases, except that he localizes the *wh*-operator at LF, in my view an unnecessary addition to syntax.

18. For example, Kamp's Discourse Representation Theory (Kamp and Reyle 1993) and related approaches such as those of Heim (1982), Verkuyl (1993) and Chierchia (1988) in model-theoretic semantics, Kuno (1987) in functional grammar, and Fauconnier (1985) and Van Hoek (1992, 1995) in Cognitive Semantics,

to name only a few. Within the general tradition of GB, one finds LF-less archi-tectures such as those of Koster (1987) and Williams (1986), a monostratal syntax in which LF = PIL (the input to Spell-Out) such as that of Brody (1995), and proposals for quantifier interpretation such as that of Lappin (1991); also within the GB tradition, Kim (1991) shows that in situ *wh* in Korean behaves more like quantification than like fronted *wh* in English. Csuri (1996) and I (Jackendoff 1992b, 1996e) make specific proposals that incorporate aspects of anaphora and quantification into the theory of conceptual structure developed in Jackendoff 1983, 1990.

Chapter 4

1. It is not clear to me why each item should require a *set* of transformations rather than one—or in fact why the transformation should be localized in the lexical item rather than in a single rule for inserting *all* lexical items. The latter, I think, is the assumption that has percolated into general practice. The difference, however, plays no role in what is to follow.

2. Halle and Marantz (1993) actually place their rule of Vocabulary Insertion at a level of Morphological Structure intermediate between S-Structure and PF. Chomsky (1979 and elsewhere) acknowledges the possibility of late lexical inser-tion, though to my knowledge he never explores it.

3. Halle and Marantz (1993) advocate half of this position: they properly desire to eliminate phonological information from syntactic structure. Phonological infor-mation is introduced by their rule of Vocabulary Insertion at Morphological Structure, a post-S-Structure level on the way to PF. They propose (p. 121) that "at LF, DS [D-Structure], and SS [S-Structure] terminal nodes consist exclusively of morphosyntactic/semantic features and lack phonological features.... The semantic features and properties of terminal nodes created at DS will ... be drawn from Universal Grammar and perhaps from language-particular semantic cate-gories or concepts." In other words, they still endorse mixed syntactic and semantic representations, which I wish to rule out.

4. Incidentally, on this formalization, the feature TOKEN and the function INSTANCE OF may possibly be regarded as coercions, not contributed by the LCS of *the* or *cat*. In a predicative or generic context, the conceptual structure of this NP would lack these elements, expressing simply a Type-constituent. (See some discussion in Jackendoff 1983, chapter 5.)

5. It is possible to see here a formal counterpart for Levelt's (1989) distinction between *lemmas* and *lexical forms* in processing. For Levelt, a lemma is the part of a lexical listing that enables an LCS (in his terms, a *lexical concept*) to be mapped into a lexical category in syntactic structure. In these terms, the lemma for *cat* is the SS-CS correspondence in (5). Levelt's lexical form is the part of a lexical listing that enables a syntactic category to be realized phonologically; the lexeme *cat* is thus the PS-SS correspondence in (5). Levelt shows experimentally that these two aspects of lexical entries play different roles in speech production. The *lexeme/lexical form* distinction of Halle and Marantz (1993) appears to be parallel.

This distinction is important because the selection of the particular lexical form for a lemma depends on the outcome of syntactic inflectional processes such as tense attachment, case marking, and agreement. See chapter 6.

6. Interestingly, Generative Semantics (McCawley 1968b) also took the view that lexical items are inserted in the course of a derivation. And Chomsky (1993, 22) proposes that "[c]omputation [of phrase markers] proceeds in parallel, selecting from the lexicon freely at any point.... At any point, we may apply the operation Spell-Out, which switches to the PF component.... After Spell-Out, the computational process continues, with the sole constraint that it has no further access to the lexicon." Here phonological and semantic material are still passed inertly through the syntax, though not necessarily all the way from initial phrase markers; as suggested in chapter 2, the uncharacterized operation of Spell-Out *might* play the role assigned here to the PS-SS correspondence rules.

7. An equivalent in the theory outlined in Chomsky 1995 might be to index each element in the numeration of lexical items that leads to the construction of the syntactic tree through Merge.

8. Parallel arguments can be constructed for two-stage theories of lexical insertion in which lexical items are inserted without their phonology (or without their inflectional morphology) in D-Structure, and the grammar then "goes back to the lexicon" at a later stage to recover, for instance, irregularly inflected forms. As mentioned earlier, Halle and Marantz's (1993) theory is a recent example. To my knowledge, though, proponents of such theories have not raised the question of how the grammar can "go back to the lexicon" and know it is finding the same item.

9. I am grateful to Urpo Nikanne for pointing out to me this class and its significance. Paul Postal and Jim McCawley (personal communication) have pointed out that some of these items do have minimal combinatorial properties (e.g. *hello there*/*here, *goodbye now*/*then*/*there, *dammit all*/*some*). I am inclined to regard these not as productive syntactic combinations but as memorized fixed expressions (see chapter 7). In other cases (e.g. *hurray for*/*against linguistics, shit on*/*with linguistics*), there is perhaps some free syntactic combination, but there is certainly no evidence for a standard X-bar schema associated with *hurray* and *shit*, or even for a standard syntactic category (see Quang 1969).

10. I am grateful to an anonymous reader for pointing out this fact. Note, however, that *hello* or any other phrase is acceptable in (9b) if uttered with some distinctive intonation or tone of voice; the sentence then draws attention to the auditory rather than linguistic characteristics of the utterance.

11. As Martin Everaert (personal communication) has pointed out, this includes cases like *His loud "yummy yummy yummy" always irritates me* and *I heard him ouch-ing his way through acupuncture*. In the first case, the phrase is a quotation, and any part of speech can go in its place, even though the position is normally a noun position. In the second case, *ouch-ing* is the consequence of the productive morphological rule that produces such coinages as *He Dershowitzed the interview* (Clark and Clark 1979). This does not necessarily show that *ouch* is a noun; perhaps it simply does not conflict with the structural description of the rule. These

are without doubt cases of enriched composition in semantics, and also perhaps in syntax.

12. There are also items that have phonological and syntactic structure but no semantics, such as expletive subjects and the *do* of English *do*-support. Empty categories that carry a θ-role, for instance PRO (if it exists), are items with syntax and semantics but no phonology.

13. I offer this argument with some trepidation. Children of course demonstrate some comprehension of syntactic structure long before they produce much more than single-word utterances. The argument to follow therefore probably should not be applied to speech production per se. Rather, it must be modulated in one or both of the following ways: (1) either it applies to the growth of language comprehension, rather than to production; or, (2) if the gap between comprehension and production proves to follow from a lag in the ability to construct syntactic trees in production, it applies to the trees actually constructed during speech production, even while perceptive trees are richer.

14. Aoun et al. (1987) propose that binding theory makes certain distinctions based on whether anaphoric elements are phoneticized in PF. However, as section 3.7 has made clear, it is equally possible in the present theory of binding to make a distinction between binding with and without accompanying overt syntax and/or phonology. Another recent proposal for the PF component is that of Halle and Marantz (1993), where, within the PF component, syntactic rules manipulate inflectional aspects of S-Structures to form Morphological Structures prior to Vocabulary Insertion. I will not deal with their proposals here, while acknowledging that the present approach needs to offer an alternative; chapter 6 gets the discussion off the ground.

15. The f-structure of LFG is made not of primitives such as NPs and VPs, but of networks of grammatical functions. I think it is therefore more properly seen as an "interlevel" between syntax and semantics, not as a part of syntax proper. In this sense the syntax proper of LFG—the c-structure—is monostratal.

16. Curiously, Chomsky (1995) explicitly disclaims trying to account for some of these aspects, for example topic/focus structure, within his minimalist architecture.

17. Even so, Chomsky sometimes still does not quite abandon D-Structure interpretation of θ-roles. For instance, in Chomsky 1986, 67, he partly justifies D-Structure by saying, "...D-structures serve as an abstract representation of semantically relevant grammatical relations such as subject-verb, verb-object, and so on, one crucial element that enters into semantic interpretation of sentences...." However, the immediate continuation is, "(recall that these relations are also indirectly expressed at S-structure, assuming traces)." In addition, he observes that "other features of semantic interpretation" are represented at LF, and by the next page asserts that "PF and LF constitute the 'interface' between language and other cognitive systems, yielding direct [*sic*] representations of sound on the one hand and meaning on the other...." In other words, in the end it has been denied that D-Structure directly feeds semantic representation, and it is presupposed that there is a strictly derivational relationship from D-Structure to both sound and meaning.

18. Chomsky is alluding in essence to RUGR when he says (1993, 10), "...
[when] H heads a chain (H, ..., t), ... this chain, not H in isolation, enters into
head-α relations." RUGR is also essentially equivalent to Brody's (1995, 14)
Generalized Projection Principle.

19. Chomsky himself (1993, 46 note 20) alludes to such a possibility of dispensing
with movement altogether, replacing it with well-formedness conditions on chains.
He argues against this possibility, on the grounds that Move α can be shown
necessary if the relation between a moved element and its trace can be disrupted or
obliterated by subsequent movement. The single example he presents involves the
adjunction of a verb to one of its functional projections, which then goes on to
adjoin to a functional projection above it. This analysis seems to me sufficiently
theory-internal—and, even within the theory, sufficiently open to ingenious options
to overcome loss of locality—that I need not answer it here. Brody (1995) however does provide discussion.

RUGR as it stands does not, I think, adequately account for pleonastic NPs
such as *it* and *there*, since they do not, strictly speaking, carry thematic or selectional roles. I leave the proper account open for the moment.

20. This section draws on the somewhat more elaborate discussion in Jackendoff
1987a, chapter 6.

21. This proposal does not preclude the possibility, suggested by Marcel Kinsbourne (personal communication), that in the actual brain the blackboards are of
flexible size and can compete with each other for space (and therefore computational resources).

Another independent alternative is to think of the blackboards as active, self-
organizing agents, that is, not to make a distinction between the medium for
working memory storage of information and the integrative processor that structures the information. Ultimately I think this is probably the right way to think of
it neurally. But since nothing I will have to say here hinges on the distinction, and
since the separation of blackboard and processor is so much easier to deal with
intuitively, I will stay with the more primitive metaphor.

22. Levelt (1989) presents strong psycholinguistic evidence that lexical activation
in production occurs in two stages, the *lemma*, or access from meaning to morphosyntax, and the *lexical form*, or access to phonology. It is not clear to me how
to interpret these results in the present approach, given that I have tried to avoid
the notion of "going back to the lexicon later" in the formal grammar. What I
think has to be sought is the proper trope on "lexical activation" in terms of the
formal model and its implementation in a processor. See section 6.4 for formal
justification of the separation of lemmas from lexical forms.

Chapter 5

1. In fact, Di Sciullo and Williams (1987) appear to presume a standard theory
of lexical insertion (or, later, a standard theory of lexical insertion moved to S-
Structure (p. 53)), since they speak of "items that are syntactic atoms (insertable in
X^0 slots in syntactic structures)" (p. 1). Although they speak of lexical VPs such as

take NP to task as listemes (p. 5), they do not address how these come to be inserted into syntactic structures. From the present point of view, this omission is significant: the insertion of phrasal listemes ought certainly to be "of interest to the grammarian."

2. Notice that the constituency of the morphophonology in (2) is not congruent with the syllabification.

I am assuming that the bracketing of the morphosyntax in (2) mirrors the semantics: 'someone who does [atomic science]'. Alternatively, the morpho-syntactic bracketing might parallel the phonology, in which case the mismatch lies between syntactic structure and conceptual structure.

3. Granted, Halle (1973) cites some odd situations in Russian in which certain case forms seem not to exist (see also Anderson 1982). I don't know what to say about them; but such cases are, I gather, quite rare.

4. What about cases in which a regular and an irregular form coexist (uneasily), for instance *dived* and *dove*? I think we have to assume that both are listed, so that they can compete with each other. See section 5.5. (This solution is advocated also by Pinker and Prince (1991).)

5. This probably entails some trick in the formalization of unification. Suppose unification of a string of phonological units (feet, segments) with a lexical item can be accomplished if linear order is preserved—but gaps are allowed, just in case they are licensed by something else. Then *automatic* would license the appropriate segments of *autofuckinmatic*, and the remaining segments would be licensed by the expletive. On the other hand, the intrusive segments in, say, **autobargainmatic* would not be licensed by anything, so the word would not be legal.

We will encounter the need for such a convention on unification again in chapter 6 in connection with templatic morphology, and in chapter 7 in connection with discontinuous idioms.

6. Anderson (1992, 64–69) argues against listing morphemes this way, on the grounds that there are instances of subtractive morphophonology, where the derived form is *smaller* than the stem, and of morphologically conditioned metathesis, where no affixal addition is feasible. See the brief remarks in section 6.2.

7. On the other hand, as Robert Beard (personal communication) has reminded me, affixes *do* share certain special properties with closed-class words such as pronouns and auxiliary verbs. For instance, closed-class words can cliticize and undergo contraction, making them look phonologically more like affixes; both closed-class words such as *it* and affixes such as structural case can be semantically empty. Even if such behavior warrants its own special corner of the lexicon, as Beard (1988) advocates, the point relevant here is that this special corner contains both affixes and words.

8. One of the reasons I was unable to make this distinction in Jackendoff 1975, I think, is that the notion of morphological blocking was not well established at that time.

9. A plausible constraint, for the most part observed in practice, is that X^0 constituents may not dominate phrasal constituents. However, Di Sciullo and

Williams (1987) argue that French compounds like *trompe-l'oeil* (lit. 'deceive the eye'), *arc-en-ciel* ('arc in sky' (rainbow)), and *hors-la-loi* ('outside the law' (outlaw)) are N^0s that dominate phrasal constituents—so this constraint might have to be relaxed (or abandoned). English counterparts are words like *mother-in-law*, *commander-in-chief*. See however Anderson's (1992, 315–318) discussion of Di Sciullo and Williams's argument.

Another case, presented by Lieber (1992), concerns constructions like *a Charles-and-Di syndrome*, *a let's-get-on-with-it attitude*, *the three-strikes-and-you're-out legislation*. She takes these to be adjectival compounds. But she presents no evidence that they are A^0s, and I suspect they are not, since they resist modification typical of adjectives, such as ??*I've never seen a more let's-get-on-with-it attitude than yours*, **John's attitude is very let's-get-on-with-it*. Also, Bresnan and Mchombo (1995) observe that the phrases that can be so used are selected from fixed expressions of the language (i.e. listemes). For example, random productive substitutions cannot be made in these phrases while preserving acceptability: ??*a Harry-and-Betty syndrome*, ??*let's-get-some-vanilla-ice-cream attitude*, ??*the four-balls-and-you-walk opportunity*. So Lieber's characterization of these cases may be too unconstrained.

There are, however, still worse cases, such as *the I-don't-have-to-tell-you-anything kind of love*, pointed out by Biljana Mišić Ilić (personal communication). I know of no discussion of these in the literature.

10. I find it reasonable, as advocated by Di Sciullo and Williams (1987), following Aronoff (1983), that there may be something of a cline in semiproductive processes, shading toward productive ones.

11. This claim should not be construed as implying that there is a strict cutoff in frequency between stored forms and forms generated on-line. Rather, I would expect a cline in accessibility for stored forms, including the usual differential in accessibility between recognition (better) and recall (worse).

12. This seems an appropriate place to comment on Hale and Keyser's (1993) analysis of such denominal verbs. Hale and Keyser propose, for instance, to derive the verb *shelve* from a syntactic structure like (i), listed in the lexicon.

(i) $[_{VP}[_{V_1}$ e] NP $[_{VP}[_{V_2}$ e] $[_{PP}[_P$ e] $[_{NP}$ shelf]]]]

The two verbs V_1 and V_2 and the preposition are syntactically empty, and "therefore" interpreted (by unstated principles) as *cause*, *be*, and *at/on* respectively. *Shelf* undergoes head-to-head movement to the P node, which in turn raises to the V_2 node, which in turn raises to the V_1 node, yielding the surface form.

This approach is subject to many of the same objections that Chomsky (1970) raised to the Generative Semantics treatment of lexical semantics. Here are some of the problems.

a. *Shelve* means more than 'put on a shelf'. One can't shelve a single pot or dish, for example; and one can't shelve books just by tossing them randomly on a shelf. This is not predicted by the syntax, so there must be some aspects of the semantics of *shelve* that go beyond the expressive power of syntactic representation. (In many of these verbs, the extra semantic material involves a characteristic

use or function, so it may be pulled out of the qualia structure of the root noun—
yet another use of qualia structure in addition to those cited in sections 3.4 and
3.5.)

b. Hale and Keyser do not address how the phonological form is realized as
shelve rather than *shelf*. This becomes more acute with verbs of removal, which
presumably have similar derivations. For instance, how is phonological structure
connected to syntax and semantics so as to get *skin* and *weed* but also *uncover* and
unmask, *declaw* and *defang*, *disrobe* and *disembowel*?

c. *Widen* and *thin* are supposed to be derived from syntactic structures similar
to (i), but with the APs *wide* and *thin* at the bottom instead of the PP *e shelf* (i.e.
'cause to become wide'). *Grow* has the same thematic roles as these verbs, as can
be seen especially from its similarity to the deadjectival *enlarge*. But there is no
adjective that can be used as the base for this structure, and the noun *growth* is
more morphologically complex and more semantically specialized than the verb
that might be supposed to be derived from it.

d. More acutely, at this grain of distinctions, *kill* has the same semantic structure as *widen*; that is, it means 'cause to become dead'. UTAH therefore requires
that *kill* be derived from the same syntactic structure. In other words, we are
directly back in the world of Generative Semantics (McCawley 1968b). Although
I agree with the *semantic* insights that Generative Semantics sought to express, the
possibility of expressing them by syntactic means has been largely discredited (e.g.
Chomsky 1970; Bolinger 1971; Jackendoff 1972). Incidentally, Fodor's (1970)
"Three Reasons for Not Deriving 'Kill' from 'Cause to Die,'" widely taken to
discredit lexical decomposition, apply equally to lexically transparent causative
relations such as transitive versus intransitive *widen* and *break*. See Jackendoff
1983, 124–126, and 1990, 150–151, for rebuttal of Fodor's arguments.

e. Hale and Keyser's proposal claims that the NP *shelf* satisfies the Location
role in *We shelved the books*. However, *We shelved the books on the top shelf* has
an overt Location, hence a double filling of the Location role. This of course violates UTAH, since it is impossible for two different NPs with the same θ-role to be
in the same underlying syntactic position. In addition it violates the θ-criterion; it
should be as bad as, say, **He opened the door with a key with a skeleton key*. But
it's perfect. See Jackendoff 1990, chapter 8, for an account of such sentences
within a lexicalist theory of verbs like *shelve*.

13. I am actually unclear whether the syntax needs to specify that the verb dominates a noun. After all, it could just be a plain verb, for all the syntax cares. One
piece of evidence that there is morphosyntactic structure comes from cases pointed
out by Pinker and Prince (1988) such as *flied out*, where the verb is derived from
the noun *fly (ball)*, in turn derived from the verb *fly*. Something is necessary to
suppress the appearance of the irregular past *flew*; Pinker and Prince claim it is the
extra bracketing [$_V$[$_N$ V]].

14. Incidentally, these forms also provide decisive evidence (I think) against a
view of lexical relations that which Chomsky has occasionally entertained (e.g.
1970). His idea is that *destroy* and *destruction*, for instance, constitute a single

lexical item, unspecified for which part of speech it is. If inserted into a V slot, it comes to be "spelled out" (by Lexical Assembly) phonologically as *destroy*; if inserted into an N slot, as *destruction*. Although this may possibly work for words as closely related as *destroy* and *destruction*, it cannot work for denominal verbs such as *saddle* and *shelve*. For one thing, it cannot account for the semantic peculiarities of these forms. More crucially, though, it cannot possibly account for the existence of more than one verb built from the same noun, as in the examples *smoke* and *roof* here.

Chapter 6

1. There are questions about whether all the morphosyntactic structure in (1) is necessary. For example, if plurality appears in the affix, must we also encode it as a feature in the upper node? I am encoding it in both places as a way to represent the effect of "percolation" of plurality up to the maximal phrase node (NP or DP), so that it can be detected by rules of agreement both inside the maximal phrase (e.g. agreement with determiners and adjectival modifiers) and outside the maximal phrase (e.g. agreement with a verb of which this is the subject). Alternatively, other solutions for "percolation" might be envisioned, and I leave the issue open. In particular, it may not be strictly necessary to encode the result of percolation in the lexical entry itself. (See Lieber 1992 for discussion of percolation; parallel issues arise in HPSG.)

Similarly, one might ask whether the extra node for the affix needs to be syntactically ordered with respect to the host. In cases where an affix is phonologically intercalated with the host, such as English expletive infixation, German past participle circumfixation (*ge-kauf-t*), and much Semitic morphology (see section 6.2), there is actually no syntactic evidence for ordering, and we may well consider the host and affix syntactically unordered. On the other hand, ordering must be stipulated if there are multiple affixes attached in a flat structure, as in (ia).

(i) a.   X   b.   X

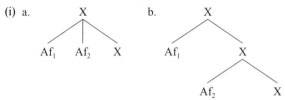

Whether there are such structures is an open question. In some cases, recursive binary branching like (ib) is motivated. However, a language with separate subject and object agreement markers on the verb (say Swahili) provides no (non-theory internal) evidence for syntactic recursion; and the complex templates associated with Navajo verbs (Spencer 1991, 208–214) are a still more extreme case.

In any event, if morphosyntactic structure can be pared down, or if it needs to be further augmented, I see no basic problems in adapting the present proposals to such alternatives.

2. Note that I do not call it the "Lexical Interface Level," as one might first be tempted to do. Remember that the lexicon is part of the PS-SS and SS-CS correspondence components, not itself a level of structure with which phonology can interface.

3. *SPE* itself did not make use of the notion of syllable, of course. However, if it had, this is how it would have been done. The case of stress, which *SPE* did treat, is similar.

4. As suggested in note 1, the morphosyntax need establish no linear order between the verb stem and the tense.

5. It is unclear to me how the index associated with the affix in syntax would then correspond to an index in SIL. Perhaps the index could be associated with the entire phonological formative, so that, for instance, the phonological form /kæts/ as a whole would be coindexed in syntax with both the count noun and the plural affix. It would then parallel the treatment of /katab/ in hypothesis 2 of (5). This solution seems congenial to Anderson's general approach.

6. As suggested in section 4.2, Goldsmith's (1993) "harmonic phonology" is another variant consistent with the present approach. Goldsmith's "M-level," the level at which morphemes are phonologically specified, appears to be LPS; his "W-level," at which expressions are structured into well-formed syllables and words, appears to be SIL; his "P-level" is PF. Instead of being connected by a derivation in the manner of *SPE*, the levels are connected by correspondence rules of roughly the sort advocated here.

One proposal that I cannot locate in this spectrum is Kiparsky's (1982) Lexical Phonology, in which some regular phonological rules apply "inside the lexicon," before lexical insertion, and some apply "outside the lexicon," after words are inserted into phrasal structures. In the present architecture, forms are not "actively derived" in the lexicon; the only rules "in the lexicon" are semiproductive rules that relate fully listed forms.

7. I have been compulsively complete; one can imagine abbreviatory notations to compress (10). Also, in this case it is not clear to me if it matters whether the F superscript is placed on the syntactic or the phonological constituent.

8. The subscripts A in the LCS of (11) are the linking indices for argument structure; they stipulate that the Thing-argument and the Path-argument must be realized in syntax. The fact that the former is realized as subject and the latter as a PP follows from the principles of linking worked out in Jackendoff 1990, chapter 11. For a more detailed treatment of GO and EXT and their relationship, see Jackendoff 1996e. As usual, readers should feel free to substitute their own favorite formalism for mine.

9. I will assume that the allomorphy of /-d/, /-t/, /-əd/ is a function of regular phonological rules of voicing assimilation and vowel epenthesis. If not, especially in the case of /-əd/, then phonological allomorphy along the lines of section 6.3 must be invoked in this entry. (A similar assumption obtains in my treatment of the LPS of the plural.)

10. This differs slightly from the treatment of *do*-support by Grimshaw (1997), who claims that *do* is a "minimal" light verb and therefore automatically fills the spot where a stranded Tense needs help. I am inclined to question her analysis, in that *do* both as a light verb and as part of an anaphor stands in only for action verbs, whereas *do*-support *do* applies to statives as well. On Grimshaw's theory, one might perhaps expect the minimal stative verb *be* to support Tense in questions with stative verbs. This suggests to me that *do*-support *do* should be listed as an allomorph of Tense, licensed in phonology just when Tense is not adjoined to a verb in syntax. However, it doesn't appear that anything much in either my analysis or Grimshaw's depends on the correct answer here.

11. Recall that the linking indices can be regarded alternatively as the endpoints of association lines. Hence reinvoking the indices x and y is in effect connecting *went* to the meanings of both *go* and *past*. (For complete accuracy, then, the indices in each form in (10) should be different.)

12. Aronoff's (1994) term *morphome* in present terms designates a set of allomorphs that may be linked to more than one LSS, for instance the set /-d/, /-t/, /-əd/, which is used not just for regular pasts but also for regular past participles and passive participles. Another example, from Beard 1987, is the set of allomorphs in Russian that can express either diminutivization or feminization.

13. In (18) the morphosyntax has been conveniently arranged so that Tense and Agreement fall under a single constituent that can be linked with the phonology in the usual way. I recognize that this is not necessarily feasible in general, in which case more elaborate linking conventions will have to be devised. The tree in (i) represents another possibility for the morphosyntax, with two linking indices simultaneously linking to the single phonological constituent. Such a structure will make the statement of lexical licensing more complex as well. I forgo the details.

(i)

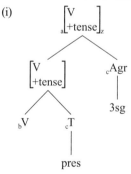

14. This form of course alternates with the special case of third person singular, (18). The two forms share the lemma for present tense, indexed by z in both structures. Presumably the zero morph is the default case, and third person singular blocks it because of its greater specificity in morphosyntax. Such blocking does not fall under either of the conditions on lexical licensing that have been stated so far; it is presumably a condition parallel to allomorphic blocking, but stated over LSS instead of LPS.

15. As mentioned in section 3.3, I have shown elsewhere (Jackendoff 1992b) that there is no evidence for embedding in the syntactic structure associated with this construction, say as in (i). Hence the double indexation is the only possible solution.

(i) $[_{NP}$ e $NP_x]_y$

Chapter 7

1. This chapter is adapted from Jackendoff 1995 and appears here by permission of Lawrence Erlbaum Associates, Inc. Most of the examples come from the *Wheel of Fortune* corpus (see sections 7.2 and the appendix), Weinreich 1969, Culicover 1967, or Wasow, Nunberg, and Sag 1984.

2. A number of her examples came from the *Wheel of Fortune* computer game; there were a few overlaps between these and the television show puzzles.

3. Another widely held view is that names are noncompositional, functioning merely as rigid designators. Brand names and organization names provide convincing evidence against this view, in that they have (semi)meaningful compositional structure. For instance, it would be rather surreal to name a linguistic society the Pittsburgh Pirates; and the point of giving musical groups names like The Grateful Dead or No Dogs Allowed is to invoke such surrealism. If names were truly nonmeaningful, this effect would be impossible.

4. An alternative account for *sell X down the river*, in the spirit of Chomsky 1993, might be a D-Structure with a Larsonian shell around the compound verb.

(i) $[_{VP}$ e X $[_V[_{VP}$ sell down the river]]]

Sell would undergo head-to-head movement (somehow escaping the next V node up, a nontrivial problem) to move to the left of its object. I leave the details of such an account to those who might find it attractive.

5. This hypothesis is worked out within Tree-Adjoining Grammar formalism by Abeillé (1995). A version of it also appears as the "en bloc" insertion of Van Gestel (1995), and it is certainly feasible within HPSG formalism.

6. This approach does not work for the few idioms that do not have identifiably normal syntactic structure. Examples are *by and large, for the most part, to kingdom come, happy-go-lucky, trip the light fantastic, every which way,* and *easy does it*—but they are not easy to come by and appear truly marginal. However, English also contains a few single words that have abnormal syntactic structure. *Enough* is a degree word that follows rather than precedes the phrase it modifies: *so tall* but *tall enough. Galore* is a quantifier that follows rather than precedes the noun it quantifies: *many balloons* but *balloons galore. Else* is an adjective (I suppose) that occurs only in the construction *Q-one/body/place/where else* and in *or else. Ago* is a temporal preposition that either follows instead of precedes its complement (*in/ after 5 years* but *5 years ago*) or else, unlike every other preposition, takes an obligatory measure phrase specifier. (The latter analysis is advocated by Williams (1994), but he does not remark on the rarity of obligatory specifiers of this sort.)

Any mechanism that deals with lexical licensing of these syntactically deviant words can likely be extended to license syntactically deviant idioms.

7. Recall that a similar assumption was made in the analysis of expletive infixation in chapter 5.

8. I am inclined to think that this class includes the expression *pet fish*, often cited (e.g. by Fodor 1996) as evidence against any sort of stereotypical meaning. The problem is that a stereotypical pet is a dog or a cat, not a fish; a stereotypical fish is a trout or a perch. Yet a stereotypical pet fish is a goldfish or a guppy, which is not stereotypical in either of the constituent categories. (Fodor presents no alternative account.) I think the answer for this case is that *pet fish* is a fixed expression (perhaps a collocation) for which one learns what the stereotypical members are. A freely produced expression of comparable structure might be *pet marsupial*, for which one has no particular special knowledge of stereotypes. Here, as in *pet fish*, the "pet" status is highly marked, since people don't usually keep marsupials as pets. For the "marsupial" part, we are likely to generate a stereotype of a kangaroo or opossum, in accordance with stereotypical marsupials. In this case, then, it looks like there is simple semantic composition of the sort Fodor argues does not exist.

9. The lexical rules for interpreting English compounds of course permit the possibility that *snowman* could mean 'man who removes snow', and one can imagine a context where such an interpretation would be plausible. But the fact that speakers of English would recognize such a usage as a neologism or a joke shows that the standard meaning must be lexically listed. As emphasized in chapter 5, this is what distinguishes a lexical rule like English N-N compounding from a truly productive rule: a lexical rule creates possibilities, but one must learn form by form which of these actually exist.

10. It is worth noting that a vast number of the metaphors cited by Lakoff and Johnson (1980) are listed fixed expressions of this character. This does not impugn the semantic analysis offered by Lakoff and Johnson, but it does raise the question of whether what they are talking about is metaphor in the literary sense. Maybe the more general term *figurative use* would be more appropriate. See Jackendoff and Aaron 1991 for discussion of other aspects of this use of the term *metaphor*.

11. Jim McCawley (personal communication) suggests that *The breeze was being shot/The fat was being chewed by two of the tavern's regular customers* is better than the examples in the text. Better, but still pretty degraded, I think.

12. Incidentally, it is not at all clear how this stipulation is to be reinterpreted within later versions of GB and especially within the Minimalist Program, where just about everything moves at some time or another during the derivation.

13. This is not to say that *all* issues in the syntactic variability of idioms can necessarily be resolved by these proposals. I have not investigated enough cases to make a strong claim. In particular, I have nothing to say about the "double" passives in *take advantage of* and *make mention of*, which are among Chomsky's most often cited examples of idioms (though see Nunberg, Sag, and Wasow 1994).

14. See Jackendoff 1990 and Carrier and Randall, in press, for arguments against other approaches to resultatives in the literature.

15. *Poss* appears as an element in the syntax. However, within the idiom itself it receives no realization in the phonology. Rather, its realization is determined by the standard PS-SS correspondence for *poss*, in particular that it combines with pronouns to produce possessive pronouns instead of the regular affix *'s*. This situation parallels the use of the lexical forms *go* and *went* in idioms (e.g. *go/went for broke*). See section 6.4.

16. Lakoff (1990) has argued for similar hierarchical relationships among more specific and more general metaphor schemas.

17. Although *in frequent touch with* occurs, ?*in occasional touch with* sounds odd, suggesting the former is an idiom on its own. Notice that there is a related "intransitive" family, for instance *for instance, in fact, of course, in part, at least,* and *on time*.

Chapter 8

1. This chapter is adapted from Jackendoff 1996d and appears by permission of the editor of *Pragmatics and Cognition*.

2. I say "essentially" here in order to hedge on possible "Whorfian" effects. There are undoubtedly expressive differences among languages in vocabulary, as well as in grammatically necessary elements such as tense-aspect systems and markers of social status (e.g. French *tu* vs. *vous*). Recent research reported by Levinson (1996) has further uncovered crosslinguistic differences in prepositional systems that affect the expression of spatial relations. But such differences must not be blown out of proportion; they are decidedly second- or third-order effects (Pullum 1991). They may create difficulties for literary translation, where style and associative richness are at stake, but no one seriously questions the possibility of effectively translating newspapers and the like.

3. At this level of generality, I concur with Fodor's (1975) Language of Thought Hypothesis. However, in other respects I disagree with Fodor; for extended discussion of Fodor's position, see Jackendoff 1983, section 7.5, Jackendoff 1990, sections 1.8 and 7.8, and Jackendoff 1992a, chapter 8. Fodor mentions my position only in Fodor 1996; his remarks address only an isolated corner of my theory of conceptual structure as if it were the entire theory.

4. Incidentally, I disagree with Bickerton's (1995) assessment that chimps lack "off-line" thinking (i.e. reasoning and planning not conditioned on the immediate environment). For instance, Köhler (1927) documents instances in which a chimp gives up trying to solve a problem, then some time later, while doing something else, displays what in a human we would call an "aha-experience," rushes back to the site of the problem, and immediately solves it.

5. Bickerton (1995) relies heavily on an assumption that a single cognitive innovation in modern humans has led to every advance over earlier hominids. Since language obviously had to have evolved at some point, he then argues that it is

implausible that any other possible independent innovation can have taken place, for instance a capacity for "off-line thinking." Though parsimonious, this assumption is hardly necessary. There are enough other *physical* differences between people and apes that it is absurd to insist that language must be the only *cognitive* innovation.

6. In a language with a productive causative morpheme, of course, this particular case would not go through; but any other inferential relationship will do as well.

7. A terminological remark. Some readers may be uneasy calling what the monkey does "reasoning" or, as Emonds (1991) puts it, "connected thought," precisely because it has no linguistic accompaniment. My question then is what term you would prefer. As Cheney and Seyfarth (1990) argue at length, no notion of "mere" stimulus generalization will account for the behavior. Rather, whatever unconscious process is responsible must logically connect pieces of information that are parallel to those expressed in (1a–e). If you prefer to reserve the term "reasoning" for a mental process that necessarily involves linguistic accompaniment, then call what the monkeys do whatever else you like, say "unconscious knowledge manipulation." In that case, my claim is that "reasoning" in your sense amounts to unconscious knowledge manipulation whose steps are expressed linguistically.

8. This linguistic consciousness is the closest equivalent in the present theory to Bickerton's (1995) Consciousness-3, the ability to report experience. More specifically, it is the way in which we *experience* our reports of our experience.

9. Block (1995) makes a distinction between what he calls Phenomenal Consciousness (or P-Consciousness) and Access Consciousness (or A-Consciousness). In effect, I am arguing here that the effects Block ascribes to A-Consciousness should actually be attributed to attention. If I read his discussion correctly, what he has called P-Consciousness corresponds fairly well to what I have called simply consciousness.

10. Damasio's (1995) "somatic marker hypothesis" is a possible exception. Damasio argues (in present terms) that certain percepts and memories are flagged by features that mark them as especially desirable or harmful, and that these enhance attention and memory recovery. He moreover proposes a brain mechanism for this flagging. These markers appear to correspond to the valuation "affective (+ or −)" in *C&CM* (pp. 307–308). However, Damasio does not identify these markers as part of a larger heterogeneous set of valuations.

11. Similar remarks apply to the term "belief" here as to "reasoning" in note 7.

12. At one presentation of the material in this chapter, a member of the audience pointed out that my argument may pertain not only to animals but also to deaf individuals who have not been exposed to language. According to this conjecture, such individuals could certainly think (and, by virtue of their larger brains, better than animals). However, they would not possess the advantages in thought conferred by language. I think I have to admit this conclusion as a distinct possibility, even if politically incorrect. If ethically feasible, it deserves experimentation. If *empirically* correct, it is just one more reason to make sure that deaf individuals are exposed to sign language as early in life as possible.

References

Abeillé, Anne. 1988. Parsing French with Tree Adjoining Grammar: Some linguistic accounts. In *Proceedings of the 12th International Conference on Computational Linguistics (COLING '88)*. Budapest.

Abeillé, Anne. 1995. The flexibility of French idioms: A representation with lexicalized tree adjoining grammar. In Everaert et al. 1995, 15–42.

Akmajian, Adrian. 1973. The role of focus in the interpretation of anaphoric expressions. In Stephen R. Anderson and Paul Kiparsky, eds., *A festschrift for Morris Halle*, 215–231. New York: Holt, Rinehart and Winston.

Allport, Alan. 1989. Visual attention. In Michael I. Posner, ed., *The foundations of cognitive science*, 631–682. Cambridge, Mass.: MIT Press.

Anderson, Stephen R. 1977. Comments on Wasow 1977. In Peter Culicover, Thomas Wasow, and Adrian Akmajian, eds., *Formal syntax*, 361–377. New York: Academic Press.

Anderson, Stephen R. 1982. Where's morphology? *Linguistic Inquiry* 13, 571–612.

Anderson, Stephen R. 1992. *A-morphous morphology*. New York: Cambridge University Press.

Anderson, Stephen R. 1995. How to put your clitics in their place. To appear in *Linguistic Review*.

Aoun, Joseph, Norbert Hornstein, David Lightfoot, and Amy Weinberg. 1987. Two types of locality. *Linguistic Inquiry* 18, 537–578.

Aronoff, Mark. 1976. *Word formation in generative grammar*. Cambridge, Mass.: MIT Press.

Aronoff, Mark. 1980. Contextuals. *Language* 56, 744–758.

Aronoff, Mark. 1983. Potential words, actual words, productivity, and frequency. In S. Hattori and K. Inoue, eds., *Proceedings of the 13th International Congress of Linguists*. Tokyo.

Aronoff, Mark. 1994. *Morphology by itself: Stems and inflectional classes*. Cambridge, Mass.: MIT Press.

Baars, Bernard J. 1988. *A cognitive theory of consciousness*. Cambridge: Cambridge University Press.

Baayen, Harald, Willem Levelt, and Alette Haveman. 1993. Research reported in Annual Report of the Max-Planck-Institut für Psycholinguistik, 6. Max-Planck-Institut, Nijmegen.

Baayen, Harald, Maarten van Casteren, and Ton Dijkstra. 1992. Research reported in Annual Report of the Max-Planck-Institut für Psycholinguistik, 28. Max-Planck-Institut, Nijmegen.

Bach, Emmon. 1983. On the relation between word-grammar and phrase-grammar. *Natural Language & Linguistic Theory* 1, 65–90.

Bach, Emmon. 1989. *Informal lectures on formal semantics.* Albany, N.Y.: SUNY Press.

Baker, Mark. 1988. *Incorporation: A theory of grammatical function changing.* Chicago: University of Chicago Press.

Beard, Robert. 1987. Morpheme order in a lexeme/morpheme-based morphology. *Lingua* 72, 1–44.

Beard, Robert. 1988. On the separation of derivation from morphology: Toward a lexeme/morpheme-based morphology. *Quaderni di Semantica* 9, 3–59.

Bellugi, Ursula, Paul P. Wang, and Terry L. Jernigan. 1994. Williams syndrome: An unusual neuropsychological profile. In Sarah H. Broman and Jordan Grafman, eds., *Atypical cognitive deficits in developmental disorders: Implications for brain function.* Hillsdale, N.J.: Erlbaum.

Berman, Steve, and Arild Hestvik. 1991. LF: A critical survey. Arbeitspapiere des Sonderforschungsbereichs 340: Sprachtheoretische Grundlagen für die Computerlinguistik, Bericht Nr. 14. Institut für maschinelle Sprachverarbeitung, Universität Stuttgart.

Berwick, Robert, and Amy Weinberg. 1984. *The grammatical basis of linguistic performance.* Cambridge, Mass.: MIT Press.

Besten, Hans den. 1977. Surface lexicalization and trace theory. In Henk van Riemsdijk, ed., *Green ideas blown up.* Publikaties van het Instituut voor Algemene Taalwetenschap, 13. University of Amsterdam.

Bickerton, Derek. 1990. *Language and species.* Chicago: University of Chicago Press.

Bickerton, Derek. 1995. *Language and human behavior.* Seattle, Wash.: University of Washington Press.

Bierwisch, Manfred, and Ewald Lang. 1989. Somewhat longer—much deeper—further and further: Epilogue to the Dimensional Adjective Project. In Manfred Bierwisch and Ewald Lang, eds., *Dimensional adjectives: Grammatical structure and conceptual interpretation,* 471–514. Berlin: Springer-Verlag.

Block, Ned. 1995. On a confusion about the function of consciousness. *Behavioral and Brain Sciences* 18, 227–287.

Bloom, Paul. 1994. Possible names: The role of syntax-semantics mappings in the acquisition of nominals. *Lingua* 92, 297–329.

Bloomfield, Leonard. 1933. *Language.* New York: Holt, Rinehart and Winston.

Boland, Julie E., and Anne Cutler. 1996. Interaction with autonomy: Multiple Output models and the inadequacy of the Great Divide. *Cognition* 58, 309–320.

Bolinger, Dwight. 1971. Semantic overloading: A restudy of the verb *remind.* *Language* 47, 522–547.

Bouchard, Denis. 1995. *The semantics of syntax.* Chicago: University of Chicago Press.

Brame, Michael. 1978. *Base-generated syntax.* Seattle, Wash.: Noit Amrofer.

Bregman, Albert S. 1990. *Auditory scene analysis.* Cambridge, Mass.: MIT Press.

Bresnan, Joan. 1978. A realistic transformational grammar. In Morris Halle, Joan Bresnan, and George Miller, eds., *Linguistic theory and psychological reality*, 1–59. Cambridge, Mass.: MIT Press.

Bresnan, Joan. 1982. Control and complementation. In Joan Bresnan, ed., *The mental representation of grammatical relations*, 282–390. Cambridge, Mass.: MIT Press.

Bresnan, Joan, and Jonni Kanerva. 1989. Locative inversion in Chicheŵa: A case study of factorization in grammar. *Linguistic Inquiry* 20, 1–50.

Bresnan, Joan, and Ronald M. Kaplan. 1982. Introduction. In Joan Bresnan, ed., *The mental representation of grammatical relations*, xvii–lii. Cambridge, Mass.: MIT Press.

Bresnan, Joan, and Sam A. Mchombo. 1995. The Lexical Integrity Principle: Evidence from Bantu. *Natural Language & Linguistic Theory* 13, 181–254.

Briscoe, E., A. Copestake, and B. Boguraev. 1990. Enjoy the paper: Lexical semantics via lexicology. In *Proceedings of the 13th International Conference on Computational Linguistics*, 42–47. Helsinki.

Broadbent, Donald E. 1958. *Perception and communication.* Oxford: Pergamon.

Brody, Michael. 1995. *Lexico-Logical Form: A radically minimalist theory.* Cambridge, Mass.: MIT Press.

Bromberger, Sylvain, and Morris Halle. 1989. Why phonology is different. *Linguistic Inquiry* 20, 51–70.

Büring, Daniel. 1993. Interacting modules, word formation, and the lexicon in generative grammar. Theorie des Lexicons, Arbeiten des Sonderforschungsbereichs 282, No. 50. Institut für deutsche Sprache und Literatur, Köln.

Bybee, Joan, and Dan Slobin. 1982. Rules and schemes in the development and use of the English past tense. *Language* 58, 265–289.

Calvin, William H. 1990. *The cerebral symphony: Seashore reflections on the structure of consciousness.* New York: Bantam Books.

Carrier, Jill, and Janet Randall. In press. *From conceptual structure to syntax: Projecting from resultatives.* Dordrecht: Foris.

Carrier-Duncan, Jill. 1985. Linking of thematic roles in derivational word formation. *Linguistic Inquiry* 16, 1–34.

Carroll, Lewis. 1895. What the Tortoise said to Achilles. *Mind* 4, 278–280. Reprinted in Hofstadter 1979, 43–45.

Carter, Richard. 1976. Some linking regularities. In *On linking: Papers by Richard Carter* (edited by Beth Levin and Carol Tenny), 1–92. MITWPL, Department of Linguistics and Philosophy, MIT (1988).

Cattell, Ray. 1984. *Composite predicates in English.* New York: Academic Press.

Cavanagh, Patrick. 1991. What's up in top-down processing? In Andrei Gorea, ed., *Representations of vision: Trends and tacit assumptions in vision research*, 295–304. Cambridge: Cambridge University Press.

Cheney, Dorothy L., and Robert M. Seyfarth. 1990. *How monkeys see the world.* Chicago: University of Chicago Press.

Chialant, Doriana, and Alfonso Caramazza. 1995. Where is morphology and how is it processed? The case of written word recognition. In Feldman 1995, 55–76.

Chierchia, Gennaro. 1988. Aspects of a categorial theory of binding. In Richard T. Oehrle, Emmon Bach, and Deirdre Wheeler, eds., *Categorial Grammars and natural language structures*, 125–152. Dordrecht: Reidel.

Chomsky, Noam. 1957. *Syntactic structures.* The Hague: Mouton.

Chomsky, Noam. 1959. Review of Skinner 1957. *Language* 35, 26–58.

Chomsky, Noam. 1965. *Aspects of the theory of syntax.* Cambridge, Mass.: MIT Press.

Chomsky, Noam. 1966. *Cartesian linguistics.* New York: Harper & Row.

Chomsky, Noam. 1970. Remarks on nominalization. In Richard Jacobs and Peter Rosenbaum, eds., *Readings in English transformational grammar.* Waltham, Mass.: Ginn.

Chomsky, Noam. 1971. Deep structure, surface structure and semantic interpretation. In Danny D. Steinberg and Leon A. Jacobovits, eds., *Semantics.* Cambridge: Cambridge University Press.

Chomsky, Noam. 1972. Some empirical issues in the theory of transformational grammar. In Stanley Peters, ed., *Goals of linguistic theory.* Englewood Cliffs, N.J.: Prentice-Hall.

Chomsky, Noam. 1973. *For reasons of state.* New York: Vintage Books.

Chomsky, Noam. 1975. *Reflections on language.* New York: Pantheon.

Chomsky, Noam. 1979. *Language and responsibility.* New York: Pantheon.

Chomsky, Noam. 1980. *Rules and representations.* New York: Columbia University Press.

Chomsky, Noam. 1981. *Lectures on government and binding.* Dordrecht: Foris.

Chomsky, Noam. 1986. *Knowledge of language.* New York: Praeger.

Chomsky, Noam. 1993. A minimalist program for linguistic theory. In Kenneth Hale and Samuel Jay Keyser, eds., *The view from Building 20*, 1–52. Cambridge, Mass.: MIT Press. Also in *The Minimalist Program*, 167–218. Cambridge, Mass.: MIT Press (1995).

Chomsky, Noam. 1995. Categories and transformations. In *The Minimalist Program*, 219–394. Cambridge, Mass.: MIT Press.

Chomsky, Noam, and Morris Halle. 1968. *The sound pattern of English*. New York: Harper & Row.

Chomsky, Noam, and George Miller. 1963. Introduction to the formal analysis of natural languages. In R. Duncan Luce, Robert R. Bush, and Eugene Galanter, eds., *Handbook of mathematical psychology*, vol. II, 269–322. New York: Wiley.

Churchland, Patricia, and Terrence Sejnowski. 1992. *The computational brain*. Cambridge, Mass.: MIT Press.

Clark, Eve, and Herbert Clark. 1979. When nouns surface as verbs. *Language* 55, 767–811.

Corballis, Michael C. 1991. *The lopsided ape: Evolution of the generative mind*. New York: Oxford University Press.

Crick, Francis. 1994. *The astonishing hypothesis: The scientific search for the soul*. New York: Scribner.

Csuri, Piroska. 1996. Generalized referential dependencies. Doctoral dissertation, Brandeis University.

Culham, J. C., and P. Cavanagh. 1994. Motion capture of luminance stimuli by equiluminous color gratings and by attentive tracking. *Vision Research* 34, 2701–2706.

Culicover, Peter. 1967. The treatment of idioms in a transformational framework. Ms., IBM Boston Programming Center, Cambridge, Mass.

Culicover, Peter. 1972. OM-sentences: On the derivation of sentences with systematically unspecifiable interpretations. *Foundations of Language* 8, 199–236.

Culicover, Peter, and Ray Jackendoff. 1995. *Something else* for the binding theory. *Linguistic Inquiry* 26, 249–275.

Culicover, Peter, and Michael Rochemont. 1990. Extraposition and the Complement Principle. *Linguistic Inquiry* 21, 23–48.

Damasio, Antonio R. 1995. *Descartes' error: Emotion, reason, and the human brain*. New York: Putnam.

Dascal, Marcelo. 1995. The dispute on the primacy of thinking or speaking. In M. Dascal, D. Gerhardus, G. Meddle, and K. Lorenz, eds., *Philosophy of language: An international handbook of contemporary research*, vol. II. Berlin: De Gruyter.

Declerck, R. 1979. Aspect and the bounded/unbounded telic/atelic distinction. *Linguistics* 17, 761–794.

Dennett, Daniel C. 1991. *Consciousness explained*. New York: Little, Brown.

Dennett, Daniel C. 1995. *Darwin's dangerous idea*. New York: Simon & Schuster.

Di Sciullo, Anna Maria, and Edwin Williams. 1987. *On the definition of word*. Cambridge, Mass.: MIT Press.

Dor, Daniel. 1996. Representations, attitudes, and factivity evaluations. Doctoral dissertation, Stanford University.

Dowty, David. 1979. *Word meaning and Montague Grammar*. Dordrecht: Reidel.

Dowty, David. 1991. Thematic proto-roles and argument selection. *Language* 67, 547–619.

Edelman, Gerald M. 1992. *Bright air, brilliant fire*. New York: Basic Books.

Emonds, Joseph E. 1970. *Root and structure-preserving transformations*. Doctoral dissertation, MIT.

Emonds, Joseph E. 1991. Subcategorization and syntax-based theta-role assignment. *Natural Language & Linguistic Theory* 9, 369–429.

Everaert, Martin. 1991. The lexical representation of idioms and the morphology-syntax interface. Ms., University of Utrecht.

Everaert, Martin, Erik-Jan van der Linden, André Schenk, and Rob Schreuder, eds. 1995. *Idioms: Structural and psychological perspectives*. Hillsdale, N.J.: Erlbaum.

Farah, M., K. Hammond, D. Levine, and R. Calvanio. 1988. Visual and spatial mental imagery: Dissociable systems of representation. *Cognitive Psychology* 20, 439–462.

Farkas, Donca. 1988. On obligatory control. *Linguistics and Philosophy* 11, 27–58.

Fauconnier, Gilles. 1985. *Mental spaces: Aspects of meaning construction in natural language*. Cambridge, Mass.: MIT Press.

Feldman, Laurie Beth, ed. 1995. *Morphological aspects of language processing*. Hillsdale, N.J.: Erlbaum.

Fiengo, Robert. 1980. *Surface structure: The interface of autonomous components*. Cambridge, Mass.: Harvard University Press.

Fiengo, Robert, and Robert May. 1994. *Indices and identity*. Cambridge, Mass.: MIT Press.

Fillmore, Charles, and Paul Kay. 1993. *Construction Grammar coursebook*. Copy Central, University of California, Berkeley.

Fillmore, Charles, Paul Kay, and Mary Catherine O'Connor. 1988. Regularity and idiomaticity in grammatical constructions: The case of *let alone*. *Language* 64, 501–538.

Fodor, Jerry A. 1970. Three reasons for not deriving "kill" from "cause to die." *Linguistic Inquiry* 1, 429–438.

Fodor, Jerry A. 1975. *The language of thought*. Cambridge, Mass.: Harvard University Press.

Fodor, Jerry A. 1983. *Modularity of mind*. Cambridge, Mass.: MIT Press.

Fodor, Jerry A. 1987. *Psychosemantics*. Cambridge, Mass.: MIT Press.

Fodor, Jerry A. 1996. Concepts: Where cognitive science went wrong. Ms., Rutgers University.

Fodor, Jerry A., Thomas Bever, and Merrill Garrett. 1974. *The psychology of language*. New York: McGraw-Hill.

Fodor, J. A., M. Garrett, E. Walker, and C. Parkes. 1980. Against definitions. *Cognition* 8, 263–367.

Foley, William A., and Robert D. Van Valin. 1984. *Functional syntax and Universal Grammar*. Cambridge: Cambridge University Press.

Frank, Robert, and Anthony Kroch. 1995. Generalized transformations and the theory of grammar. *Studia Linguistica* 49, 103–151.

Franks, Bradley. 1995. Sense generation: A "quasi-classical" approach to concepts and concept combination. *Cognitive Science* 19.

Fraser, Bruce. 1970. Idioms in a transformational grammar. *Foundations of Language* 6, 22–42.

Garrett, Merrill. 1975. The analysis of sentence production. In Gordon H. Bower, ed., *Psychology of learning and motivation*, vol. 9, 133–177. New York: Academic Press.

Gee, James, and François Grosjean. 1983. Performance structures: A psycholinguistic and linguistic appraisal. *Cognitive Psychology* 15, 411–458.

Goldberg, Adele. 1992. In support of a semantic account of resultatives. CSLI Technical Report No. 163, Center for the Study of Language and Information, Stanford University.

Goldberg, Adele. 1993. Making one's way through the data. In Alex Alsina, ed., *Complex predicates*. Stanford, Calif.: CSLI Publications.

Goldberg, Adele. 1995. *Constructions: A Construction Grammar approach to argument structure*. Chicago: University of Chicago Press.

Goldsmith, John. 1976. Autosegmental phonology. Doctoral dissertation, MIT. Distributed by Indiana University Linguistics Club, Bloomington.

Goldsmith, John. 1993. Harmonic phonology. In John Goldsmith, ed., *The last phonological rule*, 21–60. Chicago: University of Chicago Press.

Gould, Stephen Jay. 1980. Our greatest evolutionary step. In *The panda's thumb*, 125–133. New York: Norton.

Gould, Stephen Jay, and Richard Lewontin. 1979. The spandrels of San Marco and the panglossian paradigm: A critique of the adaptationist programme. *Proceedings of the Royal Society* B205, 581–598.

Grimshaw, Jane. 1979. Complement selection and the lexicon. *Linguistic Inquiry* 10, 279–325.

Grimshaw, Jane. 1990. *Argument structure*. Cambridge, Mass.: MIT Press.

Grimshaw, Jane. 1997. Projection, heads, and optimality. *Linguistic Inquiry* 28.

Gross, Maurice. 1982. Une classification des phrases "figées" en français. *Revue Québecoise de linguistique* 11, 151–185.

Hale, Kenneth, and Samuel Jay Keyser. 1993. On argument structure and the lexical expression of syntactic relations. In Kenneth Hale and Samuel Jay Keyser, eds., *The view from Building 20*, 53–109. Cambridge, Mass.: MIT Press.

Halle, Morris. 1973. Prolegomena to a theory of word-formation. *Linguistic Inquiry* 4, 3–16.

Halle, Morris, and Alec Marantz. 1993. Distributed Morphology and the pieces of inflection. In Kenneth Hale and Samuel Jay Keyser, eds., *The view from Building 20*, 111–176. Cambridge, Mass.: MIT Press.

Halpern, Aaron. 1995. *On the placement and morphology of clitics.* Stanford, Calif.: CSLI Publications.

Hankamer, Jorge. 1989. Morphological parsing and the lexicon. In William Marslen-Wilson, ed., *Lexical representation and process*, 392–408. Cambridge, Mass.: MIT Press.

Heim, Irene. 1982. The semantics of definite and indefinite noun phrases. Doctoral dissertation, University of Massachusetts, Amherst.

Henderson, Leslie. 1989. On mental representation of morphology and its diagnosis by measures of visual access speed. In William Marslen-Wilson, ed., *Lexical representation and procees*, 357–391. Cambridge, Mass.: MIT Press.

Herskovits, Annette. 1986. *Language and spatial cognition.* Cambridge: Cambridge University Press.

Hinrichs, Erhard. 1985. A compositional semantics for Aktionsarten and NP reference in English. Doctoral dissertation, Ohio State University.

Hirst, Daniel. 1993. Detaching intonational phrases from syntactic structure. *Linguistic Inquiry* 24, 781–788.

Hofstadter, Douglas R. 1979. *Gödel, Escher, Bach: An eternal golden braid.* New York: Basic Books.

Huang, C.-T. James. 1982. Logical relations in Chinese and the theory of grammar. Doctoral dissertation, MIT.

Inkelas, Sharon, and Draga Zec, eds. 1990. *The phonology-syntax connection.* Chicago: University of Chicago Press.

Jackendoff, Ray. 1972. *Semantic interpretation in generative grammar.* Cambridge, Mass.: MIT Press.

Jackendoff, Ray. 1974. A Deep Structure projection rule. *Linguistic Inquiry* 5, 481–506.

Jackendoff, Ray. 1975. Morphological and semantic regularities in the lexicon. *Language* 51, 639–671.

Jackendoff, Ray. 1976. Toward an explanatory semantic representation. *Linguistic Inquiry* 7, 89–150.

Jackendoff, Ray. 1983. *Semantics and cognition.* Cambridge, Mass.: MIT Press.

Jackendoff, Ray. 1987a. *Consciousness and the computational mind.* Cambridge, Mass.: MIT Press.

Jackendoff, Ray. 1987b. On beyond zebra: The relation of linguistic and visual information. *Cognition* 26, 89–114.

Jackendoff, Ray. 1990. *Semantic structures*. Cambridge, Mass.: MIT Press.

Jackendoff, Ray. 1991. Parts and boundaries. *Cognition* 41, 9–45.

Jackendoff, Ray. 1992a. *Languages of the mind*. Cambridge, Mass.: MIT Press.

Jackendoff, Ray. 1992b. Mme. Tussaud meets the binding theory. *Natural Language & Linguistic Theory* 10, 1–31.

Jackendoff, Ray. 1993a. *Patterns in the mind*. London: Harvester Wheatsheaf; New York: Basic Books.

Jackendoff, Ray. 1993b. The role of conceptual structure in argument selection: A reply to Emonds. *Natural Language & Linguistic Theory* 11, 279–312.

Jackendoff, Ray. 1995. The boundaries of the lexicon. In Everaert et al. 1995, 133–166.

Jackendoff, Ray. 1996a. The architecture of the linguistic-spatial interface. In Paul Bloom, Mary A. Peterson, Lynn Nadel, and Merrill F. Garrett, eds., *Language and space*, 1–30. Cambridge, Mass.: MIT Press.

Jackendoff, Ray. 1996b. Conceptual semantics and cognitive semantics. *Cognitive Linguistics*, 7, 93–129.

Jackendoff, Ray. 1996c. The conceptual structure of intending and volitional action. In Héctor Campos and Paula Kempchinsky, eds., *Evolution and revolution in linguistic theory: Studies in honor of Carlos P. Otero*, 198–227. Washington, D.C.: Georgetown University Press.

Jackendoff, Ray. 1996d. How language helps us think. *Pragmatics and Cognition* 4, 1–24.

Jackendoff, Ray. 1996e. The proper treatment of measuring out, telicity, and perhaps even quantification in English. *Natural Language & Linguistic Theory* 14, 305–354.

Jackendoff, Ray, and David Aaron. 1991. Review of George Lakoff and Mark Turner, *More than cool reason. Language* 67, 320–338.

Jaeger, J., A. Lockwood, D. Kemmerer, R. Van Valin, B. Murphy, and H. Khalek. 1996. A positron emission tomographic study of regular and irregular verb morphology in English. *Language* 72.

Joshi, Aravind. 1987. An introduction to tree-adjoining grammars. In Alexis Manaster-Ramer, ed., *Mathematics of Language*, 87–114. Amsterdam: John Benjamins.

Julesz, Bela. 1971. *Foundations of cyclopean perception*. Chicago: University of Chicago Press.

Kamp, Hans, and U. Reyle. 1993. *From discourse to logic*. Dordrecht: Kluwer.

Katz, Jerrold. 1966. *The philosophy of language*. New York: Harper & Row.

Katz, Jerrold, and Paul M. Postal. 1964. *An integrated theory of linguistic descriptions*. Cambridge, Mass.: MIT Press.

Kayne, Richard. 1994. *The antisymmetry of syntax*. Cambridge, Mass.: MIT Press.

Kim, Soowon. 1991. Chain scope and quantification structure. Doctoral dissertation, Brandeis University.

Kiparsky, Paul. 1982. From cyclic phonology to lexical phonology. In Harry van der Hulst and Neil Smith, eds., *The structure of phonological representations.* Dordrecht: Foris.

Koenig, Jean-Pierre, and Daniel Jurafsky. 1994. Type underspecification and online type construction in the lexicon. In *Proceedings of the West Coast Conference on Formal Linguistics.* Stanford, Calif.: CSLI Publications. Distributed by Cambridge University Press.

Koffka, Kurt. 1935. *Principles of Gestalt psychology.* New York: Harcourt, Brace & World.

Köhler, Wolfgang. 1927. *The mentality of apes.* London: Routledge & Kegan Paul.

Koster, Jan. 1978. *Locality principles in syntax.* Dordrecht: Foris.

Koster, Jan. 1987. *Domains and dynasties.* Dordrecht: Foris.

Krifka, Manfred. 1992. Thematic relations as links between nominal reference and temporal constitution. In Ivan Sag and Anna Szabolcsi, eds., *Lexical matters,* 29–54. Stanford, Calif.: CSLI Publications.

Kroch, Anthony. 1987. Unbounded dependencies and subjacency in a tree adjoining grammar. In Alexis Manaster-Ramer, ed., *Mathematics of language,* 143–172. Amsterdam: John Benjamins.

Kuno, Susumu. 1987. *Functional syntax.* Chicago: University of Chicago Press.

Lackner, James. 1985. Human sensory-motor adaptation to the terrestrial force environment. In David J. Ingle, Marc Jeannerod, and David N. Lee, eds., *Brain mechanisms and spatial vision.* Dordrecht: Martinus Nijhoff.

Lakoff, George. 1987. *Women, fire, and dangerous things.* Chicago: University of Chicago Press.

Lakoff, George. 1990. The invariance hypothesis: Is abstract reasoning based on image schemas? *Cognitive Linguistics* 1, 39–74.

Lakoff, George, and Mark Johnson. 1980. *Metaphors we live by.* Chicago: University of Chicago Press.

Lamb, Sidney. 1966. *Outline of Stratificational Grammar.* Washington, D.C.: Georgetown University Press.

Landau, Barbara, and Lila Gleitman. 1985. *Language and experience: Evidence from the blind child.* Cambridge, Mass.: Harvard University Press.

Landau, Barbara, and Ray Jackendoff. 1993. "What" and "where" in spatial language and spatial cognition. *Behavioral and Brain Sciences* 16, 217–238.

Langacker, Ronald. 1987. *Foundations of cognitive grammar.* Vol. 1. Stanford, Calif.: Stanford University Press.

Lappin, Shalom. 1991. Concepts of logical form in linguistics and philosophy. In Asa Kasher, ed., *The Chomskyan turn,* 300–333. Oxford: Blackwell.

Lees, Robert B. 1960. *The grammar of English nominalizations*. The Hague: Mouton.

Legendre, Geraldine P., Paul Smolensky, and Colin Wilson. 1996. When is less more? Faithfulness and minimal links in *wh*-chains. In *Proceedings of the Workshop on Optimality in Syntax*. Cambridge, Mass.: MIT Press and MIT Working Papers in Linguistics.

Lerdahl, Fred, and Ray Jackendoff. 1983. *A generative theory of tonal music*. Cambridge, Mass.: MIT Press.

Levelt, Willem. 1989. *Speaking: From intention to articulation*. Cambridge, Mass.: MIT Press.

Levelt, Willem, and Linda Wheeldon. 1994. Do speakers have access to a mental syllabary? *Cognition* 50, 239–269.

Levinson, Stephen. 1996. Frames of reference and Molyneaux's problem: Cross-linguistic evidence. In Paul Bloom, Mary A. Peterson, Lynn Nadel, and Merrill F. Garrett, eds., *Language and space*. Cambridge, Mass.: MIT Press.

Lewis, David. 1972. General semantics. In Donald Davidson and Gilbert Harman, eds., *Semantics of natural language*, 169–218. Dordrecht: Reidel.

Lewis, Geoffrey. 1967. *Turkish grammar*. Oxford: Oxford University Press.

Liberman, Mark, and Alan Prince. 1977. On stress and linguistic rhythm. *Linguistic Inquiry* 8, 249–336.

Lieber, Rochelle. 1992. *Deconstructing morphology: Word formation in syntactic theory*. Chicago: University of Chicago Press.

Macnamara, John. 1978. How do we talk about what we see? Ms., McGill University.

Macnamara, John. 1982. *Names for things*. Cambridge, Mass.: MIT Press.

Marantz, Alec. 1984. *On the nature of grammatical relations*. Cambridge, Mass.: MIT Press.

Marantz, Alec. 1992. The *way*-construction and the semantics of direct arguments in English: A reply to Jackendoff. In Tim Stowell and Eric Wehrli, eds., *Syntax and semantics*. Vol. 26, *Syntax and the lexicon*, 179–188. San Diego, Calif.: Academic Press.

Marin, O., E. Saffran, and M. Schwartz. 1976. Dissociations of language in aphasia: Implications for normal function. In S. R. Harnad, H. S. Steklis, and J. Lancaster, eds., *Origin and evolution of language and speech*. *Annals of the New York Academy of Sciences* 280, 868–884.

Marr, David. 1982. *Vision*. San Francisco: Freeman.

Marslen-Wilson, William, Lorraine K. Tyler, Rachelle Waksler, and Lianne Older. 1994. Morphology and meaning in the English mental lexicon. *Psychological Review* 101, 3–33.

May, Robert. 1985. *Logical Form: Its structure and derivation*. Cambridge, Mass.: MIT Press.

McCarthy, John. 1982. Prosodic structure and expletive infixation. *Language* 58, 574–590.

McCarthy, John, and Alan Prince. 1986. Prosodic Morphology. Ms., University of Massachusetts, Amherst, and Brandeis University.

McCawley, James D. 1968a. Concerning the base component of a transformational grammar. *Foundations of Language* 4, 243–269.

McCawley, James D. 1968b. Lexical insertion in a transformational grammar without Deep Structure. In B. Darden, C.-J. N. Bailey, and A. Davison, eds., *Papers from the Fourth Regional Meeting, Chicago Linguistic Society*. Chicago Linguistic Society, University of Chicago.

McGurk, H., and J. Macdonald. 1976. Hearing lips and seeing voices. *Nature* 264, 746–748.

Mel'čuk, Igor. 1995. Phrasemes in language and phraseology in linguistics. In Everaert et al. 1995, 167–232.

Minsky, Marvin. 1986. *The society of mind*. New York: Simon & Schuster.

Morgan, Jerry. 1971. On arguing about semantics. *Papers in Linguistics* 1, 49–70.

Newmeyer, Fritz. 1988. Minor movement rules. In Caroline Duncan-Rose and Theo Vennemann, eds., *On language: Rhetorica, phonologica, syntactica: A festschrift for Robert P. Stockwell from his friends and colleagues*, 402–412. London: Routledge.

Nikanne, Urpo. 1996. Lexical conceptual structure and argument linking. Ms., University of Oslo.

Nunberg, Geoffrey. 1979. The non-uniqueness of semantic solutions: Polysemy. *Linguistics and Philosophy* 3, 143–184.

Nunberg, Geoffrey, Ivan Sag, and Thomas Wasow. 1994. Idioms. *Language* 70, 491–538.

Oehrle, Richard T. 1988. Multi-dimensional compositional functions as a basis for grammatical analysis. In Richard T. Oehrle, Emmon Bach, and Deirdre Wheeler, eds., *Categorial grammars and natural language structures*, 349–390. Dordrecht: Reidel.

Ostler, Nick. 1979. Case linking: A theory of case and verb diathesis applied to Classical Sanskrit. Doctoral dissertation, MIT.

Otero, Carlos. 1976. The dictionary in a generative grammar. Ms., UCLA.

Otero, Carlos. 1983. Towards a model of paradigmatic grammar. *Quaderni di Semantica* 4, 134–144.

Partee, Barbara H. 1995. The development of formal semantics in linguistic theory. In Shalom Lappin, ed., *The handbook of contemporary semantic theory*, 11–38. Oxford: Blackwell.

Perlmutter, David, and Paul M. Postal. 1984. The 1-Advancement Exclusiveness Law. In David Perlmutter and Carol Rosen, eds., *Studies in Relational Grammar* 2, 81–125. Chicago: University of Chicago Press.

Perlmutter, David, and John Robert Ross. 1970. Relative clauses with split antecedents. *Linguistic Inquiry* 1, 350.

Pinker, Steven. 1989. *Learnability and cognition: The acquisition of argument structure.* Cambridge, Mass.: MIT Press.

Pinker, Steven. 1992. Review of Bickerton 1990. *Language* 68, 375–382.

Pinker, Steven, and Paul Bloom. 1990. Natural language and natural selection. *Behavioral and Brain Sciences* 13, 707–726.

Pinker, Steven, and Alan Prince. 1988. On language and connectionism: Analysis of a parallel distributed processing model of language acquisition. *Cognition* 26, 195–267.

Pinker, Steven, and Alan Prince. 1991. Regular and irregular morphology and the psychological status of rules of grammar. In Laurel A. Sutton, Christopher Johnson, and Ruth Shields, eds., *Proceedings of the Seventeenth Annual Meeting of the Berkeley Linguistics Society*, 230–251. Berkeley Linguistics Society, University of California, Berkeley.

Pollard, Carl, and Ivan Sag. 1987. *Information-based syntax and semantics.* Stanford, Calif.: CSLI Publications.

Pollard, Carl, and Ivan Sag. 1994. *Head-Driven Phrase Structure Grammar.* Chicago: University of Chicago Press.

Prasada, S., S. Pinker, and W. Snyder. 1990. Some evidence that irregular forms are retrieved from memory but regular forms are rule-generated. Paper presented to the Annual Meeting of the Psychonomic Society, New Orleans.

Prince, Alan, and Paul Smolensky. 1993. Optimality Theory: Constraint interaction in generative grammar. Ms., Rutgers University and University of Colorado.

Prince, Ellen F. 1995. On the limits of syntax, with reference to Topicalization and Left-Dislocation. To appear in P. Culicover and L. McNally, eds., *The limits of syntax.* San Diego, Calif.: Academic Press.

Pullum, Geoffrey K. 1991. *The great Eskimo vocabulary hoax.* Chicago: University of Chicago Press.

Pustejovsky, James. 1991a. The generative lexicon. *Computational Linguistics* 17, 409–441.

Pustejovsky, James. 1991b. The syntax of event structure. *Cognition* 41, 47–82.

Pustejovsky, James. 1995. *The generative lexicon.* Cambridge, Mass.: MIT Press.

Quang Phuc Dong. 1969. Phrases anglaises sans sujet grammatical apparent. *Langages* 14, 44–51.

Randall, Janet. 1988. Inheritance. In Wendy Wilkins, ed., *Syntax and semantics.* Vol. 21, *Thematic relations*, 129–146. San Diego, Calif.: Academic Press.

Rosen, Carol. 1984. The interface between semantic roles and initial grammatical relations. In David Perlmutter and Carol Rosen, eds., *Studies in Relational Grammar 2*, 38–77. Chicago: University of Chicago Press.

Rosenzweig, Mark R., and Arnold L. Leiman. 1989. *Physiological psychology.* 2nd ed. New York: Random House.

Ross, John Robert. 1967. Constraints on variables in syntax. Doctoral dissertation, MIT.

Rothstein, Susan. 1991. LF and the structure of the grammar: Comments. In Asa Kasher, ed., *The Chomskyan turn*, 385–395. Oxford: Blackwell.

Rumelhart, David, and James McClelland. 1986. On learning the past tenses of English verbs. In James McClelland, David Rumelhart, and the PDP Research Group, *Parallel distributed processing: Explorations in the microstructure of cognition.* Vol. 2, *Psychological and biological models*, 216–271. Cambridge, Mass.: MIT Press.

Rumelhart, David, James McClelland, and the PDP Research Group. 1986. *Parallel distributed processing: Explorations in the microstructure of cognition.* Vol. 1, *Foundations.* Cambridge, Mass.: MIT Press.

Ruwet, Nicolas. 1991. *Syntax and human experience.* Chicago: University of Chicago Press.

Sadock, Jerrold M. 1991. *Autolexical Syntax.* Chicago: University of Chicago Press.

Sag, Ivan, and Carl Pollard. 1991. An integrated theory of complement control. *Language* 67, 63–113.

Schenk, André. 1995. The syntactic behavior of idioms. In Everaert et al. 1995, 253–271.

Schreuder, Robert, and R. Harald Baayen. 1995. Modeling morphological processing. In Feldman 1995, 131–154.

Searle, John R. 1983. *Intentionality.* Cambridge: Cambridge University Press.

Searle, John R. 1992. *The rediscovery of mind.* Cambridge, Mass.: MIT Press.

Selkirk, Elisabeth O. 1982. *The syntax of words.* Cambridge, Mass.: MIT Press.

Selkirk, Elisabeth O. 1984. *Phonology and syntax: The relation between sound and structure.* Cambridge, Mass.: MIT Press.

Shieber, Stuart. 1986. *An introduction to unification-based approaches to grammar.* Stanford, Calif.: CSLI Publications.

Shieber, Stuart, and Yves Schabes. 1991. Generation and synchronous tree adjoining grammars. *Journal of Computational Intelligence* 7, 220–228.

Skinner, B. F. 1957. *Verbal behavior.* New York: Appleton-Century-Crofts.

Slobin, Dan. 1966. Grammatical transformations and sentence comprehension in childhood and adulthood. *Journal of Verbal Learning and Verbal Behavior* 5, 219–227.

Smith, Neil V., and Ianthi-Maria Tsimpli. 1995. *The mind of a savant.* Oxford: Blackwell.

Spencer, Andrew. 1991. *Morphological theory.* Oxford: Blackwell.

Steedman, Mark. 1990. Gapping as constituent coordination. *Linguistics and Philosophy* 13, 207–263.

Steedman, Mark. 1991. Structure and intonation. *Language* 67, 260–296.

Stemberger, Joseph Paul, and Brian MacWhinney. 1988. Are inflected forms stored in the lexicon? In Michael Hammond and Michael Noonan, eds., *Theoretical morphology: Approaches in modern linguistics*, 101–116. San Diego, Calif.: Academic Press.

Swinney, David. 1979. Lexical access during sentence comprehension: (Re)consideration of context effects. *Journal of Verbal Learning and Verbal Behavior* 18, 654–659.

Talmy, Leonard. 1978. The relation of grammar to cognition: A synopsis. In D. Waltz, ed., *Theoretical issues in natural language processing 2*, 14–24. New York: Association for Computing Machinery.

Tanenhaus, Michael, J. M. Leiman, and Mark Seidenberg. 1979. Evidence for multiple states in the processing of ambiguous words in syntactic contexts. *Journal of Verbal Learning and Verbal Behavior* 18, 427–440.

Tenny, Carol. 1987. Grammaticalizing aspect and affectedness. Doctoral dissertation, MIT.

Tenny, Carol. 1992. The aspectual interface hypothesis. In Ivan Sag and Anna Szabolcsi, eds., *Lexical matters*, 1–28. Stanford, Calif.: CSLI Publications.

Tenny, Carol. 1994. *Aspectual roles and the syntax-semantics interface*. Dordrecht: Kluwer.

Terrace, Herbert. 1979. *Nim*. New York: Knopf.

Trueswell, John C., and Michael K. Tanenhaus. 1994. Toward a lexicalist framework for constraint-based syntactic-ambiguity resolution. In Charles Clifton, Lynn Frazier, and Keith Rayner, eds., *Perspectives on sentence processing*, 155–179. Hillsdale, N.J.: Erlbaum.

Ullman, M., and S. Pinker. 1991. Connectionism versus symbolic rules in language: A case study. Paper presented at the Spring Symposium Series of the American Association for Artificial Intelligence, Stanford.

Ungerleider, Leslie G., and Mortimer Mishkin. 1982. Two cortical visual systems. In David J. Ingle, Melvyn A. Goodale, and Richard J. W. Mansfield, eds., *Analysis of visual behavior*, 549–586. Cambridge, Mass.: MIT Press.

Vandeloise, Claude. 1991. *Spatial prepositions: A case study from French*. Chicago: University of Chicago Press.

Van Gestel, Frank. 1995. En bloc insertion. In Everaert et al. 1995, 75–96.

Van Hoek, Karen. 1992. Paths through conceptual structure: Constraints on pronominal anaphora. Doctoral dissertation, University of California, San Diego.

Van Hoek, Karen. 1995. Conceptual reference points: A Cognitive Grammar account of pronominal anaphora constraints. *Language* 71, 310–340.

Van Valin, Robert D. 1994. Extraction restrictions, competing theories, and the argument from the poverty of the stimulus. In Susan D. Lima, Roberta L.

Corrigan, and Gregory K. Iverson, eds., *The reality of linguistic rules*, 243–259. Amsterdam: John Benjamins.

Verkuyl, H. J. 1972. *On the compositional nature of the aspects*. Dordrecht: Reidel.

Verkuyl, H. J. 1993. *A theory of aspectuality: The interaction between temporal and atemporal structure*. Cambridge: Cambridge University Press.

Wasow, Thomas. 1977. Transformations and the lexicon. In Peter Culicover, Thomas Wasow, and Adrian Akmajian, eds., *Formal syntax*, 327–360. New York: Academic Press.

Wasow, Thomas, Geoffrey Nunberg, and Ivan Sag. 1984. Idioms: An interim report. In S. Hattori and K. Inoue, eds., *Proceedings of the 13th International Congress of Linguists*. The Hague: CIPL.

Weinreich, Uriel. 1969. Problems in the analysis of idioms. In Joan Puhvel, ed., *Substance and structure of language*, 23–81. Berkeley and Los Angeles: University of California Press. Reprinted in *On semantics* (edited by William Labov and Beatrice Weinreich), 208–264. Philadelphia: University of Pennsylvania Press (1980).

Wexler, Kenneth, and Peter Culicover. 1980. *Formal principles of language acquisition*. Cambridge, Mass.: MIT Press.

Wilkins, Wendy, and Jennie Wakefield. 1995. Brain evolution and neurolinguistic preconditions. *Behavioral and Brain Sciences* 18, 161–181.

Williams, Edwin. 1981. On the notions "lexically related" and "head of a word." *Linguistic Inquiry* 12, 245–274.

Williams, Edwin. 1985. PRO and subject of NP. *Natural Language & Linguistic Theory* 3, 297–315.

Williams, Edwin. 1986. A reassignment of the functions of LF. *Linguistic Inquiry* 17, 265–300.

Williams, Edwin. 1994. Remarks on lexical knowledge. In Lila Gleitman and Barbara Landau, eds., *The acquisition of the lexicon*, 7–34. Cambridge, Mass.: MIT Press.

Wittgenstein, Ludwig. 1953. *Philosophical investigations*. Oxford: Blackwell.

Wrangham, Richard W., W. C. McGrew, Frans B. M. de Waal, and Paul G. Heltne, eds. 1994. *Chimpanzee cultures*. Cambridge, Mass.: Harvard University Press.

Zaenen, Annie, Joan Maling, and Höskuldur Thráinsson. 1985. Case and grammatical functions: The Icelandic passive. *Natural Language & Linguistic Theory* 3, 441–484.

Zwicky, Arnold, and Geoffrey K. Pullum. 1983. Phonology in syntax: The Somali optional agreement rule. *Natural Language & Linguistic Theory* 1, 385–402.

Index